COMING OF AGE

COMING

of

AGE

The Sexual Awakening
of Margaret Mead

DEBORAH BEATRIZ BLU

Thomas Dunne Books ♞ St. Martin's Press

THOMAS DUNNE BOOKS.
An imprint of St. Martin's Press.

COMING OF AGE. Copyright © 2017 by Deborah Beatriz Blum. All rights reserved. Printed in the United States of America. For information, address St. Martin's Press, 175 Fifth Avenue, New York, N.Y. 10010.

www.thomasdunnebooks.com
www.stmartins.com

Designed by Steven Seighman

Margaret Mead photograph courtesy of the Barnard Archives and Special
Collections.

The Library of Congress Cataloging-in-Publication Data is available
upon request.

ISBN 978-1-250-05572-9 (hardcover)
ISBN 978-1-4668-5949-4 (e-book)

Our books may be purchased in bulk for promotional, educational, or
business use. Please contact your local bookseller or the Macmillan
Corporate and Premium Sales Department at 1-800-221-7945, extension
5442, or by e-mail at MacmillanSpecialMarkets@macmillan.com.

First Edition: July 2017

10 9 8 7 6 5 4 3 2 1

For the men in my life . . . Dale, Tommy, Andre, and Theron

CONTENTS

AUTHOR'S NOTE

*This last night of waiting for mail is dreadful. I can't read,
I can't write coherently. I can't sit still. This sad passivity
of the last three weeks is doomed to burst tomorrow—and
into what new encompassing gloom I wonder.*

—MARGARET MEAD

The importance of letters—for Margaret Mead and her intimates—
cannot be overstated.

For individuals who were venturing off to faraway and untraveled lands, alone and without a roadmap, letters were a lifeline home.
At a time when the telephone was a relatively new invention and long-
distance calling did not exist, they had no other way to emotionally connect themselves except through the written word. Letters were the way
they recounted their experiences, explored their innermost thoughts,
exorcized their demons, and made love.

During the 1920s, the time it took a letter to find its way by rail to a
remote outpost could be three weeks, by ocean liner six. For the individuals who populate these pages—Luther Cressman, Ruth Benedict,
Edward Sapir, and Margaret Mead—the arrival of the mail was often
cited as the most anticipated moment of the day. Margaret Mead made
a habit out of saving every letter she received—save for the bundle she
ceremoniously set fire to on a beach in Samoa in January of 1926.

Now, nearly one hundred years later, I, too, have gained my own ap-
preciation for these letters. Through them I have been able to enter the
world of the young Margaret Mead, to get to know her as she was coming of age, in the years before she became famous.

Mead's correspondence, missives that number in the thousands—

both written by her and written to her—is housed in the U.S. Library of Congress. Most are handwritten, some scrawled in haste, in misery, or erotic passion. As a collection they reveal a side of Mead that she successfully hid from the world during her lifetime and for many years after her death. Thanks to the advent of digital photography, I have been able to store them in my own computer, decipher them, and study them.

What follows is a story told by Mead and her closest confidants. Anything between quotation marks is based on the written record. Scenes and dialogue have been reconstructed out of the actual words and memories of the participants.

Sometimes sleep will not descend upon the village until long past midnight; then at last there is only the mellow thunder of the reef and the whisper of lovers, as the village rests until dawn.

—MARGARET MEAD, *COMING OF AGE IN SAMOA*

Margaret Mead, senior class photo, from the Barnard College yearbook, 1923.

I

——

SHOOTING STAR

She was hitching her wagon to a star, and I felt grateful I had never stood in her way. . . .

—LUTHER CRESSMAN

August 1925

On the third of August, 1925, a Southern Pacific passenger train streaked across the Arizona desert. Inside the dining car a girl in pale-colored silk sat eating breakfast. Her name was Margaret Mead and she was traveling alone, en route to California, where she was to catch the SS *Matsonia,* the first of two steamers that would take her to the South Seas.

Known among her friends as extravagantly talkative, Margaret was quiet now, gazing out at scenery that was passing by in a blur. Her mind was full of what had just happened, and what was to come.

Margaret's light brown hair, cut short in a bob, was unruly, the bridge of her nose lightly freckled. At just over five-foot-two, and weighing not quite one hundred pounds, she looked more like an eleven-year-old child than a twenty-three-year-old woman. Accustomed to being underestimated, she had long ago decided it didn't matter. As soon as she spoke it was apparent from her Main Line accent and the hint of command in her voice that she was, in reality, a young lady who knew what she was about.

Raised in the privileged environs of Bucks County, Pennsylvania, and recently married to her childhood sweetheart, Margaret had never spent a night alone in her life, yet now she was at the beginning of a journey that would span nine thousand miles. Once she reached her destination— American Samoa—she would spend the better part of a year separated from family and friends. Sometimes, though she was loath to admit it, she went numb at the thought.

Breakfast finished, Margaret took out her writing case and began a letter to one of her preferred confidants:

Dear Grandma . . . Ruth left me last night at Williams and in three hours I shall be in Los Angeles and see Uncle Leland, I hope. We had gorgeous weather all the way across the desert, almost cold, even in the day time.

For the last two years Margaret had been working toward her doctorate in anthropology at Columbia University in New York City. When faced with choosing a culture on which to base her professional career, she said she had no intention of being like the rest of the women in the department who were content to study the American Indian. She wanted to go to Polynesia. Nearly everyone she knew had said no, the South Pacific was impossible. Young ladies, traveling on their own, simply did not go there.

Her letter continued:

We saw many Indians baling alfalfa into square blocks, and we marveled that the alfalfa was green. Blue and red and yellow are the colors of this country; green is swallowed up when it does occur. The cattle and horses are lean and lost looking, gaunt and gray on the barren lands. But the trees bloom, Grandma, all of them, pines and junipers and all. Think of a little tree that smells like an evergreen and has daisies on it. And there are also delicate scarlet flowers, growing unexpectedly in the waste land.

Everyone had said the enterprise carried too many risks. Margaret could not speak a word of the native language and the tropics were treacherous. But Margaret was adamant, and stubborn. She prevailed and now, in a mere four weeks, she would begin fieldwork in Samoa to observe the way that adolescent girls in a primitive culture differed from their counterparts in America. It was not for nothing that, as a child, her determination had earned her the nickname "Punk." She was also known to be irrepressibly curious.

Ruth and I got different things out of the Grand Canyon, but we both loved it. She was the most impressed by the effort of the river to hide, a torturing need for secrecy which had made it dig its way, century by century, deeper into the face of the earth. The part I loved the best was the endless possibilities of those miles of pinna- cled clay, red and white, and fantastic, ever changing their aspect under new shadowing cloud. One minute I saw a castle, with a great white horse of mythical stature, standing tethered by the gate, and further over, a great Roman wall.

Margaret did not realize it, could never have guessed it, but those words that she'd just put to paper, the ones that alluded to the "endless possibilities" before her, were prophetic. That quality she exhibited, the ability to engage with the life around her, to respond to events as they were unfolding and turn the moment to her advantage, was a gift, one she was armed with as she set out to confront the unknown.

IT WAS A JOURNEY THAT HAD BEGUN FOUR YEARS EARLIER

ONE FOR MY LADY LOVE

Darling mine . . . , You are made up of . . . pretty eyes that shine with happiness of love, two red lips that tell me you love me and give me yourself in their kisses, two pretty white arms that I love to feel around me . . . and a beautiful soft delicate rounded body full of mystery and strange fascinating power.

—LUTHER CRESSMAN

December 1921

With a rush of wind and sleet pushing at his back, the young man opened the heavy door and stepped inside. Shaking a layer of snow off his coat, feeling the warmth of the room, and seeing the floor-to-ceiling shelves of books, he felt happy.

Luther Cressman, a lean, clean-shaven twenty-five-year-old, had rushed from his class at the General Theological Seminary on West 21st Street, to reach his favorite bookstore before closing time. Brentano's, on Fifth Avenue, between 48th and 49th Streets, boasted the city's most complete collection of the classics, some even in their original Greek.

The smell of the books, the texture of their leather bindings, the varied thickness of the volumes, all of this created in Luther a feeling of well-being.

As he made his way down the aisle, Luther's head was still filled with the ideas he'd just been listening to, a lecture on Saint Thomas Aquinas, delivered by the elderly Father Arthur Jenks.

The experience, strangely mind-numbing and inspiring at the same time, had ended with an Aquinas quote that caught Luther's fancy: "If the highest aim of a captain were to preserve his ship, he would keep it in port forever." On the way out of class Luther had told his friend Holly, "I am going to write a paper for Jenks that will make his hair crack . . . I shall give him an earful."

Now, intent on making good on that promise, he headed for the history section.

Some minutes passed before the lights dimmed. Luther looked up to see the clerk crossing the floor, moving from tidying up the islands of books. Tucking a book under his arm and grabbing up another, Luther made his way to the cash register.

"One for myself," said Luther, placing a collection of essays by the pacifist Romain Rolland on the counter, "and one for my lady love," putting a slim volume of Sappho's poetry on top of it. "I couldn't resist."

Luther had a cleft chin and a high domed forehead topped with dark coppery-colored hair. His narrow face had a solemn aspect until something or someone grabbed his attention, then he was quick to break into an easy grin. But the most striking thing about his appearance were his eyes. It wasn't the color, which was a muddy blue-gray and indistinct, but the quality of his gaze. His fiancée, Margaret, called them "kind eyes."

Luther was the son of a country doctor, one of six brothers, all raised in Montgomery County, Pennsylvania. Born in 1897, he'd grown up at a time before telephone lines had been strung and when people still traveled by horse and buggy. As a boy he had especially enjoyed accompanying his father on house calls:

> I remember when in high school we had a terrible blizzard and papa could not get out. He had a typhoid patient out at Pughtown and had to go see him. We started on foot. The snow came in from that ridge of hills and stung the face like hail. It was drifted so that there wasn't any road. We just went, he and I.

Leaving Brentano's now Luther was on an equally important mission. He was on his way uptown, traveling by subway, to reach the infirmary.

For the last two weeks Luther had been worried about Margaret. She was very sick. The night she fell ill he'd been with her, and when she complained about how sore her throat was, he'd felt her forehead and it almost burned his hand. He'd half carried her over to Brooks Hall, the Barnard College infirmary. While they were in the waiting room he noticed that an angry red rash had spread across her cheeks. Then a nurse slid a thermometer under her tongue and a few minutes later announced that Margaret's fever was 103 degrees.

They'd led Margaret off to an examination room. Finally the nurse had come out, shaking her head. "Miss Mead has scarlet fever," she said. "She'll be with us for a while, I'm afraid."

By the end of the week, five other cases of scarlet fever had been confirmed and Miss Abbott, Barnard's assistant dean, was calling the girls the "Scarlet Six." They were to remain in the infirmary for at least six weeks under "strict quarantine," by order of New York's Board of Health.

Everyone knew that scarlet fever often damaged the heart and could even be fatal. What no one had dared yet say was that six cases, popping up at once, was a full-fledged epidemic, a potential catastrophe for the college. Hoping to keep a lid on the hysteria, Miss Abbott had written to parents, assuring them that "all sorts of investigations are being made by the college and health authorities to try to trace this germ to its source."

For Luther, the next stretch of days had seemed interminable.

At the end of the first week the nurses had reported that Margaret was still running a high fever, unable to eat solid foods or even swallow water. There was nothing any of them could do beyond plumping her pillows and applying cool compresses to her body. Luther knew that Margaret was in a fight for her life until the infection reached its crisis point, when her body's natural defenses would either kick in or fail.

Quite naturally, Luther had found it impossible to do much of anything, let alone concentrate on the research paper he was supposed to be writing for Father Jenks. He sent Margaret two letters a day, but she was too sick to answer.

Then on Christmas day, Margaret's mother telephoned. They had just received a telegram from Margaret:

Dear family cannot contaminate the telephone am doing swimmingly and simply drowned with letters and flowers the family ink bottle seems to have run dry yours with love and no germs.

It seemed that the worst was over, or so they all thought, but the quarantine was still in effect. Margaret wasn't allowed visitors, nor could she talk on the phone.

Greatly relieved, Luther was yearning for the sight of her, and her touch:

My arms ache for you, my lips are burnt for lack of your kisses, my body is weary with wanting you and my whole self is crying and longing and impatiently waiting for you, you, my own dearest love.

Margaret had always been his closest confidant. A few years earlier, when Luther had first started to contemplate a life in the clergy, Margaret had convinced him that the Episcopal Church might suit him better than his family's Lutheran faith. With her encouragement he'd enrolled at General Theological Seminary. Since then her influence over him had only increased. Recently she'd bragged to her mother: "You should see how far Luther has swerved toward the left wing since last winter. He no longer boasts an inflexible moral code nor a single reactionary principle, thank heaven."

While Margaret may have applauded Luther's move to the left, the Brothers at the seminary reacted differently. Luther told Margaret, "They have me down for a Bolshevik Red, Communist, Socialist or what not here—I guess I can stand it though. You watch me stand it."

Now, emerging from the subway stop, looking at the snow swirling around him, Luther found himself thinking once again about fate, and how it had swept him up in a maelstrom of events, events that all revolved around the Great War, as everything had in those days before he'd met Margaret.

Newspapers in the fall of 1916 had run story after story describing how the trenches in France were filling with corpses. Between July and November, over 400,000 British soldiers were wounded or killed in the fields along the Somme River.

During the spring of that year Luther had been in school at Penn State studying Ancient Greek, hearing about Heinrich Schliemann's excavation of Troy, and reading the plays of Sophocles. He was nineteen years old and those ancient tales, extolling the virtue of the great heroes of the battlefield, mixed with the news from overseas, lent the Battle of the Somme an even greater poignancy.

Full of idealism, Luther was determined to prepare himself for future service. That summer he enrolled in the Citizens Military Training Camp at the Plattsburgh Barracks in New York. After four weeks of field maneuvers that entailed slogging through the mud with full packs, and firing a Springfield rifle at targets at five and six hundred yards, Luther was commissioned to first lieutenant in the Cadet Regiment. In March of 1917, he wrote to his parents to ask for permission to enlist in a specialized naval unit. Two weeks passed and he still had not received a response. Then a letter came from his mother saying that their family home had burned to the ground.

Everything was gone. Mrs. Cressman needed him to come home to help run the family farm for the summer. His elder brother George was already there.

Sensitive to his parents' loss, both economic and emotional, Luther agreed. By Monday morning he was working as a farmer, cleaning out the barn, spreading manure on the field he would soon be plowing. His brother George was teaching science at the local high school in Doylestown. When the school principal asked George to give the commencement address he agreed and, borrowing their father's motorcar, brought Luther along for the occasion.

Before the evening ceremony Emily Mead, the mother of a girl in one of George's classes, invited the two young men to supper. Luther and George drove through the gentle rolling hills of Buckingham Township, then up a long dirt road lined with poplar trees to a faded white Georgian house. Luther was introduced to Emily's husband, Sherwood Mead, a university professor, and their eldest daughter Margaret, who appeared to be about sixteen.

Luther sat down to a rather tasteless plate of roast chicken, a dish that became even less appetizing when Professor Mead exhibited his caustic sense of humor, making derisive comments about the "folly of young men who were determined to enlist." While Sherwood was busy talking, taking thinly veiled potshots at George and Luther, Luther's gaze settled on Margaret. He was surprised to find her looking straight at him.

By December of 1917, Luther, George, and their parents had moved into a rented farmhouse in Pughtown.

With Americans now fighting overseas, all the talk at the Cressmans' table was about joining up. Fearing that the family might not be together again for a while, Mrs. Cressman summoned all her sons home for Christmas. To counterbalance the "heavily male contingent" she asked George to invite his "bright young student" Margaret, and her classmate, Esther, the sheriff's daughter, for Christmas lunch.

After the meal the brothers took their guests outside to French Creek, where the snow was deep and the ice was hard. Esther, a "thorough extrovert, was full of fun and laughter and willing to try almost anything, . . . quite the perfect foil for the rather intellectual Margaret."

Luther found himself skating with Margaret. With hands crossed, they circled the pond again and again. Luther pointed out a group of young children playing Crack the Whip.

"Look at that little fellow," he said, pointing to a small boy at the end of the line, now sitting on his bottom on the ice. "He's the lash. That's just what I always was. I used to clean up yards of ice and not with my skates."

Margaret laughed.

Pressing his luck, Luther took a gamble and started telling Margaret the story of Antigone, his favorite character in Sophocles' play by the same name. Antigone was willing to go to her death in defense of her beliefs; she was, in Luther's mind, "a timeless heroine." He was gratified to see that Margaret seemed to respond to the story.

A few nights later, on New Year's Eve, Margaret returned to the farm to visit with Luther. Bundled up against the cold, they set out on a walk toward Daisy Point. Stars sparkled in a black sky.

After about half a mile, they turned back. "We had said little, but our bodies by some subtle means exchanged messages as we walked arm in arm, our shoes crunching the dry snow in the bitter cold."

Seeing that they were almost home, Luther stopped. He turned Margaret toward him. For a moment they stood facing one another. "I love you, Margaret," he said, stepping forward to embrace her.

She lifted her veil worn against the cold. "I love you, too, Luther," she replied.

They kissed.

"Does this mean we're engaged?" she asked.

"I think it does," Luther said. "I really think so."

"I do, too," said Margaret.

For these two innocents, he just twenty years old, she barely sixteen, it was a kiss that sealed a secret, an engagement that they would keep hidden from family and friends.

They walked back to the farm, both awestruck by the enormity of what had just happened.

Luther did not delude himself about the obstacles that lay in their path. They both knew that he would be going off to war soon.

After college graduation Luther attended an ROTC camp. Trained for individual combat, the cadets were taught how to use bayonets by confronting bloodless, inanimate dummies on stakes. Commands were shouted, meant to drive them forward. "Grunt when you shove your bayonet into his guts, twist it."

In all this Luther excelled. The school-type exams designed to measure proficiency in the required skills identified him as an exemplary soldier. He was instructed to report to the Field Artillery Officers' Training School at Camp Taylor in Kentucky. Steeped as he was in humanistic values, this prospect presented an insoluble moral dilemma:

> We found ourselves part of a great machine organized for destruction. The object to be destroyed was always spoken of as the "target." . . . The sensitive and imaginative among us could not help but find conflict between the utter brutality of the behavior for which we were being trained and the moral values on which our lives were based.

For Luther, "The haunting question of 'Why did one, I, have to kill?'" would not go away. Finally, he decided that, at war's end, he would devote himself to the ideal of *eliminating* war. He would study for the ministry, for the priesthood of the Episcopal Church.

Then the influenza of 1918 struck, a pandemic responsible for fifty million deaths worldwide. Reaching Camp Taylor, it spread through the barracks where Luther was stationed, sending four out of five men either to the hospital or to their grave. In an effort to control the disease, the commanding officer quarantined all personnel for six weeks. By the time the danger of contagion lifted, the Armistice had been signed; the war was over.

Luther was free to be with Margaret.

Now, on this December night in 1921, the street lamps were glittering when Luther arrived at Brooks Hall. Walking through the wide portico into the lobby he was again dusting the snow off his coat. The night-duty nurse sat behind a desk by the elevator. His heart sank when he saw that it was Miss O'Connor, who, he suspected, "thinks I am mostly a bother." She and all the others knew him as "Margaret Mead's young man," a faithful visitor to Brooks Hall, even though he was barred from speaking to her or even advancing beyond the lobby.

Luther walked up to Miss O'Connor's desk. "Miss O'Connor," he said, "I hope I didn't shock you the last time I was here. When I said you should tell Margaret to tell her devils to go home."

"Goodness, Mr. Cressman. If you want to talk about devils, don't we all know what that's about. We know how active she wants to be. And how difficult it is for her."

"Here's something she might like," said Luther, handing over the book of Sappho's poems he'd bought at Brentano's.

Once outside on the sidewalk, he leaned back, feeling the snow lightly falling on his face. Craning his neck so he could see up to the seventh floor and the hallway where Margaret was installed, he spotted forms walking back and forth. He imagined Margaret in her nightgown and repeated to himself the words he had uttered so often in letters, "Dearest little girl, I love you, I love you, I love you."

Standing under a street lamp so that he was illuminated in a pool of light, he waved his hand high over his head, waiting, watching for a sign of recognition coming from the seventh floor. When he got no response he raised his arms again and waved them in great, sweeping exaggerated circles. Still he got nothing back.

On the sidewalk, people rushed past him, their heads down, avoiding the snow.

He started to wave again, but became self-conscious. It was foolish to continue making a spectacle of himself.

Then he saw one of the forms toss her hair in that spirited way Margaret had of announcing herself, with her chin lifted and her head slightly cocked.

He felt a rush of excitement.

Standing stock-still he stared up at the window. All of a sudden he didn't care if people looked at him because he was sure that this time he was seeing Margaret. And, oh, it was good to see her again. Then he thought he saw her looking straight at him. The light behind her made her hair look like a golden mist.

He thought to himself, "Now, that is the hair and face that I love to kiss and I shall soon be doing it again."

A while later, after he'd been sufficiently chilled, Luther walked on Broadway to 116th Street. He went down the stairs into the subway station. Once down on the platform, waiting for the train, he suddenly realized that he felt "all hot and cold and weak." On the train he started a letter:

Didn't you see me wave my hand to you . . . I raised it several times to my hat but I watched for a wave of recognition from you and though you looked at me I could not see you wave your hand. There were too many people around for me to do much conspicuous waving towards a girls' dormitory. I had everybody passing by looking up as it was but I did not care for I saw you.

By the time he got home it was late. He left the letter, unfinished, on his desk. The next morning he added a few sentences:

I dreamed about you last night. You could not guess what it was about either, I bet. You were not out of quarantine but somehow I was living near you and you came to my room for—guess what! To cut your hair! Can you imagine it! I did it too. I like such dreams.

GIRLS, UNMARRIED AS YET

I wish that you wouldn't tell me all the bribes that Dadda concocts because you know that I can't accept them, it would be a moral defeat for me to give up and come home. I am going to finish this year out. It wouldn't be worth anything to me if I didn't.

—MARGARET MEAD

March 1922

Margaret surveyed herself in the full-length mirror that hung on her closet door. She was dressed in the outfit that Mrs. Stengel, her mother's dressmaker, had made for her—a sensible navy blue tailored suit, appropriate for the month of March and the importance of the occasion.

Straightening her eyeglasses, taking in the overall effect, she sighed.

From the next room she could hear peals of laughter. Her roommates were yelling and talking, all at once. "Quiet ladies," came Léonie's voice, rising above the others, "I want to read you something. This is serious."

Turning back to the mirror, the task at hand, Margaret's gaze settled on her hairdo. Her hair, long, wavy, and honey-colored, was ordinarily her best feature. As a little girl, this was the hair her grandmother had lovingly brushed every night before she went to bed. For years she'd worn it loose and over her shoulders, but now, in deference to the seriousness of the occasion, the final debate of the year between Barnard and the girls from Wellesley, she had arranged it in an elaborate coif, a concoction that had taken nearly an hour to effect. The style—parted down the middle and wound over wire "cooties"—was not flattering.

While she didn't look her best, the hairstyle, Margaret reasoned, wasn't going to matter—it was going to be what she did onstage. For such a slip of a girl she had a remarkably powerful presence—and she knew it. She'd once said to a friend, "If I were a man, I would probably be one of those bantam fighters. . . . I think of myself as being small and fighting back . . . and so I speak with the voice of someone who is David vis-à-vis Goliath."

The year was 1922, and Margaret Mead was a junior at Barnard College in New York City. Ever since she'd transferred to Barnard the year before, she'd shared a dormitory style apartment at 606 West 116th Street with four other girls. Although the roommates had been thrown together by chance, she and the others—Léonie Adams, Pelham Kortheuer, Deborah Kaplan, and Bunny McCall—got along quite famously. Margaret had immediately taken charge of the room, selecting fabric for a new set of drapes, organizing formal afternoon teas, and introducing her roommates to Luther's friends at the seminary.

She was immensely happy.

Every letter home bubbled over with news of whichever matinee she'd just seen, from *Madame Butterfly* to *Hedda Gabler,* or the special little bookstore that she and Luther had discovered, or the outing they'd made to Coney Island. She told her mother, "I don't see how I ever could have gone anywhere else. To be up in here in this wonderful place and part of this great cosmopolitan university. . . . I just love it, love it, love it."

Margaret had the plain but endearing face of an eager schoolgirl. With blue eyes, set under eyebrows that were unfashionably thick, and a prominent chin, she exuded a bit too much determination to be called pretty. She took her grades very seriously and was in the habit of reporting all her academic triumphs to "Dadda," the name she called her father, Sherwood Mead, a professor at the Wharton School of Finance and Commerce.

She was also known to have strongly held opinions, and in spite of having a penchant for delivering these in a bossy tone, her diminutive size caused friends and family to address her in letters as "Girlie," "Little Girl," or "Dear Little Mar." Dadda, however, had gone one step further and named her "Punk."

Margaret had come to New York at a time when young ladies, including all of her roommates, were rebelling against the institution of marriage. They prided themselves on being what the magazines called "flappers," girls who drank, smoked, and dressed like tomboys. They sat up late into the night discussing how James Joyce's *Ulysses* had been unfairly banned and agreeing that the so-called Bolshevik takeover was a bunch of reactionary propaganda.

And while these girls might have dreaded ending up old maids every bit as much as their mother's generation had, they maintained they were *not* attending the university merely to find a husband. It was not commitment they were after, but romance and adventure. They idolized the Greenwich Village poet Edna St. Vincent Millay for applauding the merits of free love, and subscribed to her motto, "My candle burns at both ends; it will not last the night."

Margaret and her roommates so personified the flapper attitude that one of Barnard's professors singled them out, remarking to Léonie Adams, "You girls who sit up all night readin' poetry come to class lookin' like ash can cats." The nickname stuck. From then on they were known around campus as the "Ash Can Cats."

Every one of them ridiculed the idea of marrying young and starting a family—everyone, that is, except Margaret. In spite of the sea change that was occurring around her, Margaret was wholeheartedly committed to marrying Luther Cressman. As far as she was concerned, "He made all the nonsense about dates—or not having dates—irrelevant."

Basking in Luther's devotion, Margaret never had to feel she was "among the rejected and un-chosen." From the safety of a secure relationship, she watched as the others surrendered themselves to the highs and lows of infatuation. While her roommates turned their dressing tables into shrines dedicated to the promise of the night, littered with pots of makeup, mascara brushes, and perfume bottles, Margaret's table was covered with books. Her vision of the future included marriage to an Episcopalian minister, setting up house in a rural parish, raising a passel of children, and immersing herself in a career, as yet to be determined.

Margaret was the only one of her friends who had not yet cut her hair in the new style, the bob. Chopped off at chin length, with a fringe of bangs over the forehead, this wildly popular hairdo was the emblem of the flapper. Above all, it was a statement of something they all believed in—a woman's right to be assertive in the world.

For her part, Margaret was not lacking in boldness, but her hair—long and golden and the only aspect of her appearance that she really liked—made a different statement. And while she was quick to make the disclaimer that she cared very little about how she looked, defiantly wearing her eyeglasses no matter what the occasion, she was loath to give up her one tenuous claim to beauty, writing home to her mother, "I haven't bobbed my hair yet because the apartment objected."

Margaret, now crossing campus, couldn't help but reflect on how different things were since she'd transferred to Barnard. Not that long ago she'd been a freshman at DePauw University in the small town of Greencastle, Indiana. Looking back, it seemed like someone else's life.

For a girl who'd grown up on a farm in Bucks County, on the outskirts of Philadelphia, DePauw had been an unlikely choice. In fact, it had never been a choice at all. When the question of what college to attend had been raised and Margaret had announced she wanted to apply to Wellesley, her mother's alma mater, Dadda had said she wasn't going to go to any college at all. His decision, he said, was based on bad news he'd received about one of his business ventures. He simply couldn't afford the tuition.

Fortunately her mother had figured out that the easiest way around Dadda's objections was to appeal to his vanity. When Emily suggested that Margaret attend *his* alma mater—DePauw—Dadda promised he would find the money to send her.

Margaret had looked forward to DePauw with excitement, and a touch of apprehension. While she could hardly wait to partake of the "intellectual feast" she imagined was waiting, her main preoccupation had been how to make friends, and lots of them. Her mother had tried to help by letting her plan her wardrobe with Mrs. Stengel and by allowing her to pick out the color scheme for her dorm room, which they had finally decided would be old rose and blue.

Once at DePauw, Margaret had immediately thrown herself into the whirl of Sorority Rush, writing to Mother:

> *The invitations to the sorority rush parties came out this morning. I received a Kappa invitation for which I understand I should be extremely grateful. . . . I'm going to their party tonight. My roommates both got Tri Delt invitations. These are not bids to enter the sorority, it's just a preliminary rush party.*

She arrived at the Kappas early, before any of the others. She was wearing a dress she had designed herself, an eccentric frock that was supposed to "represent a field of wheat with poppies against a blue sky." The skirt, made of a stiff silver-green material, was accordion-pleated; the blouse was a loose-fitting, diaphanous affair, cut from Georgette crêpe.

Margaret and the other rushes mingled in the foyer, before they were guided down the receiving line of sorority sisters and into the parlor. Seated on a straight-backed chair, Margaret sipped tea and kept up a constant flow of small talk. Caught up in the excitement of the moment, she failed to notice how the girls were reacting.

Apparently, the Kappas found Margaret's Main Line accent affected, her dress unfashionable, and her lack of makeup an unforgivable social gaffe. It was not until five days later that she learned she was one of only a handful of freshman who had not received an invitation to join a sorority. Ostracized by the popular girls, excluded from the fraternity parties, she could look forward to spending her weekends alone in the dorm.

It was the first time in her life she had experienced organized rejection. The pain was intense. When she turned to her parents, Dadda refused to coddle her:

> Don't let this fraternity thing get on your nerves. If you do good work and make yourself strong in your class, they will be fighting for you before the year is out. I hope you will throw them all down and do it publicly, that is, if you are sure they are as snobbish or as clannish as you say. I am disturbed that you pay any attention to the matter.

Margaret was not appeased. As the weeks dragged on and her letters dwelled on how lonely she felt, her father wrote again:

> Mar . . . Really, I can't make you out but I have an abiding faith in your ability to get what you want, if not in one way, then in another. The only way to get what you want is to find out who has the disposal of it, then bring pressure to bear on that person.

Still miserable, Margaret looked forward to only one thing—spending Christmas with the family. And she was desperate to go home for Christmas. Then her father dropped a bombshell. Writing her that money was short, he said he couldn't afford to bring her back.

Margaret immediately turned to her mother. "Please let me come

home. We have sixteen days now and surely that is long enough to justify the journey. Please, mother, I never was so homesick in my life."

Then Dadda sent another letter suggesting that if the DePauw experience was *that* unsatisfactory, perhaps she should consider coming home
at Christmas and staying for good. She could enroll at the University of
Pennsylvania and spend the spring in town.

Margaret rallied with a storm of protest.

> *Dear Dadda . . . I am not to be tempted. Has not long acquaintance*
> *with me convinced you of that? All the alluring things you propose,*
> *through mother, are lovely of course. I would like nothing better*
> *except to finish what I've begun. I stay here the rest of the year, and*
> *nothing, not being allowed to come home at Christmas, or the pros-*
> *pect of a winter in town will make me change my mind.*

Telling her parents that "it would be a moral defeat" to give up and
come home, she finished out the year. Only when her final exams were
behind her did she put in an application to transfer to Barnard, the
women's college affiliated with Columbia University.

Although neither she nor her father acknowledged it, they had come
to an understanding: she had earned the right to study in the same city
as her beau, Luther Cressman. Now, two years later and looking back
on all of it, Margaret was quite pleased with the way she'd comported
herself. She didn't realize it, but Dadda was, too.

On this blustery March day, Margaret made her way across campus,
toward Barnard's small Brinckerhoff Theatre. With her arms clasped
around her, she put her head down and marched forward into the
wind.

Three weeks earlier, when the subject of the debate had been posted,
Margaret had been thrilled. The topic, "Resolved that European Immigration should be further restricted," was one that engaged her interest.
America, in her mind, had always been a land of immigrants, and should
remain so. As the most humane country in the world, wasn't it incumbent upon the United States to welcome all who sought a better life? She
immediately announced, "I'm going out for the negative." But when the
teams received their assignments, Barnard had been selected to represent

the affirmative. It would be her job to argue for a tight quota on immigration. In a letter home she wrote that she "did not believe in a restrictive immigration policy" and complained that debate practice was "crawling along," adding, "I have such a strong emotional bias it is extremely difficult for me to get up any interest in the matter." Her father, however, dismissed her misgivings, and congratulating her on being chosen to compete in the final debate, told her to "write out every possible argument of the other side" and to make her rebuttal "snappy."

For as long as Margaret could remember, Dadda had coached her in the art of public speaking. In high school, before every competition, they'd gone to work on her delivery.

Dadda, his legs propped up on an ottoman, sat in his chair. Margaret stood in the center of the room, facing him. As soon as she started, Dadda would yell, "Look me in the eye! Pick someone to speak to!" He told her the first rule of public speaking was to avoid "the lawn sprinkler method." He never wanted to see her "scatter her words" over an audience.

Thanks to Dadda's coaching, Margaret had come to understand that the success of one's presentation had as much to do with body language as it did with the content that was delivered.

Today's debate, the final competition between the squads from Barnard and Wellesley, was the most important of the year and, considering Margaret's emotional bias, it was going to be challenging. She was resolved to view the event as a contest, not as an expression of her personal point of view. She had written to her mother, "Goodness knows whether I'll do well or not, but I'd like to have you and Dadda here."

Once inside the auditorium Margaret took her place among her teammates. The Wellesley girls were already assembled. The Chair directed the speakers to move to the stage.

A girl from Wellesley spoke first: "The time once was when we welcomed to our shores the oppressed and downtrodden people from the world over, and they came to us because of oppression at home and with the sincere purpose of making true and loyal American citizens."

When it was time for her to speak Margaret rose from her chair and walked to the podium. She looked out at her audience, cleared her throat. "It is time that we act now, because in a few short years the damage will have been done. The endless tide of immigration will have filled our country with a foreign and unsympathetic element."

The words tasted bitter as she spoke them. Reminding herself that public speaking was play-acting, she went on, "Those who are out of sympathy with our Constitution and the spirit of our government will be here in large numbers, and the true spirit of Americanism left us by our fathers will gradually become poisoned by this uncertain element."

As she surveyed the faces that looked back at her, Margaret found she wasn't nervous. She found that her voice, surprisingly, did not waver. She felt in command of her facts. She felt she knew more than her opponents. When she returned to her chair and sat down, she allowed herself to take a deep breath. She was pleased with both her performance and herself.

Then it was all over, and the audience was clapping. There were a few nervous minutes while the judges conferred. Then the decision was announced.

The judges had voted unanimously for the Wellesley team.

Margaret rose from her seat and began to shake hands with the victors. She couldn't get over it. How was it possible? Her body felt cold and clammy; she noticed she was shivering. As she walked through the auditorium she overheard someone say that Barnard had all the facts, but had fallen short on style. Someone else said the Barnard girls should have worked harder to master the technique.

Was it true? she asked herself. Had *she* fallen short on technique? Was her delivery weak? Had she been slumped over while she was speaking?

Suddenly she was conscious of her hair, which had been coiled in place all day. Reaching up she began to yank out the bobby pins, one by one, letting the hair tumble down.

When she returned to the apartment all the girls were gone except for Léonie, who was sitting at the kitchen table, bent over her typewriter, furiously pounding the keys. Margaret kept her face averted as she moved to hang up her coat.

"I'm nearly finished with my article," Léonie called out.

Margaret heard a bang as Léonie slapped the carriage return. Walking past her and going into the bedroom Margaret threw down her jacket and began unbuttoning her blouse.

Then she felt someone's shadow behind her and heard Léonie's voice. "Listen to this. Coolidge actually singles out Barnard from all the other schools. Barnard, can you believe it? He says, 'You can't go through Barnard without knowing the principles of socialism.'"

Margaret looked in the mirror and saw Léonie's reflection looming over her, holding a cigarette in one hand and waving a typewritten page in the other.

Léonie thrust the paper toward her. "Tell me what you think of this as a title, 'Cheer up, Mr. Coolidge'?"

Taking the paper, Margaret began to read.

Léonie's editorial was the rebuttal to an opinion piece written by Vice President Calvin Coolidge, published earlier that week in *The Delineator*, a woman's magazine. Titled "Are the Reds Stalking Our College Women?" it alleged that anarchists and radicals were overrunning the nation's best colleges and endangering America's young women. The imagined foes, as conjured up by Coolidge, were spreading a gospel that was "hostile to our American form of government, to the established personal right to hold property and the long recognized sanctions of civilized society."

Margaret and her roommates had pronounced the Coolidge piece laughable. All week long they'd read parts out loud, reacting with jeers and derision. As far as they were concerned, there were no agitators on campus, unless they themselves were the agitators.

Now Léonie—known around campus as a rebellious spirit and a budding poet—had taken on Coolidge. Recently named the editor of *The Barnard Bulletin*, she intended to run her editorial on the front page.

For Margaret, the coincidence was more than ironic. While Léonie had been concentrated on framing an attack against Coolidge, Margaret had spent the day defending him and applauding his restrictive immigration policy, a policy that was—as far as she was concerned—paranoid, reactionary, and wrong.

That night Margaret and Luther went to dinner at Galati's. They had planned to try for last-minute seats to see Katharine Cornell in *A Bill of Divorcement*, but Margaret's head hurt too much to sit through a play.

Knowing her as he did, Luther was not surprised that Margaret was taking her defeat so hard. Margaret was nothing if not determined—and competitive.

Through dinner Margaret pondered the loss, revisiting those pivotal moments in the debate, trying to identify the point when things had gone wrong.

"What didn't I do?"

"You had the weaker argument," said Luther.

"Yes, but I *knew* how to present it. At least I thought I did."

"Maybe it's not losing that bothers you," he said.

"What do you mean?"

"Maybe it's being on the wrong side."

"You always refuse to understand how a debate works. I *have* to be on whatever side they assign me to."

"Yes, and you have to exploit whatever weakness you can find in the other side, even if you don't believe it."

"That's politics," she said.

"Well?"

"Well, nothing. That *is* politics."

Margaret went back to the apartment feeling glum. When she stepped through the door, she found the lights out, the rooms empty. All the girls were out.

She hadn't liked what Luther had said and she didn't accept it. She was good at public speaking, at debating, and that talent might get her somewhere if she went into politics.

She moved on into the bedroom she shared with Léonie.

On Léonie's side of the room, clothes and undergarments were heaped on the floor, strewn about on every available surface. Cigarette stubs filled the ashtray. The desk where Léonie wrote her verse was buried under piles of books and crumpled papers. Apparently, the disorder left Léonie unfazed.

Léonie's verse was so good it had already been published in the highly respected poetry journal *The Measure*. As far as Margaret was concerned, to be recognized as a poet was to achieve near mystical stardom. This was due in part to the cult of personality that had sprung up around the soldier-poets of the Great War, and in part because writing poetry was one of the few endeavors in which women were allowed to shine. Amy Lowell's name was familiar to every English major and Edna St. Vincent Millay's voice, low and timorous, was as recognizable as her shock of red hair. Now Léonie—one of Margaret's own roommates—seemed to be on the verge of joining this elite sisterhood. Margaret was the first to give her credit, saying, "Léonie is a real poet; none of the rest of us is a real anything yet," but that didn't make her success any easier to accept. Léonie's poetry gave her a celebrity status that Margaret desperately wanted for herself.

Margaret had to wonder, however was Léonie able to pull serious work out of the chaos of her life, the infatuation, the ecstasy, and the heartbreak that always seemed to trail in her wake? For a girl as conscientious as Margaret, who relied on self-will and determination, Léonie's success was maddening.

That night in bed, Margaret's thoughts returned to the question of her future. The talk with Luther had left her even more confused. He had forced her to acknowledge that debating was dishonest.

Without the debate squad, she would be cut adrift. She needed a focus for her prodigious energy. Believing that a unique talent *must* be lurking within her, she was impatient to identify it. As one friend had said, she was "like a missile waiting to be directed."

By the time she closed her eyes, she'd come to the same conclusion she'd reached on many other nights: that no one—not Dadda, not Grandma, and not even Luther—was going to set her on her path. That was something she was going to have to discover for herself.

The pair of scissors in the barber's hand was silver, sharp, and shiny.

Margaret sat in a swivel chair in the barber's shop, looking out the big plate glass window. She wore a smock over her dress and her dark golden hair was spread like a canopy over her shoulders.

The barber grabbed a handful of hair and pulled it taut.

Scissors make a distinct sound as they cut through hair, a crisp slicing sound, very final. The sound seems even more distinct when the hair in question falls to a girl's waist and hasn't been cut in years.

Margaret watched clumps of it fall to the floor.

Suddenly she thought about her grandmother, her tiny little grandma who ruled the family with her kindness. When Margaret was a little girl, she used to love to sit at Grandma's dressing table, with its frosted glass jar full of cold cream and the hand-painted handkerchief box. There, every night before bedtime, Grandma brushed her hair and told her stories of what it had been like for her, growing up.

She told me about . . . Great Aunt Louisian, who could read people's minds and tell them everything they had said about her and who had been a triplet and so small when she was born that she would fit into a quart cup . . . and about the time . . . Lida cut off [Louisian's] . . . curls, and said, "Now they won't say 'pretty little girl' anymore."

———

Margaret looked down at the pile of hair accumulating around her feet. Straightening the spectacles on her nose as the barber turned her chair toward the mirror, she looked at her reflection.

The heaviness had dropped away from her.

She reached up to feel the short blunt ends of her hair. They felt healthy and strong. She stared at herself. Her newly shorn locks stuck out around her face, untamed, unruly, and boyish. The scissored-off hair would be easy to take care of, certainly a plus.

Now, like Aunt Louisian, no one was going to call her "pretty little girl" anymore.

Yes, somehow this new haircut was going to be more in keeping with who she was, and with the person she wanted to become.

A COURSE IN OLD MAIDS

So much of the trouble is because I am a woman. To me
it seems a terrible thing to be a woman. There is one crown
which perhaps is worth it all—a great love, a quiet home,
and children.

—RUTH BENEDICT

November 1922

On the days she was teaching, like she was scheduled to do today, Ruth Fulton Benedict made a point of walking the full forty blocks from Columbia University to the American Museum of Natural History. She traveled first down Broadway, and then cut across at 86th Street over to Central Park West. The purposeful rhythm of her long, athletic stride, the swing of her arms, the feel of the air against her face, all calmed her nerves, helped her to mentally prepare. Good, hard physical exertion—whether it be rowing, hiking, or chopping firewood—was the thing she'd always relied on to focus her mind.

Today Ruth was scheduled to take a group of anthropology students through the Museum's Plains Indian Hall. As one of only three PhD candidates in Columbia's Department of Anthropology, she had been asked to help Professor Franz Boas teach his introductory course.

Ruth was thirty-five years old, tall and slender, with an athletic grace. Upon first meeting she projected an outward calm, causing one female colleague to say she "resembled the platonic ideal of a poetess." Yet there was tentativeness to her nature, a hesitancy that always seemed to dog her. When she dropped by the anthropology office, her colleagues pronounced her a disappointment. Rather than engage in department gossip, she held herself apart, responding to their overtures by nodding assent or offering a vague noncommittal smile.

On this November morning, Ruth was doing her best to mask her discomfort. Even though the dimly lit hall, with its cool marble columns and lofty depths provided cover, she found the prospect of delivering a lecture daunting. What was so difficult, she wondered, about standing in front of a dozen young people, many of whom were actually receptive, to talk about a subject she knew like the back of her hand? Whether it be the Sun Dance of a Cheyenne brave or the consecration of a Pawnee tribal bundle, these were rituals that sprang from a world she had made her own.

Ruth stopped in front of a tall, sun-bleached pole cut from pine, an artifact from a Cheyenne Sun Dance, and turned to face the students. "Today we must ask, what was the Vision Quest, and how was the Vision obtained?"

A few of the students opened their notebooks and began to take notes.

"In spite of a diversity of local setting," said Ruth, "the tribes of the Plains all sought communication with the Spirit. That Spirit might be some animal, bird, or voice. And the thing that spoke to the suppliant—animal, bird, or voice—that thing became his 'Guardian Spirit.'"

As usual, Ruth's explanation was coming in fits and starts but this morning, as she attempted to describe the Vision Quest, she seemed even more uncomfortable, at times pausing so long between thoughts the more sensitive of her students felt embarrassed for her.

Ruth, unaware that she was having an effect on her students, would have been stunned to know that any of them worried about her lack of composure. As it happened, however, one of them did. A diminutive girl was registering her concern by nudging her elbow into the side of a classmate.

Facing the tall pine pole, totally focused on its function, Ruth was endeavoring to bring to life the Cheyenne Sun Dance. "Whenever the Cheyenne came together," she said, "it was common to see men torturing themselves." She herself had no trouble imagining the glistening bodies of the braves, swinging in the baking heat and rising dust, and she wanted her students to see the image, too. With her head leaned back, she pointed up, to the long strips of rawhide that dangled from the top of the pole. "Sometimes they would retire to a lonely hill where they were pierced and tied and suspended from poles, poles just like this one."

Moving on, Ruth stopped in front of an illuminated case that held ceremonial objects, including a knife and a dozen sharply pointed wooden pegs. "Dr. Grinnell, in *When Buffalo Ran*, gives us the only concrete description we have of what happened at the start of the Sun Dance."

She opened a thin book to the passage she had marked:

> *A suppliant goes out to a lonely part of the prairie on the day selected, accompanied by the person who is to tie the thongs for him. Pins and knife are consecrated by prayer and held toward the sun and sky. . . . He is then tied to the pole by means of wooden pins driven through the flesh.*

Some of the students gasped. The wooden pegs, arranged so neatly in the case, had suddenly taken on a new meaning.

"It's important to note," continued Ruth, "for the Cheyenne, the use of torture in the Vision Quest, is strongly established."

"Excuse me, Mrs. Benedict," someone said.

Ruth turned to see who had spoken.

"Mrs. Benedict? About these rituals," and then the girl said something Ruth didn't quite catch.

Ruth looked at the girl who had asked the question.

"Mrs. Benedict, can you give us the names of other anthropologists who've done the studies?"

Smiling quizzically, Ruth groped to retrieve the girl's name—it was Margaret Mead. The truth was Ruth could give this student many references if only she'd heard her question clearly, but she hadn't. A childhood case of the measles had left Ruth partially deaf. Usually she was able to compensate by lip-reading but in the dim light of the exhibition hall this was impossible.

Now, unaware that Margaret—her question unanswered—felt snubbed, Ruth walked on to the next display case. Nodding toward a set of steel pins, she said, "The Blackfoot practiced another custom called 'Feeding-the-sun with-bits-of-one's body.' According to Dr. Wissler, 'The skin is pricked up by a splinter or sharp knife, and a coin-shaped piece cut from beneath.'"

The hall was quiet as the students, understanding what the inherent use of the steel pins must have been, took notes.

Not one of them, including the girl who radiated such purpose, could have guessed that their teacher had not arrived at her topic by chance.

Ruth's interest in the infliction of self-torture was rooted in her own life experience, brought on by a cascade of tragedies that had overwhelmed her childhood.

Ruth Benedict had been born Ruth Fulton in New York City in 1887. Her father, Frederick Fulton, a homeopathic physician who specialized in the study of tumors, was stricken with a debilitating illness by the time she turned one. As best the medical experts could surmise, Dr. Fulton had been infected with a mysterious bacterium while working in the operating theater. Within two years he was dead. Ruth retained only one memory of him as a "worn face, illuminated with the translucence of illness and very beautiful."

Ruth's mother Beatrice—left to care for Ruth and a newborn daughter—descended into a prolonged state of mourning. She had little energy for a child who was not responsive to direction. Not realizing that Ruth's inattention was caused by impaired hearing, Bertrice was quick to interpret her behavior as willful disobedience.

For her part, Ruth resented her mother's "cult of grief" and reacted by throwing tantrums. Her mother was determined to subdue Ruth's violent temper. Their struggle, which went on for years, culminated in an event that had an almost medieval quality when, according to Ruth, her mother "forced her to kneel with a candle on a cold floor until God granted her prayer that she would never again lose control of her temper."

It was around this time that Ruth established a rule for herself that was to persist throughout her life. She made it a "taboo" to express emotion in front of anyone, even when she was in physical pain. Maintaining a distance from other human beings made her feel comfortable. She was to say that during childhood she couldn't remember "any longing to have any person love me."

If Bertrice hadn't been so preoccupied she would have realized that her daughter was withdrawing deeper and deeper into her own world. She was, however, focused on the need to make a living and, as a single mother, was pursuing the only career open to women—teaching. All of her sacrifice seemed worth it when—in 1905—her two daughters were awarded full scholarships to attend Vassar College.

Vassar, the preeminent institution of higher education for women, was situated on the Hudson River, two hours north of New York City.

In order to get there, Ruth and her sister Margery took the train to a depot in the gritty industrial town of Poughkeepsie, and from there were conveyed by carriage past several mansions perched high above the Hudson. Their driver made a point of letting them know that these estates belonged to American royalty, families not unlike the Roosevelts and the Vanderbilts. Later, Ruth came to understand that the college administrators, who had been entrusted with the sacred task of turning out finished ladies, were intent on guiding their charges toward a version of that gilded future.

At Vassar, sequestered within a medieval quad, shaded under old-growth pines, the girls were fed a curriculum that included Greek, Latin, history, and a smattering of the sciences. It was just enough education to enable a young woman to shine in high society before she matriculated to her real career, that of becoming the wife of a wealthy man and the mother of his children.

In 1911, two years after graduation, Ruth moved out to California to stay with Margery, who by now was married and living in a modest bungalow near Pasadena, a town to the northeast of Los Angeles.

The arrangement suited them both. Ruth was adrift, and Margery needed help caring for her two babies. There, amongst citrus groves and stately mansions, Ruth observed yet another culture that was built on wealth and power. Within a year she had secured a job teaching English literature at the exclusive Miss Orton's Classical School for Girls.

It was during this period that Ruth began to keep a journal. In it she acknowledged her fight with anxiety and depression saying, "I seemed to keep my grip only by setting my teeth and playing up to the mask I had chosen." In another entry she elaborated on how her mask functioned:

> *What was my character anyway? My real* me *was a creature I dared not look upon—it was terrorized by loneliness, frozen by a state of futility, obsessed by longing to stop. No one had ever heard of that* me. *If they had they would have thought it was an interesting pose. The mask was tightly adjusted.*

It was in this journal that Ruth constantly returned to her concern over the future. The problem, as she saw it, was that she had been born a woman. She bemoaned the "terrible destiny" that dictated what her quest must be—finding the "right man." She mocked her circumstances, saying, "we women . . . have not the motive to prepare ourselves for a 'life-work' of teaching, of social work—we know we would lay it down with hallelujah in the height of our success, to make a home for the right man."

Yet, in spite of all her defiant words, Ruth was still held in the yoke of society's conventions, consumed with the question that invariably loomed up in the life of a young woman: when would she make the transition from maidenhood to marriage? Or, heaven forbid, would the unthinkable occur, would she miss this crucial passage, only to be relegated to the category of "old maid" or "spinster"? For in Ruth's universe, these were the only terms that were available to describe a woman over the age of thirty who had failed to secure a husband.

One evening, on the way home from school, Ruth walked several blocks with Miss Van Rossum, another teacher at the Orton School. The street lamps had just come on, then the lights inside the bungalows followed. Miss Van Rossum sighed. "There are so many homes. There ought to be enough to go around."

Ruth surveyed the houses, glowing with life and movement inside. It was a far cry from what Van Rossum would find when she arrived at her rented room.

That night over dinner with Margery and her husband, Bob, Ruth brought up the unmarried teachers she'd met at Miss Orton's school.

"I don't want to end up like them," said Ruth. "The spinsters."

Margery looked up from her plate. "Why should you?"

"There are three at school," said Ruth.

Margery laughed. "It's your course in old maids."

"It really isn't a joke at all. It's quite tragically serious," said Ruth. "They retell all their old conversations with men, ones that they had twenty years ago. Conversations that of course might have developed into love affairs, if they'd allowed the men the liberty."

Margery and Bob exchanged glances.

"One is supposed to believe they're not old maids by necessity. All except Miss Van Rossum," said Ruth. "She told me no one ever let her suspect that he was ever even interested. It's she who is really tragic."

Ironically, just at the point Ruth was calculating the odds of becoming a spinster, she was also fending off the attentions of a serious suitor. His name was Stanley Benedict, the older brother of Agnes Benedict, a friend from Vassar.

Stanley was a professor of biochemistry at the Cornell Medical

College in Manhattan, and his field of research—the ability of chemicals to inhibit the growth of cancer cells—bore an uncanny similarity to the work her father had done with his own patients.

After Ruth had left for California, Stanley had taken up the challenge, bombarding her with letters. Yet it was precisely this ardor, so strongly expressed, that frightened Ruth. She remained unyielding and impassive.

Much like Artemis, the Greek goddess of the hunt—that fleet-footed virgin—she embodied a quality of inaccessibility.

And then, writing in a letter, Stanley demonstrated that he had an understanding of the real Ruth, the one she hid from the world:

> And Ruth—your mask is getting thicker and thicker—I could see that it is—and that's all wrong. . . . You shouldn't have to wear it at all, for it's certain to grow to be a part of you if you do—and then you'll be altogether alone, and it's so wrong for you Ruth.

In June of 1914, Ruth Fulton returned to New York to marry Stanley Benedict. She was twenty-seven years old.

In some ways, married life turned out to be more agreeable than Ruth ever dreamed possible. The demand for intimacy—which had terrified her during the courtship—was gone. Stanley was so engrossed in his work he barely had time to spend with her, and when he did, he didn't expect her to engage in a cloying or demonstrative show of affection.

They settled down in Bedford Hills, a bedroom community within commuting distance of New York City. On weekdays, Stanley traveled into the city, to his research lab. Ruth envied the intensity with which he threw himself into work, which contrasted so greatly with her own vague restlessness, or what she called "the ennui of life without purpose." She spoke to Stanley about her discontent:

> Last night Stanley and I talked. We hurt each other badly, for words are clumsy things, and he is inexorable. . . . I said that for the sake of our love—our friendship, rather—I must pay my way in a job of my own. I would not, would not drift into . . . boredom.

Stanley didn't understand why she was so dissatisfied, and said "whatever the job," she might find it would not hold her.

Then, after several years together, when she still remained childless, she began to obsess over having a baby. This yearning frightened Stanley, who warned her that a child wouldn't fix things.

Finding herself more and more distanced from Stanley, Ruth turned to writing, completing several biographical sketches about "restless and highly enslaved women of the past," including one on Mary Wollstonecraft, an eighteenth-century advocate for women's rights. She was unable to find a publisher for any of them. Then, in 1919, Ruth drifted into a course that was being offered at the progressive New School for Social Research in lower Manhattan. The class, taught by Elsie Clews Parsons, a well-married patron of avant-garde causes, was called "Sex in Ethnology" and it opened Ruth's eyes to what was a brand-new field of study—anthropology. The next semester, Ruth enrolled in a second class, this one given by Alexander Goldenweiser, a provocative thinker who was not afraid to relate the study of cultural behavior to psychoanalysis.

Ruth's experience at the New School stirred something in her that she had been seeking without ever realizing it—a connection with a community of individuals who shared her worldview. Finally a discipline had presented itself that she wanted to pursue.

With the encouragement of Parsons and Goldenweiser, Ruth sought the advice of Franz Boas, the head of the Department of Anthropology at Columbia University and the acknowledged leader in the field.

By 1920, Dr. Franz Boas had been directing ethnographical doctoral dissertations for nearly twenty years, ever since he'd introduced anthropology as a field of study at the university. During that span of time he'd shaped an entire generation of ethnographers, men who accepted his idea that it was crucial to make a record of cultures and languages that were on the verge of extinction. Beginning in 1908, he'd helped his most promising disciples secure jobs at universities and museums across the continent. They in turn disseminated his ideas and many, like Alfred Kroeber, at the University of California at Berkeley, established their own anthropology departments.

At sixty-two years of age, Boas's once black hair was gray and his right check was twisted by a palsy. In spite of the ravages of time, his "whole face and head had in them something aquiline, resolute, decisive and poised." Although short of stature, his presence was formidable. His German accent and stern demeanor made him seem unapproachable.

According to Alfred Kroeber, Boas went about the business of teaching with an "icy enthusiasm."

Either in spite of that quality or because of it, graduate students gravitated to Boas. It was well known that he was able to perceive in them innate talents that even they did not know they possessed. He used his insight to match individuals with the topics that most interested them. Not only did this habit win him the undying loyalty of his students, it also produced good work.

When Dr. Boas first sat down with Ruth Benedict to discuss a possible area for graduate work, they agreed that for her initial research she would study diverse forms of religious experience. This could be done in the library. She need not go into the field, something she was reluctant to do. She could read the accounts that had been recorded by missionaries and the early ethnographers, some dating back as far as 1850, written by men who had spent time on the central plains, living among the Blackfoot, Cheyenne, and the Dakota. Several of the early ethnographers had even cultivated close relationships with "informants"—individuals who had been willing to provide information—who had taken them into the sacred circle so they could witness the Vision-Quest ritual in its purest form.

On most days Ruth worked out of the small reading room on the third floor of the Museum of Natural History. Usually she was the only student using the facilities. Government publications and dusty professional journals lined the shelves, each volume a dark olive green, with the date of publication printed on its spine. She came to appreciate this body of literature as a nearly complete account of Native American spiritual life, as it had been perceived by the first generation of ethnographers. Over time she began to recognize connections between apparently disparate tribes, covering a vast geographical area. A pattern emerged, which gave shape to her thesis that Plains Indians had used self-inflicted torture to aid them in their quest to achieve a visionary experience.

Two weeks before Christmas of 1921, Ruth completed a lengthy paper called "The Vision in Plains Culture." Her thesis boldly set forth the importance of the vision:

> *Not only the means of obtaining the vision . . . but the events of the vision itself . . . ceremonial procedure, healing powers, success in*

battle and control of the weather . . . were standardized over thou-
sands of miles, east and west, and north and south.

The paper described the dynamic between the suppliant who sought
the vision, and the Guardian Spirit who had the power to confer it. In
some tribes, such as the Crow, this relationship was so intimate that the
initiate believed the Spirit had "adopted" him. Ruth wrote movingly
about the tenderness of this spiritual bond, saying, "The power that ap-
pears to the Crow addresses him in set words, 'I make you my son.'"

Boas was impressed enough to suggest she send a copy to the *Amer-*
ican Anthropologist, the discipline's most highly regarded journal.

Eight months later, on a hot morning in July, Ruth Benedict climbed
the stairs to the fourth floor of Schermerhorn Hall, hoping to see
Dr. Boas. His office door was closed, no light emanated through its
frosted glass pane. As she turned to go, a voice stopped her.

"Mrs. Benedict, a letter came for you."

It was Esther Goldfrank, the secretary who did all of Dr. Boas's typing.

Reaching out, Ruth took the letter. She felt at once that the envelope had some heft to it. She noticed on the top right corner a long row
of Canadian stamps. Dropping the envelope into her briefcase she descended the stairs. Only when she was outside did she examine it.

The return address indicated that the letter had been sent by Edward
Sapir. She could hardly believe it.

The name Edward Sapir was well known to Ruth even though she'd
never met the man. For the last decade Sapir had been in charge of ethnographic studies for *all* of Canada. A brilliant linguist, he'd mastered
more than twenty of the Native American languages, a nearly impossible feat. At only thirty-eight years old, he was considered Boas's most
brilliant protégé.

Ruth tore open the envelope and pulled out a thick wad of folded
pages, twelve in all.

"Dear Mrs. Benedict, I read your paper yesterday in one breath, interrupted by supper, most necessary of distractions, only," it began. "Let
me congratulate you on having produced a very fine piece of research.
It makes a notable addition to the body of historical critiques that anthropology owes to Boas."

This validation, coming from a total stranger, and one who stood at

the pinnacle of their profession, was the most meaningful acknowl-
edgment Ruth had ever received. Although much of its content was a
running monologue that allowed Sapir to demonstrate his *own* brilliance,
Ruth still felt as if he was granting her admission into an elite fraternity. His praise, and the conspiratorial tone he adopted, seemed to say
they were on equal footing.

Over the next weeks and months, Ruth did everything she could to
learn more about Edward Sapir. She read his books, sought out his essays, made inquiries about his marriage, and learned that, from time to
time, he made trips to New York, the city where he had been raised.

He was, according to rumor, the man who was destined to take over
the department when Boas retired.

Then, right before Christmas break, Esther Goldfrank gave her the
news that, sometime in January, Edward Sapir would be coming to New
York.

As Ruth walked through the museum hallway, lost in thought, a voice
jolted her out of her reverie.

"Excuse me, Mrs. Benedict."

Ruth turned around.

"Mrs. Benedict," said the girl, "I hope you're going to tell us more
about the Sun Dance?"

Ruth stared back. It was Margaret Mead, the small girl who was always trying to demonstrate that she knew more than the others. Next
to her was a quiet dark-haired girl whose name she couldn't remember.

"Actually," said Ruth, "I have something for you," and she undid the
clasp of her briefcase. Reaching inside, she pulled out a reprint of her
article from the *American Anthropologist*.

"Have a look at this," Ruth said.

She handed Margaret the reprint. It was the first time she'd shared
her scholarship with a student.

"Oh, thank you," said Margaret, exchanging a glance with her classmate. "I'll read it tonight."

Ruth walked off quickly, leaving the two girls to ponder the meaning of the special gift she'd bestowed on Margaret.

THE PROMISE OF HIS BIRTH

Sapir . . . is by far the most brilliant among the young men.

—Franz Boas

January 1923

An agitated Edward Sapir, fresh off the train from Ottawa, led his wife, Florence, through Penn Station. Even though he'd splurged and purchased first-class tickets, their bunks had been exceedingly uncomfortable and the sound of Florence's wet cough, punctuating the darkness in unpredictable spasms, had kept him awake for hours.

As they made their way through the crowded station, the sight that greeted him was disconcerting. Right in front of his eyes, as tall as a full-grown man, was a placard that warned: "SPIT SPREADS DEATH." The letters, all in caps, in a stark and leering black font, emphasized the gravity of the message. Other signs, "Offenders Are Liable for Arrest," were posted everywhere.

Ever since medical science had established that tuberculosis was a highly contagious disease, TB patients had been exiled to a life of quarantine within the four walls of the sanitarium. However, many of the chronically ill resisted treatment, either because they couldn't afford it or they didn't want to leave the home they shared with loved ones. These sick still circulated among the healthy, hiding their telltale cough and dodging the accusing stares of suspicious strangers.

So far no qualified physician had officially diagnosed Florence as tubercular. A doctor in Ottawa, whom Edward distrusted, had said he *thought* he heard it in her chest, but Edward had rejected his opinion.

Now that they'd arrived in New York, where medical care was more advanced, they were sure to receive a reliable diagnosis.

Once out on the street, Edward's ears filled with the noisy racket of foreign tongues, the shouts of newsboys and vendors, the familiar sights and smells. He was thrilled to feel the dullness of Canada dropping away. Glancing over at Florence, seeing her face coming alive, he knew that she felt that way, too, and with that understanding came a resounding wave of guilt.

Suddenly, feeling as though he bore a heavy responsibility for Florence's ill health, all he wanted was to escape. He wanted to run from her sickness, the melancholy that surrounded her, the defeat they were forced to confront in every doctor's office. He wanted to rush off to a café, to sit over coffee, listen to the latest gossip, engage in conversation with a colleague who had half a brain. He wanted to talk about books or politics or psychotherapy. He was sick to death of the endless platitudes, the limp niceties that passed for conversation in Ottawa.

What Edward wanted was, for the moment, secondary. Tomorrow was Florence's appointment with the vaunted Dr. Howard Lilienthal, chief of Thoracic Surgery at Mount Sinai Hospital. It had taken Edward nearly two months to secure this consultation, and he'd only managed to do so because Franz Boas had been able to pull some strings.

Lilienthal was going to look at the X-rays, examine Florence, listen to her chest; certainly he would be able to prescribe the correct course of treatment.

Edward Sapir had been born in 1884, in the village of Lauenburg, Prussia. His parents were Lithuanian Jews who conversed in Yiddish and German. At age seven, Edward was expected to learn to read Hebrew, which he did by sitting at his father's side while the older man translated the Old Testament, pointing to the letters with his finger as he intoned the words in a melodic voice.

Edward's father, Jacob, may have taught him Hebrew, but he did so not because he was religiously observant, but because of he was fascinated by the musicality of the ancient language. Jacob's passion was the sound of the human voice. His own singing voice was so pure, and his love for the operatic compositions of Mozart and Verdi so strong, that he auditioned twice, both times without success, for the Berlin Opera.

In 1889, joining the wave of Jewish immigrants leaving Germany, Jacob came to America, where he found work as an itinerant cantor.

It was music, banged out on the piano, written down as a fanciful composition, or expressed by the voice, that shaped the young Edward's mind. As a boy he was never forced to practice, but was allowed to come to music on his own, which he did because his father made it fun. Edward reveled in sound, which even when expressed as the mathematical patterning of notes on a page was a composition he could *hear*. Later, Edward would credit much of his success to music, saying that it had produced in him a gift for mimicry, and had turned him into an "auditory learner," the trait that enabled him to shine in the classroom.

In the academic sphere, Edward's achievements were near legendary. On New York's Lower East Side his mother and father were known not by their own names, but as the "parents of Edward Sapir." At age fourteen he won the citywide Pulitzer competition, which awarded him entrance into the prestigious Horace Mann High School. Instead, he completed grades eleven and twelve at a public high school and used the prize money to pay for his undergraduate studies at Columbia University.

Edward was a good-looking young man who wore his thick dark hair swept back and a trifle too long. Dressed in clothes that were expensive but rumpled, he projected the aura of a Jewish intellectual of the bohemian sort. Pale eyes danced behind a pair of rimless glasses, seeming to say he was concentrated on lofty thoughts, and yet, despite his reputation as a genius, he did not seem to take himself seriously. His laugh came easily, often at his own expense. It was this habit of self-deprecation that most endeared him to family, friends, and women.

While at Columbia the list of languages that Edward mastered was long and varied, and included Middle High German, Old Saxon, Swedish, Danish, Dutch, Icelandic, Persian, and Sanskrit. He was fond of saying when introduced to a foreign tongue, he felt compelled to conquer it. He enjoyed sounding out new accents, rolling the music of them around in his mind, then speaking them out loud, making them his own. Like his father, he had a rhythmic voice, which he "modulated in pitch and loudness with great effectiveness." It wasn't long before his effortless grasp of a new language equaled that of a native speaker's, leaving many in his classrooms, including his professors, green with envy.

It was in the fall of 1903, that Edward first learned of a seminar in American Indian Languages that was to be taught through the Department of Anthropology. What most intrigued Edward was that the class promised to introduce him to a family of *unwritten* languages. While he had been vaguely aware that some primitive tribes still communicated only through speech, never developing a system of writing, he had never thought it possible to study one of those exotic tongues. He suspected that, for him, picking up the sounds and syntax would not be difficult.

The first class of the semester met at the home of Dr. Franz Boas, who lived on West 82nd Street. For Edward, it would be the first time he would be attending a class inside a professor's house.

Edward rang the bell and found himself face-to-face with a typical-looking German housewife of his mother's generation. She introduced herself as Marie Boas and led him into a dimly lit parlor. A brocade-patterned wallpaper lent the room a formal feeling. Edward noticed an upright piano in the corner with sheet music open on the music rack. He thought of sitting down to play, but resisted the impulse. When the others arrived, Dr. Boas invited them to join him at the oval-shaped dining table. A plate of *apfelstrudel,* neatly divided, sat at its center. Edward helped himself to a slice. The young man seated next to him grinned. Edward turned in his direction and the man introduced himself as Frank Speck.

Edward said, "Do you like puns?"

"If you're thinking about my name," said Frank, "there's not a single one I haven't heard."

Edward liked him immediately.

When Boas began speaking he said, "It's only a question of a few years, when everything reminding us of America as it was at the time of its discovery will have perished." He went on to tell them about the Vanishing Tribes Project.

If Edward thought he'd be learning the grammar or syntax of an ancient tongue, he was mistaken. Boas was stressing the urgency of their work as young "anthropologists," telling them that the tribes spoke languages that had been brought to their "polished and idiosyncratic perfection without the benefit of pen on paper." He explained that these living languages were orally learned and transmitted. Because they were languages that had no written form, they were destined to die with their last speakers.

Edward thought about his own childhood, how he'd sat next to his father and read the Torah in a language that was several thousand years old. His Hebraic ancestors had developed a written language at a time when their enemies, the Philistines, had not. Consequently the Jewish people had been able to leave *their* side of the story for posterity. The Philistine side had never found representation. This same thing was about to happen in the struggle between the white man and the Indian.

"The time is late, the dark forces of invasion have almost done their ignorant work of annihilation," said Boas. He told them he'd seen "with his own eyes" what the construction of the railroads and the inexorable push of settlers heading west had done to the natives.

The young men sitting around the table took in the gravity of the situation.

"Your generation may be the last that will be able to collect the data which will form the basis of the early history of America." Boas passed around a typed sheet that listed the eleven western states and the ninety-five tribes that demanded attention.

Later, as he made his way to the streetcar, Edward was exhilarated. Boas had told them of his own youth, of the year spent with the Eskimos on Baffin Island in the Arctic Circle, of subsisting on seal meat and sleeping in igloos. These fantastic tales, Edward reasoned, were what the life of an anthropologist was all about. Suddenly the possibility of a career that held more than earning a doctorate in Indo-European languages and teaching college-level German had been opened. Edward— like the other young men who had sat around the table—felt himself swept up in a heroic endeavor.

He didn't know that the career of Dr. Boas had been marked by great struggle, that for years, his professor had been forced to suffer any number of deprivations, including the delay of marriage and family, constant job insecurity, and the restrictions of living within a greatly reduced budget. Edward was unaware that the discipline that Boas now promoted—North American anthropology—would subject him to the same struggles.

Two years later, in June of 1905, Professor Boas gave Edward his blessing to make his first trip into the field. Boas choose the destination, an

Indian settlement close to The Dalles, along the Columbia River Gorge. This area, known for its abundant salmon runs, had been an important Native American trading post for hundreds of years. That was before the fur traders, Methodist missionaries, and settlers brought with them a wave of unknown diseases and decimated the population. In 1855, the U.S. government forced the local tribes—the Wasco and the Wishram Chinook—to sign treaties ceding their land, and resettled them onto the Yakima and Warm Springs Reservations.

During his first week on the reservation Edward identified an informant, a seventy-year-old Wishram named Louis Simpson, who although "impatient and somewhat self-willed," had a lovable personality, "owing chiefly to his keen sense of humor."

All had gone well until Edward made an attempt to use the contraption Boas had foisted on him—a new mechanical device called the phonograph. Boas had told him the phonograph would provide something amazing—an audio recording of a language that would soon be lost.

The phonograph player weighed thirty-five pounds and resembled an enormous metal conch shell. From the moment Edward set eyes on it, he knew that using it would be a nightmare. He was forced to lug the damn thing nearly two miles through the reservation, down narrow rutted lanes that were littered with rotting fish heads and broken bottles. When he arrived at Louis's shack, he had trouble getting it started.

Finally, he was ready for Louis to tell his tale:

> A certain old man was sitting in the trail with his penis wrapped around him just like a rope. And then Coyote passed on by him and went on, a little beyond. He saw some women jumping up and down in the water. And then he thought, "I shall borrow from the old man his penis." Coyote went over to him and said, "Friend, would you not lend me your penis . . . ?"

Suddenly Edward was aware that the cylinder, revolving in its box, didn't sound right. He motioned to Louis to stop. When he cranked the cylinder to listen to the recording he heard only static.

For the next hour Edward tried to get the phonograph to work. The holder and the needle inside it were broken. In retrospect, perhaps he'd jarred the mechanism when he set the case on the ground, or maybe when he fumbled with the needle he'd knocked it out of alignment.

Two hours later, sitting on the banks of the Yakima River, Edward considered what to do. He'd have to request replacement parts, which would take months to reach the reservation. He had no choice but to write to Boas, to explain why there would be no recordings of Louis Simpson reciting his Coyote tales, in a language that would soon be gone.

By the end of the summer, Edward had developed a great fondness for the Wishram Chinook. He appreciated their bawdy sense of humor. He'd filled many notebooks with their Coyote tales. In spite of the fiasco with the phonograph, Boas congratulated him for "getting such good information out of the few people who are left."

By 1907, Edward had completed his course work, and the time had come for Dr. Boas to exert his full efforts to help his star pupil find work. However, in a field that promised adventure and status, the competition was fierce. It was two years before Edward received an offer for permanent employment.

Thanks to Boas's recommendation, Edward was made the chief of anthropology within the Geological Survey of Canada. At the age of twenty-six, he was in charge of ethnology, archaeology, physical anthropology, and linguistics for all of Canada. He set about remaking the department. In an academic world where employment opportunities were scarce, he suddenly found himself in the enviable—and often difficult—position of doling out jobs to his friends. Talented colleagues such as Paul Radin, Alexander Goldenweiser, and Frank Speck were among the recipients of plum freelance assignments. By populating the drafty corridors of Ottawa's Museum of Man with like-minded friends, he created an island of New York intelligentsia.

One of his Canadian colleagues was not pleased. Marius Barbeau, who had been hired prior to Edward's arrival and had been assigned to work directly under him, derisively referred to this spate of hiring as "Sapir's Jewish period." Barbeau went even further, saying, "When you have a Jew you have something like a blot of oil, you see it spreads."

It was hardly unexpected, but Edward's ascendance to a position of power in Ottawa changed his life. The first thing he did was bring his parents to Canada. He then began to think about establishing his own household. In 1911, he fell in love with Florence Delson, a striking brunette who combined a European sophistication with a flirtatious nature. She also happened to be his second cousin.

Frank Speck, a friend accustomed to enjoying Edward's full confidence, was stunned when he heard that Edward had eloped. He wrote to Edward, demanding details.

A few weeks later, Frank received the following response:

> *As to your well meaning attempt to find out whether I am really in love, I suggest that you leave the whole matter in my hands. I shall only say that Florence Delson is absolutely penniless, much to my delight. Someday, when you have learned how to behave, I may try to have you see her.*

Clearly, Edward was smitten.

By the time the Sapirs arrived in New York City in January of 1923 to consult with Dr. Lilienthal, Edward and Florence had been married for twelve years. Florence was thirty-two years old, and had already waged an eight-year battle with chronic lung disease. She no longer had the physical stamina to walk the length of even one block, nor was she able to mother their three children. Understandably, her protracted struggle to regain her health had upended her emotional stability.

As it was on most days, the waiting room of Dr. Lilienthal's Lexington Avenue office was full. As chief of Thoracic Surgery at Mount Sinai Hospital, the doctor's services were constantly in demand. Lung ailments topped the list of the era's chronic, often fatal infections and Lilienthal could claim responsibility for several significant breakthroughs in the field. In 1910, he had performed the first operation under the use of endotracheal anesthesia and in 1914 he claimed the first successful pulmonary resection for suppurative lung disease.

After a two-hour wait, Edward and Florence were ushered into Lilienthal's office. The doctor was sitting behind his polished mahogany desk, reading Florence's file.

"The good news," Lilienthal told them, "is that the laboratory results show no evidence of the tubercle bacilli in the sputum, only local bacterial flora."

Switching on a light behind the view boxes, X-rays of Florence's lungs were illuminated.

Lilienthal contemplated the white shapes and dark shadows.

"Right here," he said, wielding a long pointer to indicate a shape, "this is a well-localized cavity filled with fluid. This is where Mrs. Sapir's body has tried to wall off an infection.

"The well-circumscribed character of the lesion," Lilienthal explained, "makes Mrs. Sapir the perfect candidate for drainage."

He told them that the way he would treat a lung abscess like Florence's was surgically. He would make an exploratory puncture with a needle and use a syringe to drain the abscess. If necessary, he would make an incision down to the ribs, and remove sections of the ribs to make the pleural cavity more accessible.

Edward looked at Florence and saw that she was fighting back tears.

"If you feel you're not ready," said Lilienthal, "there are less extreme measures you can try."

Pausing for a moment he asked, "How are your teeth?"

Edward was puzzled, and could see that Florence was, too.

"Tooth decay is the cause of many infections," said the doctor, "including those in the lungs."

Florence was embarrassed. Like the children of many immigrants, dental hygiene had not been part of her upbringing. Many of her teeth were rotted by decay.

"Something to consider," said Lilienthal, "is to have your teeth extracted."

"The ones with cavities?" asked Florence.

"No," said Lilienthal, "all of them. Every last one. It's something we often recommend."

6

—

A GLASS FULL OF CYANIDE

*She thought it took courage to die and she wanted to prove
that here at last was one thing she could do.*

—Margaret Mead

January 1923

It was late January 1923, and Margaret was in the midst of finals for the fall semester of her senior year. Earlier that day she'd written to her mother to report, "I still have two more exams and I've gotten one mark, the only A in Mental Measurements."

Tomorrow was the most important final of all, the one in Anthropology.

It was an essay test, scheduled to last three hours, and Margaret intended to fill a stack of blue books with what she knew. Around Barnard she was known as the girl who took in a full bottle of ink when she sat for an exam, and took out an empty bottle when she was done.

Margaret's need to excel, which never abated, was not without consequences. Her mother blamed it for causing all of her physical symptoms. The most serious of these were the shrieking pains in her arms. Recently diagnosed as neuritis, an inflammation of the nerves, the doctor had told her there was nothing she could do beyond supporting the aching limb in a sling. And while Emily Mead may have attributed her daughter's condition to stress, some of the Ash Can Cats saw it differently. One girl, upon hearing that Margaret had been in a chaste relationship for five years, exclaimed, "No wonder your arm hurts!"

Over the course of the semester, Anthropology had emerged as Margaret's favorite class. Not only was Dr. Boas the most profound thinker she'd ever encountered, but his teaching assistant, Mrs. Benedict, continued to astonish with her thoughtful and provocative comments. Once Margaret had gotten past the woman's drab attire, she'd realized that Mrs. Benedict was a well-bred, subtly elegant lady. If pressed, Margaret might even admit to harboring a schoolgirl crush.

Always looking for ways to outperform her classmates, Margaret endeavored to impress Mrs. Benedict. Writing home she said, "The rest of the section is so dumb that I talk to her and walk with her. And having read the 'Men of the Old Stone Age' I shone when we gazed at Paleolithic remains." When she learned that Mrs. Benedict was in the habit of walking from Columbia down to the museum, Margaret plotted to intercept her, convincing her friend and classmate Marie Bloomfield to come along.

But poor Marie! Marie had not been able to complete her classwork, nor was she going to sit for tomorrow's exam. For the last three weeks she'd been sick with the measles and quarantined in the school infirmary.

A quiet, dark-haired Jewish girl with sensitive brown eyes and amorphous facial features that merged together like cookie dough, Marie was "awkward . . . intellectually eager but stiff and unresponsive to any kind of physical affection." Moved by the girl's loneliness, Margaret had decided to take Marie under her wing. When she learned that Marie was an orphan, and that her closest relative was an older brother, seventeen years her senior, Margaret had become even more protective.

Over time Margaret heard stories from Marie about her childhood, stories that would be boring if they weren't so sad. Marie had come from the town of Elkhart Lake, Wisconsin, where her parents had run the Hotel Schwartz, a rambling white clapboard establishment built around a communal dining hall. When Marie turned sixteen her parents sent her off to the Downer Seminary in Milwaukee, ostensibly so she would get a better education. What they didn't tell her was that they were too ill to care for her. Before Marie's eighteenth birthday both her mother and father were dead. Leonard, her older brother, was named her legal guardian, and it was he who had arranged for Marie to attend Columbia.

Leonard Bloomfield, it turned out, was an anthropology professor himself, one of Dr. Boas's earliest disciples. Margaret found Marie's stories about this eccentric older brother to be quite entertaining. One family legend had to do with the time that Leonard, then a young scholar in his twenties, had come home for the High Holidays. Rather than converse with his relatives, he had disappeared into the hotel basement to shampoo his parents' Irish setter. The family upstairs could hear him through the floorboards, talking to the animal, saying, "You are a dummkopf. You are not a bit of use and a great botheration," all of which he intoned in a lyrical and tender voice. The sound of the "dog's tail thumping in repeated blows like thunder," wild with joy, could be heard as well.

Now Marie was sick and Margaret had been forced to go to the library with another classmate. There would be no Marie at the test tomorrow. Marie always seemed to have rotten luck.

Right before going to bed, Margaret wrote to her parents to say, "I've never studied so much for an exam in my life. Eleanor Phillips and I had the whole library out . . . and we read each other extracts from each volume."

On the day of the final, the lecture hall was filled to near capacity. At the front of the room, Margaret could see Mrs. Benedict and the two other teaching assistants huddled around the white-haired Professor Boas.

The Anthropology Department had only one full-time faculty member and that was Dr. Boas. Old, German, and exacting, with a wiry physique that practically gave off sparks, Boas was profoundly intimidating. Standing before a full lecture hall, "occasionally he would look around and ask a rhetorical question which no one would venture to answer." Margaret "got into the habit of writing down the answers to these questions and then showing them to Marie when she turned out to be right."

Margaret had heard fantastic stories about the old man. He had "a visage seamed and scarred from numerous rapier slashes," which people said he'd acquired as an undergraduate in Heidelberg. According to one source, Boas had been taunted by anti-Semitic insults and had challenged his attackers to a duel. Now, forty years later, he was known to be a pacifist, but no less confrontational. During the Great War his controversial antiwar sentiments had put him at odds with many of his colleagues. The resulting hard feelings were said to linger.

Suddenly Margaret felt a gentle tap on her shoulder. She turned. Mrs. Benedict was standing behind her.

Mrs. Benedict leaned down and whispered, "You're excused from the exam."

Uncomprehendingly, Margaret continued to look up at her.

Mrs. Benedict whispered again, "You're excused."

When Margaret still said nothing, Mrs. Benedict added, "Dr. Boas excused you. For your helpful participation in class discussions." Inclining her head in the direction of the exit doors she said, "You're free to go."

Margaret began to collect her belongings. When she looked again at Mrs. Benedict, she could swear she saw her teacher give her a wink. Walking out the door of Schermerhorn Hall into the bright and frosty sunlight, she felt dazed. Although she'd received many academic accolades, none had been so unexpected.

The person she really wanted to tell was Marie. Only Marie would understand the enormity of this honor. Marie, however, was confined to the infirmary and wouldn't be released for days. Margaret would have to settle for reporting the news to her parents:

> *This morning was the Anthropology exam and Boas excused three people from the class of fifty, from the exam in recognition of their helpful participation in class discussion. I was one of them. . . . I'm really very thrilled because I admire Boas so much and also it helps my arm out to be saved from a three hour exam.*

A few days later Miss Abbott, the assistant dean, informed Margaret that there was no one to bring Marie back from the infirmary. Margaret realized that she had to offer "to take some responsibility for her."

Miss Abbott told Margaret to go over late in the morning, reminding her that Marie would have a big suitcase, one that was too heavy for the girls to manage alone.

With Luther in tow, Margaret arrived at Brooks Hall. It wasn't long before the elevator door opened to reveal a haggard Marie.

Luther jumped up from his chair. "I'm sure you're ready to leave this place," he said, reaching for her suitcase.

As they walked back to the dorm, neither Marie nor Luther spoke. Margaret filled the vacuum by telling stories about mutual friends and the stress finals were putting them through. One named Lee Newton had become "hysterically blind" while taking her physics exam and was waiting for a visit from Margaret.

Marie seemed to have little interest.

Unable to contain herself, Margaret said, "I was excused from the Anthropology final."

Marie looked at her.

"Dr. Boas said it was in recognition of my helpful participation in class discussions."

Margaret was about to elaborate on exactly how Mrs. Benedict had relayed the news when she felt Luther's hand on her arm, stopping her.

Once in the dorm room, Margaret and Luther helped Marie unpack her clothes. Promising to check on her later that weekend, they said their good-byes.

Margaret was to learn what happened next from Louise Rosenblatt.

A few days later, on Sunday morning, Louise Rosenblatt headed down to brunch. Sunday was the morning the Barnard cafeteria served freshly baked cinnamon rolls and she wanted to get one before they disappeared.

The daughter of Jewish socialists from Atlantic City, Louise had become close with Margaret ever since the two girls had discovered they held the same left-wing political sentiments. Now a member of the Ash Can Cat's extended family, Louise socialized with many of the girls in Margaret's circle.

Carrying her tray into the dining hall, Louise looked around for where to sit. The other Ash Can Cats had not yet returned from semester break save for Marie Eichelberger, the girl Margaret referred to as "the little freshman," and others called "Margaret's slave." Louise made her way to Eichelberger's table.

During the course of their conversation Eichelberger mentioned that Marie Bloomfield had recovered from the measles and was back from the infirmary. Deciding to pay Marie a visit, the girls bused their dishes and headed over to the dorm.

Louise knocked on Marie's door. When there was no answer, she knocked again. "It's early," said Louise. "I doubt she's gone anywhere."

Louise knocked again and then tried to open the door. It was locked.

Alarmed, Louise banged on the door. The girl who lived next to Marie came outside. She told them there was a connecting door between her room and Marie's.

The three girls entered Marie's room. The shades were down, the curtains drawn. The dark room was stuffy with heat.

There, in bed, lay Marie.

Louise edged closer. Marie's face was white with a slight blue cast. Her lips were parted in a stiff grimace and were dotted with flecks of dried spittle. Her skin was stiff and cold.

It was obvious that she was dead.

On the bedside table was a book that was opened and turned upside down as if to mark a page. It was *The Journal of a Disappointed Man*, by a young Englishman named W. N. P. Barbellion, who had four years earlier, with a theatrical flourish, taken his own life. Before his death Barbellion had written, "To me the honour is sufficient of belonging to the universe—such a great universe—and so grand a scheme of things. Not even Death can rob me of that honour."

On February 8, *The New York Times* ran Marie's obituary:

> *Honor Student at Barnard, Takes Poison in Brooks Hall. Marie Bloomfield, 18 years old . . . was found dead in bed last night, dressed in nightgown and bathrobe. A glass half-filled with liquid that looked like water stood on a table beside her bed.*

The next day Margaret heard that Marie had killed herself and that the police had identified the liquid in the glass by her bedside as cyanide.

That night she wrote to her mother:

> *Poor little lonely thing! I was the best friend she had in college and I never loved her enough. She was just one of the group of younger girls and often I did not have time for her. This last weekend however—I went down and brought her home from the hospital. She left the "Little Book of Modern Verse" which I gave her for Christmas all marked up—showing quite clearly her purpose. . . . She was so inextricably bound up with our lives that it's very hard to go on without her.*

Although Margaret had not been the one to discover Marie's body, in the aftermath of the tragedy she took charge as if she had. When Marie's brother, Leonard, came to Barnard to collect Marie's belongings, it was Margaret who met him at the dorm and filled him in about the last days of his sister's life.

In the aftermath of the suicide, it wasn't only Leonard Bloomfield who wanted to talk to Margaret. She also received a summons from Virginia Gildersleeve, Barnard's imposing dean.

Dean Gildersleeve was known around campus as a champion of women's rights. Margaret—who knew how to curry the favor of administrators of this ilk—expected a warm reception.

When Margaret entered the office she found the dean sitting behind her desk reading a typed report. Gildersleeve removed her spectacles, placed them on her desk, and studied Margaret. "How are you holding up?"

"It was such a shock," said Margaret. "I loved her very dearly and I miss her frightfully, more and more every day."

"Yes, I'm sure that's true," said the dean, putting her glasses back on and returning to the report that lay open on her desk.

"Marie's death is spread all over the papers," said Margaret. "Her face stares up at me from trampled newspapers on the subway floor."

Gildersleeve looked up and grimaced, her lips settling into a tight seam that bisected her face. "I understand that Marie was a melancholy girl, perhaps not emotionally stable."

"She could never be convinced that she was not totally inadequate and doomed to failure," said Margaret.

Gildersleeve stared at her.

"She thought it took courage to die."

A look of disapproval spread over the dean's face. "When a young lady does something like this," said Gildersleeve, "it's not normal."

Margaret stared back at her. It was starting to dawn on her that the dean may have already formed an opinion that had little to do with the real Marie. She might even expect a response from Margaret that she could not give.

By the time Margaret rose from her chair to leave, she'd resolved not to give in to Gildersleeve's unspoken demand that she characterize Marie's suicide as the act of a deranged girl.

In the days to come Margaret was overcome by uncontrollable crying fits.

Her grief was punctuated by the arrival of a small envelope of very fine paper stock of an indistinct ecru color. The back was embossed with "R F B," initials that belonged to Ruth Fulton Benedict.

She slit it open, pulling out the card that was inside.

"My dear Margaret" it said,

You will be needed by the other girls to the limit of your strength, and if there is anything in the world I can do to leave you freer, send me word, or if you can get away come yourself. I've nothing all day that can't be put off. I shall be thinking of you today—and wishing people could be of more use to each other in difficult times.

Mrs. Benedict wanted to see her. She held up the card, felt its texture between her fingertips. Folding it back up, she tucked it into her handkerchief box for safekeeping.

PAPER DOLLS

Bought jam and cards! I must remember afterwards how simple happiness is—I don't want anything more or different at such times

—RUTH BENEDICT

February 1923

Ruth banged out through the back door, letting it slam behind her. She didn't care if the noise annoyed Stanley. She needed to feel the freezing air, needed to clear her head. She marched toward the woodpile.

As long as Ruth was doing the expected, tending to Stanley's comfort by seeing to it that domestic tasks were done to his liking, he was content. However, now that she'd become absorbed in the research for her thesis, he'd withdrawn. He found small things to criticize, like her tendency to jot down ideas on scraps of paper and leave them in untidy piles on various surfaces. The way he talked to her was harsh, often in a tone that was dismissive and scornful. Just as he had once ignored her deep yearning to conceive a child, he now ignored her desire to find meaningful work. Without giving her a reason, he had moved his clothes out of their closet and retreated to the other bedroom.

She wrote in her diary, "Stanley finds me sexually undesirable . . . the situation has tended to fixate my interest on him as perhaps a more normal relation might not have."

And Stanley seemingly couldn't put his disapproval into words. There had been a time, early in their marriage, when it had been different. He had been responsive. Now, rather than engage with her, he barricaded himself in his darkroom, tinkering with his camera, developing negatives.

A silence hung between them that she couldn't bear.

"The greatest relief I know," she wrote, "is to have put something in words, no matter if it's as stabbing as this is to me; and even to have him say cruel things to me is better than utter silence."

Why was it that Stanley should experience her increasing independence of mind as so abhorrent? *He* had work that absorbed him. *He* had the camaraderie and respect of his colleagues. Why couldn't *she* try for the same? Why did he fail to see the fairness of that equation?

She pulled the embedded axe from the stump. Lifting a log from the woodpile she set it on the stump and, standing with her legs wide apart, lifted the axe up over her head and swung it down. The log failed to split. She swung again, this time hearing a resounding crack.

That New Year's Day of 1923 she made the following notation in her diary: "A good day to sit by one's own fire and look out at the rain and at the whipping trees. Toward sunset, cleared under gale from northwest— walked in its teeth as far as sleeting roads allowed."

When she returned she found Stanley sitting by the fire. He barely spoke to her. She made tea and toast and they played Go Bang, a Japanese board game similar to Checkers.

For Ruth, the new year brought with it a sense of anticipation for what was to come, the feeling that she had something of her own to work toward, that she wasn't just mourning the child that could never, and would never, be conceived.

Months earlier she had embarked on her dissertation, expanding on the ideas she'd begun in her first paper on the Guardian Spirit in North America. Once again, she'd limited herself to a library project. Recognizing that the Museum of Natural History had become her second home, and that many hours were lost in the commute between Bedford Hills and Manhattan, she'd asked Stanley to give her enough money to rent an apartment near Columbia.

The apartment was really a room, a ten-by-twelve-foot box with one window that looked out onto the wall of another building, a dozen feet away. Its wooden floors were so worn they'd splintered, its bathroom down the hall shared with three other residents. To Ruth the space was perfect. She liked the look of the walls, an ancient white with hairline cracks running through the plaster. She liked the steaming radiator, with its peeling paint and sputtering noise. And she didn't mind the shared bathroom with its stained toilet bowl and bare lightbulb hanging from a cord. On the weekends she traveled home by train to Bedford Hills, and found she could appreciate the commodious house with three fire-places that she shared with Stanley.

On some nights she would awaken from sleep, filled with a vague fear. She would lie in bed, her heart beating fast, as the anxiety came into focus. What if her gamble failed?

Stanley didn't make it any easier. On the mornings in Bedford Hills, she'd enter the kitchen to find him already seated at the breakfast table, eating his oatmeal, silent and glum.

Sometime in early January she wrote a verse about the state of their marriage:

We'll have no crumb in common
In all our days
A dream come true by naming it together;
Nor go full-fortified
From touch of lips.

Like the rest of her literary efforts Ruth kept this verse hidden. She stashed it away with her other poems, all penned under the pseudonym "Anne Singleton," a name that reflected her need for independence.

In January of 1923, Dr. Boas announced that he was moving the location of the weekly anthropology lunches from the old Endicott Hotel to the Stockton Tearoom on West 109th Street. This simple establishment with pale yellow walls and linoleum floor offered an all-you-can-eat buffet at a reasonable price.

Ruth arrived at the Stockton about twenty minutes late. The large room was filled with long tables, all occupied. Spotting her colleagues, she filled a plate, then squeezed into a seat next to her fellow grad student Gladys Reichard. It wasn't long before she thought she heard, through the mix of conversation, the voice of Edward Sapir. Peering down the long table she saw him at the far end, next to Marius Barbeau, his colleague from Ottawa.

When the meal was over and the dishes were being cleared, Edward was suddenly there, standing over her. "Mrs. Benedict," he said, "do you mind if I sit down?" He pulled out a chair. "How is your mythological research coming along?"

"Slowly, very slowly," she said, flattered that he remembered what she was working on.

"I, too, am moving slowly. I'm preparing a detailed text analysis on Sarcee Myths." And then, showing his gift as a mimic, perfectly imitated the mannerisms of "Herr Professor Boas," saying in a stern voice, "Mr. Sapir, your handbook on the grammar is long overdue."

"Yes," Ruth acknowledged. "Dr. Boas *is* very demanding."

Edward moved his chair a little closer. His voice, when it came, was low and rich. "You produce a very fine piece of research," he said. "Why wouldn't you do mythology to the bitter end and actually prepare the full concordance we need so badly?"

Ruth said nothing.

"There is room somewhere for psychology," said Edward. "Not just as something that is incidental, but as a powerful cultural determinant."

At a loss for words, she just stared.

"While I am talking," Edward said with a laugh, "you probably have half done the job already. Really, I seem to waste a stupendous amount of time in various miscellaneous and ill-assorted activities."

Ruth, suddenly aware of the time, looked at her watch. "Oh dear," she stammered, "I must be on my way down to the museum. The students will be waiting." As she was packing her book bag she told him about the section she was teaching in the afternoons.

When she stood up he rose also. "Please," he said, "let me accompany you. If you can bear my black mood, that is."

He helped her into her coat.

"I want to see what a *real* museum collection looks like these days," he said as they walked toward the door. "Our own museum is so woefully depleted."

They walked along the west side of Central Park. She listened as he told her that during the war the Canadian government had withdrawn its support for anthropology and now, even five years after the war's end, they had not restored his funding. Ottawa's exhibition cases sat empty, with many of the collection's best artifacts packed in crates, covered by old gray horse blankets.

Then he surprised her. "My wife, Florence, is very ill again, he said. "I'm obliged to find lodging for her in the city."

"How difficult for you," said Ruth, "and for the children."

"We've found a good doctor here. My mother's brought our six-year-old, Helen, down. The plan is that when I return to Ottawa, Florence and Helen will remain here."

They walked along.

"I'm wondering if you could watch Helen while I search for lodging for the two of them?" He paused. "I know it's a lot to ask."

Ruth was flattered.

She glanced in his direction. The arrogance in his eyes seemed to mask some unspoken pain. She found herself wanting to hear him laugh again.

She agreed to help in whatever way she could.

That night she wrote in her journal, "Bought jam and cards! I must remember afterwards how simple happiness is—I don't want anything more or different at such times."

Helen, the little girl, sat on Ruth's bed, her overcoat still buttoned. She looked wide-eyed and fearful, a sweet little thing who exhibited none of her father's self-assurance.

Ruth gently helped her out of the coat and hung it in the closet.

With this visit in mind, Ruth had gone to the Five and Dime to purchase supplies that Helen might like. She brought them out now, a stack of colored construction paper, a bottle of glue, a pair of scissors.

Getting down on her hands and knees, Ruth spread them out on the floor and patted a spot next to her for Helen to sit down.

They spent the morning cutting out paper dolls, making a set of six. Ruth suggested drawing a "printed menu" so the dolls could decide what they wanted to eat for lunch. They illustrated the menu to look like the ones handed out in the dining car of a Pullman, just like the one Helen had taken from Ottawa to New York. After lunch Ruth helped Helen back into her coat and the two ran across the icy street to the soda fountain where they had arranged to meet Edward. He was ten minutes late. When he arrived, he ordered a hot fudge sundae for Helen, with two long silver spoons.

Between mouthfuls of ice cream and warm chocolate sauce, Edward told Ruth that when he had accepted his job in Ottawa, a decade earlier, it had held great promise. He had been given free rein to organize a program of ethnology for all of Canada. Then Canada had entered the war and budget cuts had hobbled his ability to launch projects. Worse, Edward had started to experience anti-Semitic resentments from the administrative staff, including from his own assistant, Marius Barbeau.

Perfectly mimicking Barbeau's French Canadian accent, Edward said, "Sapir spends all of his enthusiasm and best energies turning this into a *Jewish* division."

Ruth could see that as a Jew trying to make his way in the academic world, Edward was every bit as marginalized as she was as a woman. But Edward, at least, had a sense of humor about it.

As they were leaving the shop, Edward said, "Tonight I'm giving a lecture at Cooper Union. I don't suppose you're free for dinner?"

Ruth felt her face flush.

She wanted to say yes, but she had already made plans to visit her sister-in-law, Agnes, and her new baby. She had no choice but to decline. At any rate, she was proud of herself for refusing the last-minute invitation.

It wasn't until the next day, on February 8, that Ruth heard the news that Marie Bloomfield, one of her students, had committed suicide. That night Ruth made the following entry in her journal:

> It's unbearable that life should be so hard for them. I know it's all wrapped up with my wish for children—and dread that they might not want the gift.—It bowls me over completely.

The next day Ruth sent a card expressing her sympathy to Margaret Mead, the only real friend Marie had left behind.

The knock, a rhythmic rapping, came at half-past six. Ruth opened her door to find Margaret standing there, a small wisp of a girl, her blue eyes fixed on Ruth, her chin jutting slightly forward.

Margaret stepped into the room and embraced Ruth, holding her tight for a moment, as if a physical connection between them were the most natural thing in the world.

Ruth pulled back.

Margaret's skin was fresh and clear, the bridge of her nose sprinkled with light freckles. The fifteen-year age difference suddenly felt like an unbridgeable chasm.

"Goodness gracious," Margaret said, "I never imagined that my first visit to you would be occasioned by something so horrible."

Ruth set out teacups, put the kettle on to boil. She placed a cardboard box from the bakery on the little table. Pulling out a chair for her guest, she made sure that Margaret was positioned to talk into her good ear.

As Margaret was breaking a scone in two, spreading butter across it, Ruth assessed the girl. Even under these circumstances she radiated optimism.

Facing life from the sunny side lay outside of Ruth's experience. Always plagued by bleak moods, what Ruth called "her blue devils," she had a sensitivity for "those who by age or sex or temperament or accidents of life history were out of the main currents of their culture." This included Marie Bloomfield. It did not include Margaret Mead.

What Margaret Mead was telling her now was disconcerting.

"Some people in the administration want me to say things about Marie that aren't true," said Margaret. "They've been determined to convince me, so that I will convince others, that Marie was insane."

"Are you kidding?" said Ruth

"She wasn't insane," said Margaret, beginning to tear up.

"No," said Ruth, "I know she wasn't."

They sat in silence for a moment. "When was the last time you saw her?" asked Ruth.

"When we took her home from the hospital. She was lonely. But I certainly didn't have any sense that she was going to *kill* herself."

"The police have identified what was in the glass," said Ruth. "It was cyanide."

"Terrible," said Margaret, her eyes starting to well up. "What a terrible way to die."

"It is a terrible way to die," said Ruth, going to her dresser to find a handkerchief.

Then Ruth told Margaret about her own childhood in Norwich, in upstate New York. One morning after Sunday School she'd found her mother waiting for her at the door, crying. Sarah, their young servant, had committed suicide. No one ever told her how or why. Even years later, Ruth's mother wouldn't talk about it. Sarah's decision to take her own life was seen as a disgrace to both Sarah's family and to the Fultons.

"Someone else from the administration is coming by tomorrow," said

Margaret. "Supposedly to see how I am." She paused. "What they really care about is keeping me quiet."

"These are the ingrained attitudes that we live with," said Ruth. She explained how in other cultures like that of ancient Rome, when the great statesman Cato killed himself, the act of taking one's own life was considered noble.

Ruth had no way of knowing if her words were making an impression. Nor could she know that later that night Margaret wrote to her mother to tell her about their tea:

> *The one exception is Ruth Benedict. She wrote me a little note and I went to see her. She was the one person who understood that suicide might be a noble and conscious choice.*

What Ruth also did not realize was that the mere presence of this girl, who she had always viewed as too sunny, too buoyant, had been a comfort to her also. Without knowing it, Ruth had finally let down her mask.

The next day Ruth was working in the small seminar room next to the Anthropology office when she looked up and saw Dr. Boas standing in the doorway. As usual the expression on his face gave away nothing of what he was thinking. He motioned for her to come with him.

Her hopes soared.

Surely he was going to bring up the job opening in the department, the one teaching position yet to be filled. She followed him into his cramped office. She knew the salary was considerably less than what any man would expect as an associate professor, but that didn't matter. She had Stanley's money to provision her.

"Sit down, Mrs. Benedict," he said.

Ruth settled into the chair.

"You know our resources are limited," Boas said. "Severely limited." She waited.

"I've had a letter from Mrs. Parsons."

He rummaged through the papers on his desk until he found it. He scanned it, and then looked up.

"Mrs. Parsons has offered a grant, a fellowship, in Southwest folklore. I thought to talk to her about you and your interests and well, she fell in with my suggestions."

"Oh?" said Ruth. Perhaps he was *not* talking about a teaching job. This other opportunity involved Elsie Parsons, the same Mrs. Parsons who had been Ruth's teacher at the New School. A wealthy matron and self-taught anthropologist, Mrs. Parsons was known for making generous donations to the department, and as long as Mrs. Parsons was willing to provide funding, she could call the shots.

He continued, "Gladys Reichard has accepted our teaching job."

Ruth stared.

He cleared his throat. "She is unmarried with no means of support."

"So that's it," thought Ruth, knowing that Boas always weighed how best to disseminate the bits of money that had been put at his disposal. Obviously he'd decided that Gladys Reichard needed the teaching job more than she did.

"Why don't you talk to Mrs. Parsons," he said. "She's expecting to hear from you."

That night Ruth wrote in her journal:

> *Worst sick headache I've had in years. I know my subconscious staged it—But really I suppose it's hanging on to the idea that I can teach at Barnard—which my conscious self has known I couldn't do, always.*

A few days later at the Stockton Tearoom, Ruth spotted Elsie Parsons presiding over one of the lunch tables. A statuesque lady, dressed in a smart suit, Elsie was blessed with pleasantly symmetrical facial features. She seemed to be thoroughly enjoying her roast beef, while the men at the table listened to what she had to say with rapt attention.

As she walked toward the table, Ruth rehearsed a greeting. As she drew closer she hesitated. Suddenly it felt like the wrong time to interrupt.

That night Ruth wrote in her journal, "Said nothing to Mrs. Parsons at lunch—nor she to me. Dr. Boas said I was to approach her."

The next day Ruth felt more courageous: "Wrote Mrs. Parsons I was interested."

Ruth spent the rest of the week in the reading room at the museum, revising a paper she was writing on the Serrano Indians of California. As she was leaving the library, she spotted, halfway down the hall, a man dressed in eccentric garb.

He noticed her, too. "Ruth," he hollered. "Lunch?"

The man was Pliny Earle Goddard, the museum's curator of Indian artifacts. From his spume of pomaded hair down to his bolo tie, it was clear this was a man who paid too much attention to his appearance.

Goddard was the boyfriend of Gladys Reichard, the same Miss Reichard who had managed to snag the department's one open teaching position.

He must be gloating.

Ruth turned toward him, a gentle smile on her lips. "Hello, Dr. Goddard."

"Library research again, Ruth? We're going to have to set up a cot for you in there," he said with a laugh as he led her toward the dining room.

That night she made the following notation in her journal:

> *Lunch with Dr. Goddard. He settled scores for my lack of attention to him this winter. Began with my felicitations on Gladys' job. He took up Dr. Boas' worry about me for me. "He said he supposed there'd always be these driblets of research but that was all he could see ahead for me."—I feel some capacity for making a place for myself, thank you! But on the elevated [train] I was weary, and plain wept with vexation.*

On the following Monday Ruth received a letter from Mrs. Parsons offering to pay her $1,000 to undertake research on Southwest mythology. She accepted. The headaches, however, did not subside. At first she couldn't understand why accepting this fellowship would cause so much stress, and then one night the anxiety came into focus.

Of course, she was silly not to have known it earlier.

The fellowship meant that she would have to do *fieldwork*. She knew Dr. Boas would expect as much from her. His methodology was built on an "insistence on inclusive and systematic field investigation."

The truth was that Ruth was terrified of leaving the cool safety of the library and going into the field—choosing a community, mixing with strangers, all the intimacy that kind of human contact would necessitate. Not to mention that a summer away doing fieldwork would threaten her already fragile relationship with Stanley.

Lunch had been eaten, her papers packed into her satchel, and Ruth was heading for the train. At home, Stanley's present—"a beautiful new Zeiss lens Kodak"—was waiting to be wrapped before she made the preparations for his birthday dinner.

The sidewalk was crowded. Ahead of her she saw a man's head poking out above the others. The hair was long around his neck, his hat tilted at an angle. The shape of his shoulders, the way he swung his arms were unmistakable. Her heart quickened.

It was not unexpected that she should see Edward Sapir here, heading for the streetcar. Ruth had marked on her calendar that Florence was leaving the hospital today. No doubt he was going to pick her up.

The last time she had seen Dr. Sapir he'd told her his wife was better, saying, "At least there's something else to think of besides life and death."

She followed him down the sidewalk, dodging pedestrians, staying far enough back so he wouldn't notice her.

Her mind raced. She could tell him that she'd finished the dissertation. Maybe he would ask to read it. After all, it elaborated on the ideas she'd explored in her "Vision" paper, the paper he'd so admired.

As she drew closer she became aware that her blouse, under her arms, was cold and clammy.

She was almost alongside him. All she had to do was reach out to touch his arm.

She slowed, and then stopped, letting him walk ahead. She watched him disappear into the crowd.

That night she recorded her near encounter in her journal:

Worked on texts AM. Out to Bedford Hills. Saw Dr. Sapir ahead of me at noon, but suddenly I didn't care whether he looked up or not. He didn't, and I went on to the train.

HELL'S KITCHEN

Three nights running before the funeral, I returned to wash dishes and offer companionship to my friends in the kitchen. I could not offer prayers; nor was I moved to.
—LUTHER CRESSMAN

January 1923

Luther and his father, Dr. George Cressman, walked at a brisk pace up the dirt road. Dr. Cressman carried a walking stick and Luther a shotgun, breech open, across the crook of his arm. Before them ran the Cressmans' favorite hound, Virgil. The dog had picked up a scent and was crying excitedly under his breath. He took off, Luther and Dr. Cressman watching him go.

Luther was happy to be back home again. Father Sparks was already talking to him about possible assignments. After he and Margaret married it would be good to live in the country. "The city changes a man," he thought, and not necessarily in a good way. He and Margaret had a lot to think about.

Luther had found an opportunity to bring up the subject with her last week after they went to a matinee of Ibsen's *Peer Gynt*. Margaret loved the play for its mixture of fantasy and realism. She said Grieg's score was haunting. Afterward, sitting in a tea shop, she'd talked about her upcoming exams and the Barrymore performance of *Hamlet* she hoped they'd be able to see, adding happily, "Such a life! I scarcely have time to breathe!"

Luther had cleared his throat. "I've been speaking to Father Sparks," he said. "The place the bishop offers is at Mansfield, in Tioga County, on the state line. There's a rectory, and a garden."

"The state line?" Margaret had said. "That's a good distance from here."

"There are a couple of places but Father Sparks said they are not nearly as good as Mansfield. The rest are all small, soft-coal towns."

"Are you sure we want to be so far from the city?" she asked.

"A Ford, a new one, is provided with the rectory. Elmira is twenty-two miles away. That's about ten dollars' worth of car fare from New York."

"Well," said Margaret, "it might be all right. But I don't know if I want to live out that far."

Walking beside his father now, with the feeling of contentment that hung between them, Luther wondered how Margaret could not like living out here. Ahead of them stretched a carpet of fallen leaves, dotted with patches of thinly crusted snow. From somewhere in the woods they could hear Virgil, his drawn-out cries coming faster and faster.

"Maybe he's got something," said Luther.

"Don't think so," said Dr. Cressman. "Just running off some steam."

They walked on, listening to the cries.

"Virge," called Luther. "Good boy! Go get 'em!"

They watched as the hound appeared, then disappeared again between the maze of gray and brown trunks.

"No matter," said Dr. Cressman, when finally they heard only silence. "Let's just enjoy the walk."

"It's great to be here," Luther said. "Sometimes when I'm in the city it seems like the wrong place to be." He glanced over at his father. What he really wanted to tell him was the change in direction Margaret's life was taking. Up until now he and Margaret had shared the same dreams: that he was to become a minister in a country parish and she a college executive. They would raise a large family of six children. Somehow that had all changed. He wasn't even sure how it had come about, or when. Now Margaret had work in the city that she wanted to pursue. While Luther had always believed that what made a strong marriage was the support each partner gave the other, he didn't know how to reconcile their diverging paths. Maybe his father could give him good council.

Instead, hesitant to bring it up, Luther said, "Papa, I went to my tenements again. It's gotten easier. They know me now. I don't dread it like I used to."

An image of the tenements, an "unbroken line of brick buildings, four or five stories high" loomed up before him. He could smell the reek of boiled cabbage and the pungent stench of the outhouses.

"That's good," said Dr. Cressman, taking his pipe from his jacket pocket, reaching in and fishing out his tobacco pouch. "I'd like to come with you, next visit."

"Father Pomeroy warned me, if I were to meet someone on the stairs to stop with my back to the wall. But I can tell you, in all my work there, no one has ever bothered me."

His father nodded.

"I have definite interests there, people I know," said Luther. "Good people."

They walked in silence while his father filled his pipe and lit it.

Finally Luther said, "Papa, do you know anything about the law here in Pennsylvania? Can a physician or a nurse give information about contraceptives?"

"Of course not," said Dr. Cressman. "It's forbidden."

By the tone of his voice it was apparent that his father agreed with the generally held opinion that the use of contraceptives was immoral.

Just then they saw Virgil coming back with something in his mouth. As he came closer they saw it was a stick and Luther laughed. Virgil came up and dropped it at Dr. Cressman's feet.

"I don't think he believes you're going to use that shotgun today," Dr. Cressman said, bending down to pick up the stick.

"Well," said Luther, returning to the topic of birth control, "some young people, just married, want to put off having children on account of financial reasons. They aren't ready yet."

Dr. Cressman grunted, then tossed the stick in a spinning arc way out ahead of them, Virgil taking off after it.

Luther had no intention of saying so, but he and Margaret had decided to put off starting *their* family for a couple of years.

That night Luther wrote to Margaret:

I went along with Papa up above the Falls of French Creek and down below Pughtown. The hills are our hills again, the cold, stark trees, a sprinkle of snow over all, and a leaden gray sky—I wish we could enjoy them together but we will soon again my dearest. And after winter spring will soon be here.

With every turn of the seasons September of 1923 drew closer, the time when he and Margaret planned to be married. But, oh, how he yearned for the touch of her:

Dearest little wife to be you are such a sumptuous sweetheart and such a treasure of a promised bride and comrade. When I am with you I do not want to say goodbye and when I am separated from you I long to be with you and to be in the glory of your presence. I am so much a part of you and you of me that it is an anomaly to be separated.

Still, there was a lingering doubt. Luther knew Sherwood Mead was not in favor of the marriage and had even tried to convince Margaret that she could do better. Not that the old man's opinion carried much weight with Margaret. Everyone knew that she made up her own mind.

Luther, however, wanted both sets of parents to be happy with the union. One night when he met Margaret after her last class, he reported that he'd talked to her mother and found her to be their ally. "She said she would cooperate by urging the *other* member of the family to see things the same way," he said. "I'd say things look pretty promising."

On January 21, 1923, Luther was ordained into the priesthood of the Anglo-Catholic Church. He told Margaret that he "looked like 'the Faustus' in his clericals." He was now, in the eyes of his church, a priest in the service of all people, all the children of the Kingdom of God. It was the culmination of four years of study at the seminary.

While Luther waited for his permanent assignment, he had decided to broaden his horizons by pursuing graduate studies in sociology at Columbia University. With the encouragement of Father Pomeroy, he chose for his thesis the life of John Wesley, an eighteenth-century Anglican cleric who had lived during the time of the Industrial Revolution. What so intrigued Luther was that Wesley, like himself, had been so disturbed by his era's horrific social conditions that he had decided to go beyond what the church was willing to provide. Moving from town to town, ministering to the poor, Wesley had become, first and foremost, a social reformer.

In the meantime, Father Sparks arranged for him to split his time between St. Clement's and another low-income parish, the small Anglican Convent of English Sisters, on the Lower East Side.

On a Monday morning in March of 1923, Luther was approached by Father Sparks, who told him that over the weekend one of their parishioners—a young man—had come to St. Clement's, desperate for help. The man's wife had gone into labor, giving birth to twins, a boy and girl, but had suffered fatal convulsions during the delivery. Luther thought he remembered her, an apple-cheeked young woman, barely twenty years of age.

He was stunned to hear that she had died.

Wanting some air, Luther walked outside the seminary's redbrick edifice, exiting through its iron gates. What bothered him most was that he actually felt a sense of relief that he had not been present when the grieving husband had come looking for help. He doubted whether he could have met the challenge of that moment. And if he really had nothing significant to say in such a situation, didn't that call into question all of his vows?

Walking up the avenue, oblivious to the rush of traffic on all sides, he felt resentment at the inequalities of life by which needed care for life's basic functions should be available to a favored few with money enough to buy it.

That night Luther put on his clerical collar and vest. It was his duty to visit the bereaved family.

As he walked in the cold along Ninth Avenue, nearing the tenements of Hell's Kitchen, Luther could smell the grainy smoke of an incinerator. In the dark he saw other fires burning in metal trash barrels. People were huddled around the barrels, holding their hands above the flames for warmth. Coming closer he found his way obstructed by a man sitting against the building, his shoeless feet sticking out before him, cracked and bleeding. Luther stepped over him, and then over a woman wrapped in a blanket.

The woman had a bottle in her mouth and was spitting something into it. She looked up at Luther. The light off the fire caught her clouded eyes. A smell that seemed to be a mixture of gin and vomit rose up off of her.

These tenements housed some of Luther's people, the families he'd gotten to know at St. Clement's. This was the first time he'd paid a visit after dark.

Indigent men and women were loitering in the doorways. On the sidewalks, around their feet, were their belongings, dark piles of filth that smelled of urine. He averted his eyes so as not to make eye contact with anyone. Then he felt something hard hit him in the back. It shocked him for a moment. He quickened his step, looking for an address on buildings that were not marked. Finally, standing on the pavement in front of what he thought to be the correct building, he looked down a half dozen steps into what was another level of hell.

He walked to the bottom, knocked on the door. While he was waiting he could see a dark ooze of sewage puddled up around the corners of the foundation. After a moment, the door opened. A stout woman motioned him to come inside.

The room fell quiet as soon as he entered.

As Luther's eyes adjusted to his surroundings, he saw the indistinct forms of several people gathered around a young man who held a bundle in his arms. Next to him an older woman held another bundle.

Luther offered a greeting, feeling a wave of intense discomfort pass over him.

Through an open door he could see a small kitchen. Scattered stacks of dirty dishes were sitting on a table and around the sink. Friends had brought food to be served with coffee or tea, but no one had bothered to wash the dishes.

Seeing how he could help, Luther slipped out of his coat and moved toward the kitchen.

Turning to the three women who were closest to him, Luther said, "Please give me an apron." When the women didn't respond, Luther said, "Washing dishes is something I am very good at."

They saw he was serious.

One of the women followed him in and handed him a long, soiled apron and, once he had it on, she tied it around his waist and then went back out to the others.

The rancid smell of old food that hadn't been cleaned in days assailed his senses. Luther stayed in the kitchen, scraping the congealed food off the plates, trying to think what else he could do. The family's muted conversation didn't give him any clues.

He couldn't stop the thoughts from coming:

What did the church have to say about this? Our social ethics classes,
showed that the church was not unaware of it, yet as far as my
seminary training went it might not have even existed. How could
I, feeling as I did, have repeated with any honesty the prayers of
consolation the prayer book provided? How could I, when perhaps
this death and all it portended need not have happened?

From time to time, one of the mourners would wander into the
kitchen and talk to him. He learned that the apartment belonged to the
parents of the dead woman. They planned to care for her babies.

For the next three nights, Luther returned to the apartment to wash
dishes. He was there to "offer companionship to my friends in the
kitchen." He felt he could not offer prayers; nor was he moved to.

On the morning of the funeral, after the Requiem Mass, Luther walked
out of St. Clement's to find a row of horse-drawn carriages standing by
the curb. Who was paying for these? Certainly not the widowed husband and his impoverished family. Coachmen were helping mourners
step up into the carriages. Luther peered into the first one and saw that
it was overflowing with members of the family. As he passed the second
carriage, its door swung open. Father Sparks was seated alone inside and
he beckoned Luther to climb in. For some minutes they waited. Then
from outside Luther heard a commotion, and a shout to start up. The
carriage pitched forward and they began their long journey from lower
Manhattan to a cemetery in the Bronx.

Some awkward minutes pass. Father Sparks was watching Luther,
his blue eyes unreadable. Finally he smiled, the pink skin crinkling
around his nose. "The family told me of your kindness, how much it
meant to them."

"I tried to do what I could," said Luther, moving back against his seat
and looking out at the Sunday morning traffic.

They continued on, mostly in silence. Luther felt his decision to help
in a lowly but useful manner had been correct. He had won back at least
some measure of his self-respect, but when he thought about what had
motivated his actions, he realized it was not his religious training, but
the ideals set by his mother and father who had served the people in
their county so selflessly.

At the cemetery, Luther walked among the graves, unconsciously taking note of the dates engraved on the tombstones. So many of them marked lives cut short. Infants and children gone before they had reached the age of three. Young women, in their twenties and thirties. How many of these poor women had died during childbirth? Had their families sufficient money to pay for prenatal care and proper food? Could these tragedies have been averted?

In the following weeks Luther continued performing the ritual of Mass, but from outside the seminary other influences were at work undermining his equanimity. His courses at Columbia raised questions about the role of the Church in regard to poverty.

Then, of course, there was Margaret. She had opened his eyes, too. He wrote to her, "I have you to thank for the incentive and the awakening to new ideas and a new world of thought . . . for my interest in the church regardless of what happens to develop."

A few weeks later, during the Evensong service at eight o'clock, Luther was assisting Father Sparks at St. Clement's. Doing more talking than sermonizing, Luther told his small congregation that he believed in the Lord's saying, "Ye shall know the truth and the truth shall set you free." With this in mind he quietly urged his listeners to stay informed.

Several people looked at him quizzically.

"Try to read more than one source of news," said Luther. "You will find that each newspaper is biased."

Following the service Father Sparks was waiting for him in the vestry. Luther was surprised.

"What were you thinking?" demanded Sparks.

Luther's face reddened.

"Don't preach any more of that New Republic stuff here," said Sparks.

Before Luther could respond, Sparks turned on his heel and walked into the dimness of the chapel.

Greenwich Village could boast many unusual establishments but, in Luther's mind, none was so special as Pagan Books. Its floor-to-ceiling shelves were bent under the weight of thousands of treasures. The velvet couches that faced each other from either side of the fireplace sagged from years of heavy use. In the late afternoon, Hudson, the shop's proprietor, served tea in chipped porcelain cups and his wife, Janet, told stories about their daughter, a would-be opera singer. In Luther's mind this was a perfect place to sit and read. Then he had brought Margaret to the shop and she had rewarded him by exclaiming that Pagan Books was her favorite bookstore in the *whole* city.

One afternoon, sitting next to one another on one of the settees, Luther lay down the book of essays he was reading.

"You will like this," he said to Margaret. "This woman Magdeleine Marx believes that in marriage, a woman needs much more than romantic love to make her happy."

Margaret slowly raised her eyes from her book. "Continuing in school is what will make me happy," she said. "We'll have to economize, so we both can continue with our courses."

"We'll make it go all right," said Luther. "I'll get thirty-six credits this year if it all goes well, then six this summer, making it forty-two. That will leave me eighteen to complete my degree. I'll be able to take a minimum and do extra work."

"So you really think we can manage?" asked Margaret.

"There's no cause for worry," said Luther. "We'll fool them all."

He laughed. "And unless one or the other should develop an aversion to it—and I don't expect to—we will be married in September."

Margaret moved closer to him, her eyes searching his face.

"Martha has a gas plate we can have," said Luther. "Everything will be okay." He threw his arm over her shoulder.

"I expect it will," she said.

He slid closer to her and said into her ear, "I love you. I love you. I love you. I love every vibrant part of your body and spirit. Not my reflection in you. Not my control over you."

In fact, Luther firmly believed that love was the only justification for marriage, and when that foundation ceased to exist, dissolution was called for. He knew that Margaret felt that way, too.

"And the last thing in the world I would want, darling, would be that you were tied to me by my affection for you," said Luther. "That in fear of hurting me—if you no longer cared for me—you would feel bound to me so that your freedom was destroyed."

"I wouldn't want you to feel that way towards me either," said Margaret, holding his gaze.

"It would be terrible," said Luther, reaching out and taking both of her hands in his, "if you felt you could not leave me for fear of hurting me."

A COTTAGE ON CAPE COD

*I'm going to be famous some day . . . and I'm going to be
known by my own name.*

—MARGARET MEAD

July 1923

After a five-year engagement, Margaret and Luther had finally
picked a date: September 3, 1923.

In the weeks and days leading up to the wedding, an assort-
ment of packages had been arriving at the Mead family home. Now, piled
high on the dining room table were the boxes, some opened, some sealed,
holding all manner of ceremonial trappings.

There were hats made of pale pink tulle to coordinate with dresses
of the same color, and parasols to match, gloves to complete the ensem-
ble, and then keepsakes to mark the day: silver lockets for each of the
bridesmaids, each with the wedding date engraved on the back, and
simple gold cuff links for the five ushers, who all happened to be Luther's
brothers.

A long cardboard box that contained Margaret's gown lay open on
the table.

Marie Eichelberger, visiting for the weekend, stood over the box, pulling open the tissue-paper sleeve that enclosed it. Marie fingered the
line of delicate seed pearls that trimmed the neck.

Margaret stood behind her, waiting for her reaction.

"Satin crêpe, so versatile. Your train should be cut from the same
material, with a full veil of tulle."

"I thought you'd like it," said Margaret.

Marie gently lifted the gown up, uncoupling it from its wrapping.

Fashioned from a satin crêpe of the palest ivory, with long close-fitting sleeves and a bodice embroidered with rose point lace, it was soft, lovely, and yet still formal. Marie approached Margaret and held it up against her body so she could see the length. The hem reached to mid-calf, classical yet stylish.

"You're going to look so charming and beautiful," said Marie. "I wish I could be here to see it."

"So do I, dear," said Margaret.

Looking at Margaret with unabashed affection, Marie said, "I haven't yet discovered the word in any language which describes *you*."

"Believe me, there are plenty," said Margaret.

Marie carefully replaced the dress in the box. Then, turning to face Margaret, now seated on the divan, she said, "If only I could manicure your hands for your wedding day."

"Margaret's slave" may have been what some of the others called Marie, but to Margaret she was nothing short of a godsend. Too busy to do so herself, Margaret had asked Marie to find a florist to design the bouquets, to order the gifts for the bridesmaids, and, in a show of real trust, to assist in organizing the seating chart for the luncheon.

For her part, Marie had learned to tolerate Luther. However, what she couldn't accept was that Margaret had other close friends. When a letter had arrived from Léonie Adams saying, "How jolly that everyone is to turn up. We all promise not to be Ash Can Cats, if we can maintain respectability throughout the ceremony," Marie had sulked all afternoon.

Just then Margaret's mother came through the door from the pantry carrying a tray laden with butter cookies and ice tea.

Margaret waited until her mother left the room. "I have something to show you," she said, as she poured the tea. Rising from the divan and walking to the corner cupboard, she retrieved a small cardboard box. She held it toward Marie. "Take one."

Marie pulled an At-Home Card from the box.

Margaret watched Marie's face.

Marie peered at the card, and then held it closer so she could examine it. On the card was printed the address of Margaret and Luther's future apartment, along with their names.

"Your At-Home Cards look a little queer," said Marie. "Look at them. Your name is all wrong."

"No," said Margaret, "my name is correct. After I'm married I'm still going to be Mead. Margaret Mead."

"Goodness," said Marie, sinking back in her chair, contemplating the card. "It looks, I don't know, a trifle immoral."

Margaret smiled.

Both girls were well aware that an At-Home Card was mightily important. Generally speaking, a personal card like this one was considered to be a measure of a young lady's character. According to Emily Post's *Etiquette* published just the year before, and a book Marie frequently referenced, "A fantastic or garish note in the type effect, in the quality or shape of the card, betrays a lack of taste in the owner of the card."

Now, though she attempted to hide it, it was clear that Marie was flabbergasted. And Margaret, for whom good manners had always been the bedrock of all social interaction, was enjoying Marie's consternation.

Margaret wanted Marie to know that, really, etiquette had no bearing in this case. Her decision to keep using her maiden name was a way to assert her core values.

She'd first started thinking about it earlier in the summer, after one of Mother's cousins from the Fogg side of the family had come for a visit. The ladies had been discussing Margaret's wedding plans when the cousin, who had always disapproved of Mother's impractical idealism and her "little independent academic projects," had turned to Margaret and in a snide voice said, "If your mother were getting married today I'll bet she'd even keep her own name."

"I resented the tone with which she was putting Mother down," said Margaret, "and I said to myself, why not?"

"Would she really have kept her own name?" asked Marie.

"I expect so," said Margaret.

"Why ever would she have done that?" said Marie.

Margaret explained that her mother had always believed that women should keep their own identity and not be submerged into a man's. That's why she gave each of her daughters only one given name, so they'd keep their surnames after marriage.

"But Luther?" said Marie. "Have you talked it over with Luther?"

"Luther approves. And the Cressmans weren't a bit shocked," said Margaret. "Mrs. Cressman told Luther it was my own business and she was perfectly willing to call me Margaret Mead."

"Well," said Marie, "I suppose it's all right because it's you."

A week later, after Marie had gone home, Margaret received a note of apology. Marie explained that the initial shock of seeing the cards had caused her to be too critical. Now that she'd recovered, she wanted

Margaret to know that she appreciated her for "being her own person." She ended the letter by saying, "Part of my college education is knowing you, anyway. Barnard or New York City hasn't broadened my ideas as much as you."

What Marie did not know was that at the dinner table, a few nights earlier, Margaret had had a similar discussion with her father, albeit a more heated one. When Dadda had objected to her keeping Mead for her last name, Margaret had ended the argument by stomping her foot and yelling, "I'm going to be famous some day. And if I'm going to be famous, I'm going to be known by my own name."

Famous one day? Where had that outburst come from? And famous for what? Margaret had no idea. Certainly her pursuit of anthropology didn't seem a likely path toward achieving that goal. She herself had said, "It is so non-lucrative that I fear I'll have to do other things first," making the joke, "I'm going to get a job giving change in the subway."

Yet Margaret was so fiercely determined to make something of herself that she made a point of working harder than everyone else. Louise Rosenblatt, also a dedicated student, once told her, "Your industry makes me feel like a good-for-nothing."

When kidded about having an unrelenting work ethic, Margaret had said, "If you'd been brought up in my family, you would, too." Much of the pressure, of course, came from Dadda. On the day she was elected to Barnard's Phi Beta Kappa chapter, Dadda was in the audience, taking great pleasure in his daughter's achievement. After the ceremony, he went up to her, grasped the key that hung on a chain around her neck, and said, "That cost me ten thousand dollars. And you know what, Mar, it was worth it!"

Two weeks before the wedding, father and daughter were seated in the study of the Meads' house. Dadda had been reading one of the serialized Westerns he enjoyed. Margaret was engrossed in her writing and didn't notice that he'd laid down the book and was watching her.

"Mar," he said, "I have a proposition for you."

Margaret looked up. She knew that tone of voice too well. "What is it?"

"I have it from Mother," he said, referring to his own mother and Margaret's grandmother, "that you're getting married because in your mind it's the expected thing to do."

Margaret assured him that Grandmother was wrong but Dadda was not to be deterred.

"My proposal," said Dadda, "is that I pay for you to take a trip around the world and give you an allowance to boot. And you don't get married."

"But I *want* to get married," said Margaret, her face growing red. Picking up her stationery and pen, Margaret rose from her chair and left the room.

Margaret was accustomed to her father's attempts to manipulate her through money. A bribe of twenty or thirty dollars in the form of a check tucked into a letter was his way of expressing love. It was also the method he used to control her. On the occasions when they reached an impasse, which happened often because both were stubborn, Dadda would offer a more robust amount. Her acceptance of his check constituted her tacit acceptance that "he who pays the piper calls the tune."

Dadda wanted veto power over her choice of a husband, and he did not like Luther. She wasn't sure why. There had been a time, in the heat of an argument, when she'd told him what she valued in Luther were those abilities that he, Sherwood Mead, lacked, like Luther's "precise physical skills, and his sensitivity to other human beings." Perhaps this was what had turned Dadda against Luther. On the other hand, it might be something else that she hadn't yet discerned.

Surprisingly, in spite of how much Grandma genuinely liked Luther, the old woman had also had a lukewarm reaction to Margaret's announcement that she planned to marry in the fall. She'd told Margaret, "He'll be riding up to marry you any time you want to in the next five years. You don't have to marry him to keep him."

Margaret, however, had a mind of her own.

On the morning of September 3, 1923, an open touring car pulled into the small village of Lahaska, Pennsylvania, and stopped in front of the town's only hotel. Inside the car were six adults, all in high spirits. The young man behind the wheel peppered the horn several times.

Upstairs, in the hotel suite, Luther Cressman was dressing. Hearing the screech of tires, and the horn, he opened the window. Looking down over the circular drive, he hollered out a greeting.

By the time he reached the bottom of the stairs, his mother and father were already standing in the lobby and two of his brothers were struggling with the luggage.

"About time," said Luther, clasping his brother George's hand and embracing him.

"Well, here we are," said George. "After all, I'm the one responsible for all this."

"Not entirely, George. Luther himself might have had a little bit to do with it, don't you think?" their mother said with a laugh.

"Wasn't easy to find this place," said Morris, setting down a suitcase.

Luther stepped back and looked them over. A thick layer of dust covered their hats and clothes and they were all laughing.

"We stopped at the Meads' for directions," said his father.

"We didn't see your little girlie though," said George, "They kept her hidden away."

What about the other Meads?" said Luther. "The older ones?"

"Oh, yes," said Morris, "if you mean the Mister, we saw *him*."

Luther led his brothers and parents into the dining room. As coffee was being poured, the hotel manager entered. He announced that a young lady was on the phone asking to speak to Luther Cressman. Luther followed the manager into his office where a receiver waited, off the hook. He picked it up.

"Luther?" demanded the voice on the other end.

"Margaret?"

"Your family's not coming to the wedding in *those* clothes, are they?"

"No, Margaret, they're not."

Out of the corner of his eye Luther could see one of his brothers on the stairs, ascending to the second floor. He said, "They're changing now."

The wedding took place at Trinity Church, just outside the village of Buckingham.

Father Pomeroy, Luther's favorite professor from the seminary, came to perform the nuptial Mass. Friends and family arrived by train and by car for the eleven o'clock ceremony, which was performed by the parish priest, the Reverend Mr. Hollah.

After the wedding everyone proceeded to the farm for luncheon. The Meads' Georgian house stood proudly on a rise above a sprawling lawn. Dotting the lawn were tables covered by white linen cloths and adorned with flower arrangements that had been designed by Marie Eichelberger's florist.

Margaret's and Luther's friends from the city mingled on the grass, marveling over the pastoral charm of the countryside. At a certain point during the festivities Luther looked over and noticed his father, off to the side and standing alone. A wave of sadness swept over him, and he thought to himself, "Damn those Meads, to them we Cressmans are outlanders."

After luncheon Margaret's mother sought out Luther and, with a conspiratorial smile, handed him the keys to Sherwood Mead's black Studebaker. She leaned over and gave him a light kiss on the cheek. Luther knew he owed her many thanks.

Enclosing the keys in his palm he turned and, dropping them into his pocket, trotted toward the back porch to retrieve their luggage. On his way he caught a glimpse of Sherwood Mead. "Hell's bells," he thought, "he sent her to DePauw so she'd forget about me and it didn't work. We love each other. *I'm the one* who understands her."

A few minutes later Luther was at the wheel, Margaret climbing into the seat next to him. Before she could shut the door, several of the children rushed forward to shower them with confetti. Margaret sent for a whisk broom to brush it out. While they were waiting she told Luther that Dr. Ostrolenk, one of the men who had partnered with Dadda in a failed business venture, had accidentally spilled coffee down the front of her dress. Luther, who had never had a high opinion of Dr. Ostrolenk, thought to himself, "That figures."

"Forget the whisk broom," Luther said. "Close the door and let's get going." He turned the key in the ignition and they were on their way.

En route through the Poconos Luther saw a policeman standing on the side of the road next to his car. Slowing down, he pulled over.

The policeman told them his car had broken down and asked for a ride into town. As he was climbing into the backseat, Luther heard him say, "I see by the evidence here that *something* has happened."

Luther turned around and, seeing confetti all over the seat, laughed. "Your inference is correct." He reached over to press Margaret's hand, and felt her pull it away.

After dropping off their passenger they drove on, eventually crossing through the Berkshires, following a road that wound through green and yellow foliage. They stopped in Boston and spent the night at a friend's apartment, with Margaret taking the living room couch and Luther sleeping on the floor. The next day they continued on to Cape Cod. They had reserved a small clapboard cottage on the beach in Hyannis. When they arrived the proprietor said that, seeing as how it was off-season, they could take the larger two-bedroom unit. Luther brought their bags in from the car, then suggested they go out to explore the beach.

Margaret told him that she was going to stay back to do some work.

Margaret stood at the glass, looking out. The sea stretched out gray and flat, projecting a lassitude that was not comforting. She opened the windows to let in the smell of the ocean. In the distance she could see Luther walking across the rocks down onto the beach. Gulls flew low over his head, squawking their shrill cries. She turned away from the window and began to unpack her belongings, putting a pile of books on the kitchen table.

Although they were not unacquainted with all matter of information about sex, both Margaret and Luther were virgins. Luther, having grown up on a working farm and observing the cycle of life, had a robust interest in sex, although he didn't discuss it with Margaret. Margaret's knowledge of sex came entirely from books written by the experts of the time. She had read Sigmund Freud, Richard von Krafft-Ebing, and Havelock Ellis.

One semester Ellis's black-market bestseller, *Sexual Inversion,* had made the rounds through the dormitory, with the girls excitedly passing the thick volume in its anonymous dark green binding from one room to the next. Margaret had pored over some of the chapters three or four times, finding interest in the definition of "inverts," or individuals who preferred sex with others of the same gender. In writing about women who were attracted to other women, Ellis had made the distinction between the "true inverts" who remained in same-sex relationships their entire lives and a second group who "developed the germs of it" when they were adolescents, usually during a "crush" on another woman, but, as they matured, passed through that stage. Margaret was heartened by Ellis's theory that temporary attraction to others of the same sex was a natural phase in a young girl's life.

In regard to sex with men, while totally inexperienced, Margaret was game to try. Again, she found Havelock Ellis and his theories interesting. Ellis's analogy was that sex was like a musical instrument that the participants learned to play. If one played with feeling and technique, achieving an orgasm was possible.

She wondered if that was true. Certainly not if you didn't have any experience. And what if she didn't like it? Or if he didn't?

Clearly, Luther did not share any of her trepidation. For the last year, he had made it abundantly clear that he was bursting with impatience to lose his virginity, after their wedding, of course. So eager was he to share a bed with his bride that he filled his letters with images of what he would do when they were man and wife:

My flesh aches for the touch of love flesh beside it with a bitter in-consolable pain. My whole being is crying for you, you, you, to kiss and caress you, to rumple your hair about and kiss it till it won't be still, to see the love in your eyes, to whisper again and again I'm yours, yours, yours. To kiss your lips till they are like two roses, to feel rest after it all calm and peaceful in my arms.

Luther was prepared for Margaret to be defensive. He tried to ease her skittishness by reassuring her that she was desirable, taking advantage of the moments when they were alone to murmur endearments into her ear. "My body is calling for yours," he'd say, "when we are . . . wife and husband, our love will be like a treasure with a hoard of gold stored up till the moment comes for its use."

Finally the waiting was to be over.

The sky was darkening as Luther returned to the cottage. His cheeks were flushed and his hair windblown. He was carrying a bottle of wine and a small package wrapped in brown wax paper and tied with a string.

Margaret was sitting at the little table reading. He noticed that she had changed into a crisp sleeveless dress. She looked as pretty as he'd ever seen her. With a flourish he unwrapped the bundle, revealing several pieces of perfectly prepared fried cod that he'd bought at a roadside stand. Margaret put plates out on the table and they sat down for a leisurely meal. Over dinner Margaret told Luther about the paper she was working on for her first graduate seminar. Pointing to an overturned volume on the kitchen counter she said, "That enormous tome is nearly impossible to wade through."

Luther reached for the book, saw it had something to do with intelligence testing and the army. "Poor little girlie," he said, "it's written by some duffer at Princeton."

Luther blew out the kerosene lamp that sat on the table and came around to where Margaret was sitting on the window seat. He sat down next to her, his leg pressing against hers. He ruffled her hair. He leaned in and kissed her neck.

She twisted her neck away from him and slid herself over on the seat. Her arms pressed down stiffly on either side of her, forming a fence around her body.

He tried again, but Margaret, holding herself away, said, "Tonight I'm going to take the other bedroom. I have some skull-splitting thinking I need to do."

Luther stared at her.

Not meeting his eyes, she said, "I have a seminar paper to write. A book report to give. It's due right after we return."

As Luther regarded her he fought to cover the pain, the humiliation. He hoped to God his face wouldn't give him away. He stood up. "Which room do you want?"

"That one," said Margaret, pointing to the smaller room, the one that did not have a view of the ocean. "I'm going to sleep in there."

Looking, he saw her valise was already sitting open on a stand at the foot of the bed.

That night they did not consummate their union.

One night sleeping alone, in separate bedrooms, turned into two.

The following day Margaret wrote a three-page letter to her mother, filling it with news about the family friends and relatives they had visited in Cape Cod. "We took Aunt Nellie, Cousin Elizabeth and Betty out in the car. Picture that! And they guided us all around Woods Hole and Falmouth." She reported that one of her cousins had flunked his college boards, and the other had taken a temporary job working on a cranberry farm. In a telling remark about how she was viewing the prospect of motherhood and the constraints it would put on her career, she said, "By the way your friends the Waibasses have a *million dollar* estate. *That's* how she can be active and still a mother!" She ended her letter with a wry jest about the monotony of the local architecture, including a pencil sketch of three box-style Cape Cod cottages, all nearly identical.

Luther did not write letters home. Even if he had someone he could unburden himself to, he was too humiliated to reveal what had happened. No one would understand anyway. He looked for chores to keep himself busy, went for long walks, and dallied over the small outdoor stands where the locals sold their wares.

The next afternoon Luther discovered a nearby farm where an old man was selling blueberries and apples. Walking among the barrels, picking out red and gold apples, he was suddenly reminded of one of his favorite Greek myths. The tale was about the maiden Atalanta who didn't want to marry. She told her father she'd only agree if he could find a suitor who could beat her in a footrace. If the suitor lost, she made her father promise that he would be put to death. Many died until a young man named Melanion thought to ask the goddess Aphrodite for help. Aphrodite gave him three golden apples. During the race Melanion dropped the golden fruit, one by one, distracting Atalanta and enabling him to win the contest.

The more Luther thought about it, the more he realized that these last few days had all been about Margaret's "fear and hostility to the commitment of marriage." He was sure Margaret was "seeking to avoid an experience and a possible emotional commitment." He also knew that it was he, more than anyone else, who appreciated Margaret, this "lovely, not beautiful, young woman," now his wife. She was "willful at times, stubborn, sometimes quixotic, never simple, brilliant, goal-oriented and her course laid out, not permitting any interference with her steady progress in that direction." He realized that they were running a race, a long-distance race. Not only would he have to pace himself, but he would also have to find golden apples to throw in her path.

The next day they drove along the Cape, looking out at the low sandy beach under the long skyline. When they reached Provincetown, Luther pulled the car over to the side of the road. He looked over at Margaret, who was staring out at the ocean. Her eyes were opaque, her chin set in a determined line.

"If this is how it's going to be," he thought, "I can stand it."

Once they were on the beach Margaret took off her shoes and walked ahead of him. Luther followed, watching as she stepped lightly over the stones, making her way down to the water's edge. She stood at the waterline, letting the waves lap around her ankles.

Crouching down on his haunches, his back to Margaret, Luther began to sort through the smooth round stones. He cupped a handful in his palm and shook them until one caught his eye. It was a translucent red gold, an agate. He plucked it from the bunch and dropped it into his pocket.

In the car driving home they remained mostly silent. The late afternoon sun slanted through the upright pines. As they neared Hyannis, Margaret quietly reached over and put her hand on Luther's pants leg. He did not look in her direction. A moment later she edged her hand up along the cloth to his inner thigh, allowing the side of her hand to rest up against his crotch.

"You'd better watch out," said Luther, "or we'll end up in a ditch."

Margaret just looked over at him, keeping her hand in place.

The small cottage was almost dark inside and it took a moment for Luther's eyes to adjust. Margaret walked toward him. Even in the near darkness he could see that her eyes were laughing. She reached for his hand and turned him toward the room where she had been sleeping. Feeling the pressure of her hand on his, hearing her low and excited laugh, he let her pull him down on top of her onto the bed.

Afterward, lying side by side, Luther could see the crescent of the moon through the small window. Margaret slept peacefully at his side.

After dinner they went into town to see *Branded*. Sitting in the darkened theater, watching the silent Western, Margaret leaned in close and whispered, "Luther?" And then in a teasing tone, "Have you put your brand on me?"

"Yes," Luther said, but thinking, "No, *you* put my brand on you."

The next few days at the cottage were more relaxing. Margaret had Luther move her suitcase into the main bedroom. In the mornings she was happy to lie in bed, listening to the waves rushing up the rocks, then receding. She allowed herself to sit for long hours at the breakfast table and talk. Luther was an attentive listener, always willing to take up her ideas with an enthusiasm that matched her own.

Even so, still there was a disconnect. She later said, "Our enjoyment of these long lazy hours did not mean that even after an engagement of five years there were not moments of strangeness and disappointment to overcome."

On the morning of their departure Luther cleaned the kitchen while Margret packed their bags. He carried their suitcases out to the car, and she followed him outside.

"I'll give the place the once-over," said Luther. As he walked back toward the door he thrust his hands into his pockets. The fingers of his right hand closed over the smoothness of the agate. His eyes took in the details of the room where he had experienced both pain and pleasure.

He noted the watercolor of the fishing boats, faded and hanging slightly askew, the window seat where Margaret had positioned herself each morning so she could look out over the flat indigo sea. Taking in a last breath of the salty air, he took the beautiful agate out of his pocket and tucked it into the corner of the windowsill, trusting it would be there when they returned.

Margaret was waiting in the car, in the passenger seat. Luther swung himself in behind the wheel. He leaned toward her and they kissed. It was a long, lingering kiss. When he pulled back he saw that her gray-blue eyes were shining. He patted her hand and, starting the motor, glanced in the rearview mirror and backed the car out of the driveway.

A WOMAN OF SPARE EFFECTS

My main difficulty with this poetry—for I have one, a slight one—is its exceeding richness. It is hard for me to feel somewhat cloyed, but that is my weakness. I feel more at home with spare effects.

—EDWARD SAPIR

August 1923

The sound of the water rippling along the sides of the canoe was soothing. Ruth was reclining in the boat, a cushion under her back, looking high up to the branches that hung over her, their intertwining leaves forming a canopy of dark green and gold. Only here at the cottage in West Alton, New Hampshire, did she feel free to enjoy this unspoiled nature.

She reached for the envelope that lay by her side and, once again, extracted the letter. Sapir's slanted cursive filled three pages. He began, "My wife wrote you, I believe, of how I broke my leg and of how they proceeded to make a piece of sculpture out of me." He went on to describe, in amusing detail, how the accident had happened. It had occurred on the first day of the family's vacation. He'd been walking through a plowed field, reading a book, when he stumbled. The next thing he knew he was in a cast. So much for his much longed for holiday on a farm in Pennsylvania, and his work with informants at the neighboring Carlisle Indian School.

She couldn't help but laugh, the mishap was so typical of Edward. Everyone knew that he was absentminded. Incapable of keeping track of the time, he always seemed to arrive ten minutes late, even to teach his own class. Behind the wheel of a motorcar, he was notorious for confusing the brakes with the gas pedal.

Ruth looked up. On the far shore of the lake a splash of scarlet sig-
naled the change of seasons. She returned to his letter:

However, all is going well apparently and I expect to be rid of the plas-
ter cast in a little over a week from now. The incident was entirely
unnecessary, barring obscure Freudian interpretations which might,
I suppose, be invented without much trouble, and kept me from
enjoying these Susquehanna Hills in the way that God, or whoever is
responsible for them, evidently intended they should be enjoyed.

That Edward Sapir—the most brilliant of all the young men—the
designated heir apparent to the throne of Franz Boas, was saying such
things to her was unimaginable.

The developing friendship with Edward had begun with the sharing
of ideas based on their mutual interest in Indian myth and ritual. In all
this, Edward had been extremely complimentary, letting her know that
her writing had inspired him. Just lately he'd gone one step further, and
suggested that perhaps it was Ruth, and not he, Edward, who was destined to take the reins from Boas.

This remark had been occasioned by a conversation they'd had the
previous spring at the Stockton Tearoom. They'd been talking about the
future of their field. Edward had said, "Possibly the only kind of work
that will ever interest the public is one the dyed in the wool anthropologists will be the least ready to support." Anthropology, he said, was the
province of a few highbrows, men who bandied ideas back and forth
under the tent of academia. It was time for this to end. What was needed
was a "shooting star"—one who could break through the firmament
and speak to a wide public.

"A shooting star . . . ," Ruth wondered. "Who might that person be?"
And would a "wide public" ever have any interest in what an anthropologist had to say? She doubted it. But maybe Edward was clairvoyant; maybe
he'd realized something she didn't yet know.

She rested his letter on her chest, dropping her hand into the water,
thrilling to the sudden shock of the cold.

Ruth was seated on a wicker chair, in the spot she favored, on the ve-
randa. Whenever she and Stanley were in West Alton, they reconvened
here at the end of the day, soaking up the last rays of sunlight.

The sleeveless cut of her cotton dress revealed the shapeliness of her arms. The pattern of tiny blueberries that crawled up her bodice made her appear cool and crisp, even on this sweltering afternoon. On the tray by her side sat a pitcher of freshly brewed ice tea and and a plate of cucumber sandwiches neatly quartered.

A problem, however, was weighing her down, so much that she could feel the tension in her shoulders and her neck.

When she had accepted the fellowship to do research for Mrs. Parsons, she had done so with the tacit understanding that her work would be based on a firsthand experience with the Zuñi. This meant fieldwork, and there was no way around it. However, as drawn as she was to understanding how ritual functioned within the Zuñi community, she was equally daunted by the prospect of going there to experience it.

What could she possibly uncover that would be more insightful than all the previous anthropologists who had gone before her, those who had observed the Zuñi when their culture was still intact?

That morning she'd written to Dr. Boas:

All summer I've worked on the mythology and I don't suppose a day has ever passed that I haven't wished fervently I could ask you some question, or wondered what you thought of some difficult coincidence in the stories. I've acquired considerable material but I haven't set to work to tabulate it yet, nor even tried to summarize anything.

This would serve as a good preface to why she'd decided not to go but she wanted to discuss the rest with Stanley. He'd know how she should frame her explanation.

When Stanley finally emerged she could see that he was more distracted than usual. She poured him a glass of tea, garnishing it with a slice of lemon. Next to him she placed a plate of perfectly arranged sandwiches.

Once settled into his chair, Stanley spread a scientific journal open on his lap. Adjusting his eyeglasses, he took a bite of a sandwich, and began flipping through the pages.

Suddenly his phrase, "It's just the nerve," rose up in Ruth's mind and she found herself struggling to maintain her composure. Those words, which he had uttered a few nights earlier, still inflicted pain. The conversation had occurred over dinner. Stanley had been cutting his meat when suddenly he put down his fork and looked at her. "It isn't any laws people need for divorce, just the nerve." When she hadn't responded, he said, "You might find a job at Wellesley, while I go to California."

At the time, Ruth had thought to herself, "He has a fixed idea, and he'll drive me to it—maybe." She had come to expect indifference from him, but not an outright challenge. He was driving her to it, all right. She was infuriated, but she wasn't about to let him know it.

Suddenly his indifference was too much to bear. Rising from her chair, she walked into the cottage. Standing over the kitchen sink, fixing her gaze on the little drooping flowers that poked their heads out from the flowerbox, she poured her tea down the drain. Only later did she express her feelings, not to Stanley, but in her journal:

> For I am smitten to my knees with longing,
> Desolate utterly, scourged by your surface-touch
> Of white-lipped wave and unquiet azure hands.

One Sunday morning Ruth took Stanley's motorcar out for an excursion. Driving down a two-lane highway for forty miles, she kept on the lookout for the Second Advent campground she'd heard about. Finally she spotted a dusty field that held about two dozen dilapidated cars and trucks.

Ruth made her way across the field, passing by rows of wooden picnic tables where women in loose housedresses were setting out bowls of food. Then she saw the supplicants, gathered in a circle around the preacher:

> The great outdoors camp ground was filled with close-lipped people
> to whom the universe was about as rich and various as it is to a cat
> after mice. It seemed to me that their souls were knotted and tied
> against the very notion of infinity. . . . No stretch of sympathy could
> conceive that finite man was here rising toward the infinite—No.

Filled with a kind of revulsion, Ruth couldn't help but think about the rigidity of her own religious upbringing, and that it was "always fundamentally a paralyzing, a limiting, a mocking finite of the infinite."

Later in the afternoon, when families were seated at the tables, eating their midday meal, an older woman motioned her over and offered to share what turned out to be the vegetarian supper that she and her sister had prepared.

"Old maids," thought Ruth, "somehow they seem to find me."

After the meal Ruth walked slowly back to her motorcar. Many of the campers were tying bundles on the tops of their automobiles, saying good-bye. She found herself contemplating the future. She was now thirty-eight years old and locked in an empty marriage. She suspected if she did venture into the field to go to Zuñi that would hasten its end. She sensed that in the near future she might have more in common with the old maids than she did even now.

Ruth hurried through the lobby of Schermerhorn Hall, then through a door to the stairwell. Margaret Mead was going to talk about comparative tattooing patterns in Polynesia. Dr. Boas had promised to attend today's presentation. Taking the stairs two at a time, she reached the fourth floor.

Ruth arrived at the seminar room to find the diminutive Margaret up on a chair, teetering on tiptoes, struggling to hang an enormous reproduction of a Polynesian design on the wall.

"Here, let me give you a hand," Ruth said, rushing to support one side of it while Margaret tacked up the other. The cardboard illustration was so large it covered the entirety of a chalkboard.

It had been Ruth who had first encouraged Margaret to pursue a doctorate in anthropology. She so believed in Margaret's ability that she had taken the unprecedented step of giving her a $300 "no strings attached fellowship." This had been just enough money to make graduate school possible. Referring to Ruth as a "fairy god mother," Margaret had sent the following note:

> Perhaps there is no accepted form for thanking someone who not only opens up all the possibilities of a life work by introducing one to it, but also makes it possible for one to go into that work—perhaps there is no form of thanks because none would be adequate.

Over time Ruth had come to realize that this young lady with the sunny disposition, when focused on a goal, was relentless in her pursuit. Margaret seemed to have an opinion about everything and had no trouble demanding attention for herself. And while this trait rubbed some people the wrong way, prompting Esther Goldfrank to call her "a pugnacious little shrimp" and others to say she "had a lot of nerve," Ruth found this assertiveness attractive. In spite of being fifteen years older than Margaret, she was genuinely starting to enjoy the girl's company.

Today was to be Margaret's debut performance as a graduate student and Ruth could see that she was quite keyed up. When Dr. Boas came through the door, the room went quiet. He bowed a formal greeting and took a seat.

At the end of the presentation, Dr. Boas was his courtly self, congratulating Margaret on her illustrations and saying he had no idea she possessed such artistic talent. As he was walking out, Margaret turned to Ruth for affirmation.

"I learned quite a bit," said Ruth, trying to hide her disappointment.

The truth was that Ruth had found it difficult to concentrate on Margaret's presentation. She'd been distracted by the delivery, with the ideas firing out like corn kernels from a popper. Because of her bad ear, Ruth had missed much of what had been said.

It was two nights later when Ruth was brushing her teeth at the washbasin that she heard the sound of knocking. Turning off the water, she listened, unsure if the knock was at her door, or down the hall. When it came again, louder this time, she wiped her hands on a towel, and unhooked the chain.

Margaret's husband was standing out in the hall.

Ruth opened the door wider.

"I am so sorry, Ruth," he said. "I know the hour is late."

"That's all right, Luther." She stepped back from the threshold so he could enter.

Luther moved into the room. He was a tall young man. His clear eyes were perfectly level with Ruth's.

"It's Margaret," he said. "She's afraid you're disappointed in her."

"Disappointed? For heaven's sake, over what?"

"The seminar report. I'm afraid she's taking it hard."

"She gave a wonderful report. A first-rate report."

"That's not the way she described it," said Luther. "She said your reaction was lukewarm."

"Oh, my," said Ruth. "Did she send you here?"

"Margaret can be intense," said Luther. "You know how she gets wrapped up in things."

Ruth stared back at him.

"I'm afraid she's hysterical. I couldn't calm her down."

"Please," said Ruth, reaching out to touch Luther's arm, "when you go home, tell her that I thought she did a first-rate job."

For Ruth it was confirmation, once again, of the intensity that lay beneath Margaret's buoyant persona.

One morning, as Ruth was walking across campus, she saw a small figure coming toward her. The little person walked with a light step as though she had no weight on her shoulders. It took Ruth a moment before she realized it was Margaret.

"My goodness, you're here early," said Margaret, changing direction to fall in with Ruth.

From Ruth's vantage point the top of Margaret's head was far below her own. "Dr. Boas is giving a lecture, why don't you come?"

"Oh, but it's his introductory course. I took that two years ago."

"He never says the same thing twice," said Ruth. "I find there's always something new to learn."

Boas's lecture that morning was, as Ruth had predicted, entirely extemporaneous and full of fresh insights. Ruth was happy to see that Margaret appreciated it, too, so much so that from that point on Margaret attended every lecture Dr. Boas gave.

On some days Ruth arrived at the Anthropology Department to find Margaret already in the seminar room, seated at the long table, a book spread open before her. Ruth would join her, and the two often worked side by side for hours, reading, taking notes, and, during breaks, swapping stories about their colleagues. They were together so much that Ruth called Margaret "her companion in harness." They found they shared a like sensibility, including a distaste for the high-handed Elsie Parsons and her protégé Gladys Reichard. It still wasn't what one would call a friendship of equals, but Ruth felt strongly enough to say of Margaret, "I say it's the zest of youth I believe in when I see it in her. Or is it that I respond understandably to admiration?"

There were other times, however, when Ruth was made uncomfortable by the adulation and by Margaret's constant need for reassurance.

Margaret was full of complaints about real or imagined physical ailments. If she wasn't talking about the ache in her arm, she was complaining about the bad case of conjunctivitis she'd picked up. Ruth could see that Margaret expected those around her to be solicitous of her fragile health, and while Ruth often acceded to these unspoken demands, saying such things as, "I can't bear to think of your arms being so hard to live with," there were other times when she found them excessive. Margaret seemed to sense that she'd become burdensome and would apologize, thanking Ruth for listening to her "tales of woe."

One day Margaret, apparently thinking about her future, turned to Ruth and asked, "How old is he?"

"Who?"

"Dr. Boas. He looks ancient."

"Well, let's see. When I started here he was sixty-two," said Ruth. "He must be nearly sixty-six."

"Oh dear." Margaret looked worried. "He does have tremendous energy, but even so, who could possibly take his place?"

"It can only be one person. Edward Sapir."

"Isn't he the head of the Anthropology Division in Canada?"

"He's the most brilliant of all the men," Ruth said, thinking that even this was an understatement.

Having Edward Sapir as an ally made Ruth feel that her achievements were not inconsequential. The contrast between Edward and Stanley, her husband, was stark. Any time she put pen to paper, it was Edward she thought of, not Stanley.

Although Edward still addressed her as Mrs. Benedict, and maintained a formal distance, he was making inroads into the part of her she'd kept hidden all these many years.

It wasn't that long ago that Edward had inquired about the poets she liked to read and she'd said, "John Donne and Walt Whitman."

She remembered how he'd lifted his brows in mock surprise and exclaimed, "Of course you do! I knew it! None of that feminine self-confessional poetry for you!"

Ruth was gratified that Edward's reaction to the women poets of the day, like Edna St. Vincent Millay, was in line with her own sensibility. He'd said:

My main difficulty with this poetry—for I have one, a slight one—
is its exceeding richness. It is hard for me not to feel somewhat cloyed,
but that is my weakness. I feel more at home with spare effects.

She exulted. She knew that—if nothing else—she herself was a woman of "spare effects."

Ruth discovered that Edward, every bit as much as she did, enjoyed obsessing over the subtle nuances of words arranged in verse: their variations, their progressions. For Ruth, as well as for Edward, poetry was an expression of man's attempt to comprehend his existence. As writers, this set them apart from those who adhered to the style that was currently in fashion, which valued an expression of earnest sincerity above all else. What Ruth had in common with Edward was that they both were searching for a way to be authentic to their perceptions.

When they talked about the creative process, his advice resonated:

The best way to write a poem is to give up looking for a subject.
Grab some phrase or sentence that you hear, if in the least striking,
tear it violently from its context, idealize it or whimsicalize or in
some other way sketch it on to a remote country, let a new setting
grow out of it at fancy's command and, at the end, if necessary, erase
the line or phrase that served as stimulus.

When it came to finding a publisher, Edward was rarely successful. He complained vehemently:

My verse comes back with the regularity of clockwork. The Strat-
ford Monthly took 4 or 5 of my verses in a lump including only one
of my recent run . . . probably without reading them. They don't pay
and probably get nothing of merit sent to them.

Ruth had been secretly thrilled that Edward had seized on "their shared sensibility," and when he announced that he had "half a mind" to send her some of his verse for comments, she said she'd be happy to take a stab at it.

The poems started to arrive, one after the other. Every week she'd find a thick envelope waiting in her mailbox. When she felt his verse was not working she tried to deliver her criticism in a gentle manner.

Other times, when she could respond with enthusiasm, she was delighted by the effect her praise had on him.

However, just because Edward was sending her his poems didn't mean that she was ready to send him hers. She had no intention of sharing her poetry with anyone. She "still believed that it was safest to keep most of her personal imaginative life to herself."

And yet, the alchemy that was at work between Ruth and Edward was having a transformative effect. It was slowly melting Ruth's steely resolve.

II

THE RIDEAU CANAL

You are right in one thing. Death for myself does not seem such an evil, then why should it for Florence?
— EDWARD SAPIR

March 1924

I t was barely 4:00 p.m. in Ottawa and the sun was already down. Streetlights emitted a sickly yellow glow along the wide and empty boulevards. Snow, gray and deep, had been plowed into murky furrows along the sidewalks. Edward stepped gingerly over the wet pile of slush that had formed in front of his walkway and entered the house. From the parlor came the faint tinkle of the piano where ten-year-old Michael was practicing a simplified version of a Mozart concerto. As Edward was unlacing his boots his mother suddenly appeared before him and started *kvetching* that Michael was not practicing with a metronome.

From another part of the house he heard Florence's voice, calling to him, weak but insistent. He padded down the hall and entered their bedroom.

Florence was awake, sitting up in bed, a white wooden tray bearing her dinner balanced on her lap, the food on her plate uneaten.

Waving her hand at the tray she said, "Can you take this away?"

He lifted the tray off the bed and placed it on the floor. Unbuttoning the top button of his shirt, he settled himself into the chair by the side of the bed.

Florence shifted to face him. "Please talk to Michael," she said. "He's upset. You know he doesn't like the metronome, but your mother won't listen."

"It's not mother that's making him," said Edward, "it's Mr. Saunders. That's how he wants him to practice."

"And he doesn't want your mother at the recital," said Florence.

"That's not something you need to worry about," said Edward. They both understood that Michael was embarrassed by his grandmother's thick Yiddish accent, which always seemed to rise above the hum of small talk surrounding Mr. Saunders's refreshment table.

Rising from the chair, Edward picked up the tray and left the room.

That night Edward made a point of sitting down at the piano with Michael to teach him the simpler bass parts for a four-handed piano piece. It was a difficult piece by Beethoven. When Michael was unable to keep up with his reading speed and finger technique, Edward exasperated, yelled, "Now I see why you need the metronome."

Michael rose from his seat, tears running down his cheeks and ran from the room.

Edward watched him go, thinking, "Now why did I do that?"

He had no right to take out his unhappiness on the children. But for Edward, life in Ottawa was like dwelling in a room in which the ceiling kept dropping, lower and lower. He just couldn't help himself.

At no time did Edward dislike Ottawa more than when it was buried under a heavy blanket of snow. This reaction, of course, had much to do with how the damp cold affected Florence. Last year, after a particularly grueling winter, she had succumbed to one fever after another. Finally, she had agreed to have all of her teeth extracted. Even though the dentist had promised she would recover within a month, she hadn't. Weak and demoralized, she slipped into a profound depression.

Edward's male colleagues thought Florence was mentally unbalanced. One such individual was Alfred Kroeber, a "lay analyst." Failing to comprehend what a ten-year battle with a chronic illness could do, Kroeber insisted that what Florence needed was to be psychoanalyzed. He recommended some sessions with William Alanson White, a high-priced psychiatrist who practiced in Washington, DC. Edward took Kroeber's advice seriously until he found out what it would cost and then he said, "I should have to mortgage my soul for 10 years or more before I got through with him."

Edward never spoke about how bad things were at home, but some of his colleagues found out anyway. Marius Barbeau knew the story. He said Edward "was much upset at the time and his wife was, too, to the point of insanity. Things had been going wrong somehow for them in their domesticity in Ottawa."

By the time the ice had thawed on the Rideau Canal, Florence was nearly suicidal. In spite of the fact that she lacked the strength to walk even one city block, she insisted she wanted to take the children for an outing in the Gatinau Hills. Edward told her that she was too ill to manage such an excursion, but one afternoon when he returned from work, she was gone, along with Michael and Helen.

Barbeau recounted the rest: "Florence had jumped into the Rideau Canal with her two children under her arms to drown herself. She loved Michael and Helen, the two who she'd tried to take to the bottom of the canal. Thank the lord they were rescued."

It was in February of 1924 that Edward and Florence decided it was worth going back to the United States to get another opinion from a respiratory specialist. While Howard Lilienthal, the expert Florence had consulted in New York, was reputed to be the best thoracic surgeon in the country, Florence hadn't liked him. She'd found him cavalier and pompous. Edward was inclined to agree.

Not long after the night of Michael's piano recital Edward wrote to Ruth, "I seem to be in very poor trim psychologically and none too good physically either. Forty is a dangerous age, is it not?"

Of course Edward knew the most challenging issue before him was moving the family out of Ottawa. It simply had to be done. Florence could not survive another winter. Yet leaving Canada necessitated finding a teaching position elsewhere, no easy matter. However, he had a plan. The annual conference of the British Association for the Advancement of Science was scheduled to take place in Toronto in August. A Canadian anthropologist would be designated to organize the anthropology presentations. Taking on such a role would give him the opportunity to elevate his profile among the American scholars who had all but forgotten him.

Late in February, Edward delivered Florence to her sister Nadya's house in Boston, where she planned to stay for several months for consultations and a round of treatments.

On the journey back to Ottawa Edward stopped in New York City. He had specifically timed his visit to New York so he could attend the weekly anthropology lunch.

Edward arrived at the tearoom late, just as several of his colleagues were rising from the table and slipping into their coats. Calling out to both Pliny Goddard and Gladys Reichard not to be in such a rush, to sit back down and have some coffee, he grabbed a menu. Wasting no time, he announced to his colleagues that he had been put in charge of the Anthropology Program for that year's meeting of scholars at the British Association for the Advancement of Science.

As he was talking, he spotted Ruth at the end of the table. She appeared to be looking at him. After he finished eating he moved to the empty chair opposite her.

"Have you heard?" he said, "I'm to be the local secretary for Anthropology at the Toronto meeting."

"Well done," she said.

"Perhaps you could get some people interested," said Edward. "We Canadians should not like to have the meeting fizzle out through lack of American cooperation. You might be able to start the ball rolling."

"I'm not sure how much influence I have."

"Don't underestimate yourself," he said. "And there will undoubtedly be railroad reductions and possibly special rates for a transcontinental trip."

"They'll certainly like that," she said, starting to rise from the table.

He stood up. "Maybe I shall get some Indian agent to stage a war dance for us."

She laughed.

"I'll walk you back." Helping her on with her coat, he added, "Anyway, you might think of a paper for the grand occasion and get others to do likewise. We must try to have a good representation."

Once outside they started to head back to campus. "So, Mrs. Benedict," he said with feigned innocence, "I see you're running a typewriter."

"I beg your pardon?"

"A typewriter," he said. "You're using a typewriter. That is sad."

She stared at him, puzzled.

"It means that you have made up your mind to address me as 'family' and you've installed a machine to do it with."

"A typewritten page is so much easier to read," she said.

"That's a poor defense," said Edward. "Don't I know that women decide in silence what they are flutteringly uncertain about with the tip of the tongue?"

Leaning in close, he said in a low, but emphatic voice, "Use a typewriter for a scientific manuscript, but not for *our* correspondence please!"

Blushing, Ruth said, "Then perhaps you should stop addressing me as 'Mrs. Benedict' and call me Ruth."

"Touché." Edward smiled. "And, oh, yes, I am old-fashioned on a few things."

When Ruth queried him on what those things might be, he didn't answer but his eyes danced from side to side and a little smile crossed his lips.

If he was flirting, he appeared not to realize it.

Others, however, did realize it, and were quick to exchange stories about his so-called naïveté. Bunny Bunzel, the department's new secretary, described him as "abnormally innocent when it came to the opposite sex," while other female colleagues said they found his allegiance to monogamy "touching."

After his return to Ottawa, in a letter written to Ruth on March 1, Edward picked up their discussion where it had left off.

"It's just like me to have to be clubbed with the obvious," he said. "I am like the sleepy Missouri farmer of the Ozarks who asks each chance comer if the Civil War is indeed at an end." And then he went further, staking claim to what he termed "the privilege" of retaining his innocence, saying, "Florence *is* quite right when she says of me that with all my Bolshevistic fanfare, I am really a most-hidebound and conventional fellow."

So far the dialogue that Edward and Ruth had established had begun and ended with a discussion of Edward's poetry. He was gratified that Ruth responded to his poems with an intensity that matched his own. Her comments were well considered, and deeply felt, everything he had hungered for from the editors who sent his verse back with "the regularity of clockwork."

So far he had not been given the opportunity to read *her* poems, nor had he been made privy to any of *her* deeper feelings, but that didn't mean he wasn't curious.

On February 27 he launched his campaign, writing, "Send your verse. I feel it in my bones that you have much to say."

On March 12, Edward wrote to Ruth, naming several of the luminaries who would be attending the conference:

> I am delighted to hear that you are coming to Toronto. Golden-weiser, Wissler, Todd and Wallis will be there, also Barbeau, Jenness, McIlwraith, and myself. By all means give me a title for a paper. Anything you are interested in. Don't just come and listen. It's much more fun making others listen.

He accepted her offer to send a good book, saying "Yes, Maugham, or anyone else you think will make me civilized."

The next week a fat parcel arrived. In it was Ruth's copy of *Of Human Bondage*, recently published, by the British writer Somerset Maugham. At over five hundred pages, the book weighed several pounds. Edward wrote a note of thanks, saying:

> Maugham's book frightens me, but I shall take your word for it and go ahead bravely. Do people really read such long novels? Remember, I do not read photographically. I have to hear every syllable!

Left in Ottawa with his mother and the children, Edward dreaded the long hours after dark. Often unable to sleep, he tried to concentrate on Maugham's story, which he found "psychologically accurate but light-weight." The thoughts that were foremost on Edward's mind, however, were not about Maugham's characters, but about Ruth's poems. He was determined to find out what went on behind her vague and fleeting smile. He sensed that she could be drawn out, the way a feral cat is tempted by a bowl of milk left day after day on the back porch. He alluded to his desire for a more reciprocal relationship:

> I wish I had a poem to send you in answer to your letter of March 24th but I haven't. I have been too horribly depressed of late to do anything. . . . You are doing a good deal of verse yourself. Won't you let me see some of it?

———

Three days later, Edward informed Ruth that Florence was better and had gone to the hospital for observation. He added that she was in capable hands. The new doctor was optimistic enough to think that she would be helped by another operation, "but not the excision the New York doctor spoke of. The latter is terribly dangerous."

From that point on, events moved swiftly. By the end of the week, the doctor cabled to say that surgery was imminent. Florence was to be admitted to the hospital and would remain there until they were ready to operate.

Edward packed his bag and, instructing his mother to forward all his mail to his sister-in-law's house in Boston, caught the next train down. Upon his arrival in Boston, he sent Ruth an account of how things stood:

> Florence has pretty regularly recurring fever and considerable pain. Some operative procedure will be necessary, I am afraid. What the doctor proposed to do so far as I understand him, is to collapse the right lung. Air injection is to be tried first (one trial has already been made, I understand) but the doctor is practically certain this will be of no real use.

A few nights later on his return to his room, Edward found a package full of mail waiting for him. The letters were a welcome distraction. One was an envelope from Ruth. When he scissored it open, out fell a note addressed to Florence, a brief letter for him, and two poems. One was titled a "Discourse on Prayer":

> And I have peace. The moon at harvest is
> Round jocund laughter on the sky,—no more;
> And I have sleepy comfort in your kiss
> That is a wind-blown flame to you.

He read it over again. He rose from his desk and paced the room. Holding the sheet of paper in his hand he went out the front door, down the stone steps, and into the night.

Later, when he returned to his desk, he wrote to thank Ruth for the letter to Florence, which he would give to her in the morning. He also said that her proposed topics for a presentation at the Toronto meeting all sounded interesting. Sounding a note of uncertainty about his own ability to attend the conference, he apologized, saying much would depend on the speed of Florence's recovery.

He ended with the following:

I find myself at last somewhat in the mood to say a few words about your poems. Have you copies of them? I will be frank enough to say that they seem a little short on technique here and there, but that's an exceedingly small thing soon remedied with practice and persistence. The main point is they show great sincerity of feeling, strikingly original imagery, and strength . . .

Edward waited on a straight-backed chair in the hallway outside the operating theater. The odor of formaldehyde, plaster of Paris, and floor wax was strong. From a far distance a rattling noise got his attention. He looked up. A nurse pushing a metal trolley was coming up the long corridor, moving toward him. The trolley's little wheels jangled as they moved over the shiny linoleum tiles. As the trolley neared he could see that it carried an odd-looking machine. The machine consisted of a large deflated cloth balloon that sprouted a red rubber tubing. The contraption was seated on a polished wooden base. Next to it were several large metal canisters that presumably held nitrous oxide.

Edward watched as the nurse rolled the trolley past him, opened the door to the operating theater, and disappeared inside.

This apparatus—the artificial pneumothorax—was the surgeon's last great hope. This was the machine that would enable the doctor to pump gas into the pleural space that enclosed the diseased lung. Once the pleural cavity was inflated, it would balloon in size and push inward against the lung, causing the lung to collapse. The theory was that a collapsed lung was a resting lung, a lung that could heal.

The doctors had told him that sometimes the presence of scar tissue made it impossible for them to inject air into the pleural space. They had warned him that if this turned out to be the case, they would need to try a more drastic approach.

Edward explained it to Ruth. "The next . . . is to remove a few ribs and collapse the lung artificially."

These few words, however, did not really convey what Florence was facing. If the artificial pneumothorax failed, the surgeon would have to reach his own hand inside the pleural cavity and apply manual pressure to collapse the lung.

"So you see poor Florence has a great ordeal before her," said Edward. "She is exceedingly brave about it all and impatient to have something radical done."

The operation seemed to go on for a very long time. The longer Edward waited, the more nervous he became. Only by holding on to the knowledge that this crisis was temporary was he able to soothe himself. Soon this would be over and they would be able to get on with their lives.

Edward stood by the side of the bed, looking down at Florence. A thick gauze wrap encircled her rib cage where the sections of ribs had been removed. The doctor told him that she had been given morphine to lessen the pain.

She looked up at him with glazed eyes.

He reached for her hand and held it.

Later that day he wrote to Ruth:

Florence had an operation yesterday—six rib sections were taken out—and while she looks pale and weak today, she did very well and says she has no pain. I hope the operation will cure the abscess, but it is too early to say anything definite yet.

Five days after the surgery Edward brought Florence back to Nadya's house. Florence was feeling well enough to announce that what she wanted, more than anything else, was to get her hair bobbed. Later that afternoon, while Edward was sitting by her side reading out loud to her from *Of Human Bondage,* Florence interrupted with another request. "Edward," she said, "do you know what I'd like to do when I'm better?"

"What?" he asked.

"Go for high tea at the Château Laurier. After the first snowfall."

The Laurier was Ottawa's grand old hotel. It overlooked the Rideau Canal. From its dining room guests were treated to a view of a winter wonderland—skaters gliding arm-in-arm up and down the glistening ice of the frozen waterway. Tea at the Laurier was always a special event.

"With the children, of course," she added. "Helen would love it."

Edward stood up and moved to the side of the bed. He gently caressed her cheek. "We will," he said, thinking how good it would be to replace that other memory of the Rideau Canal with this one.

Looking down at her wan, but still beautiful face, Edward resolved that he had to find another job, even if it meant a cut in pay and status. He simply could not subject Florence to another winter in Ottawa. That evening, Edward watched Florence joke with her sister as she had in the old days. His wife's exuberance made her look like a young girl again.

Later that night he wrote to Ruth. He had more to say about her poems:

There is a mannerism of yours. An apologetic, conditional style of utterance. It is in your speech and letters, but eschew it in verse. You have more defiance than you allow yourself to express. You must scale off the crust of protective coloration. If you are not careful, you will become mincing, like Henry James.

He was careful to leave her with a word of praise. "There. You must send more. And certainly you must work. I wish I had your delicacy of feeling. . . . It would be unforgiveable if you didn't."

Edward awoke from a dream. In it he had been back at the Algonquin Provincial Park walking with Florence and Michael toward the entrance of Camp Pathfinder. No sooner had they seen the cabins than Michael had taken off at a run. Edward and Florence followed slowly behind. Just then Edward saw Taylor Statent, the camp's director, walking toward them. Edward was embarrassed because he'd not yet paid for Michael's camp session. Before Mr. Statent could raise the subject, Edward reached into a bag and carefully withdrew a large bundle wrapped in brown paper. He held it out to Mr. Statent. Statent took it out of the paper. It was an authentic headdress, once worn by a Sarcee chief. The kind one could only see in a museum. The feathers were uniform, dove gray in color. It was majestic. Edward had correctly surmised that if anyone would be willing to barter, it was Pathfinder's director.

That's where the dream ended. It had been so vivid, replaying events just as they had happened the previous summer, all except for the fact that Florence had been with them. She hadn't. She'd been too sick to accompany him when he'd taken Michael to camp. Maybe the dream was a good omen.

Still groggy, Edward rose from his bed and went in to check on her.

When he entered the room it was too dark to see. He listened for her breathing, and was relieved because he could hear it coming in an unforced and steady cadence. He gently closed the door.

He wrote to Ruth:

Mrs. Sapir is still very weak and has a good deal of fever. She had some very bad days lately but is apparently doing better now. The doctors give me to understand that she will without much doubt get over the operation itself. Meanwhile the operative wound naturally prevents the pad from being tightened all it should be for proper collapsing of the lung, so that the effect of the operation on the lung abscess cannot be properly judged for some time.

The next morning when Edward looked into the bedroom the sight before him startled him. Florence was asleep, her body rising and falling with shallow, rapid breaths. But it was not that. It was that her form looked fuller, as though inflated.

He moved closer.

Her skin was pink, an unnatural pink, and crinkled. The texture looked something like an inflated balloon that had lost some of its air. This wasn't right. He touched her cheek. It was hot, much too hot. Seeing that she was still asleep, he turned and went out the door, closing it gently behind him. He stood there for a moment, his heart pounding, not sure what to do. He went to the kitchen and in a hoarse voice asked Nadya to come take a look. She followed him back into Florence's room.

They stood over the bed. Nadya touched her cheek. With effort, Florence raised her arm up into the air. She cried out in a feeble warble, "Oh please, oh please . . ."

Edward looked to Nadya. "What should we do?"

Florence cried again, "Please, please help!"

The arm was bloated, the skin too hot.

"Oh, dear God," said Edward.

The doctor was called but within a few hours Florence was dead. A few days later, on April 24, Edward wrote the following to Ruth:

The operation was in vain. Poor Florence breathed her last early Monday morning. A general sepsis had set in. My mother and all the children are here now.

In early May Edward returned to Ottawa. Upon entering his neighborhood he was confronted by that riot of color that accompanies a Canadian spring. Housewives were in their front yards, dressed in gay cotton dresses. Many were crouched in their flowerbeds, planting seeds or tending to the young buds that were already pushing their way up. Several of his neighbors called out to him as he passed.

Once on his front porch, Edward noticed that the shoots had come up in Florence's flowerboxes. Entering the parlor he found the room lighter than he remembered it, presumably because his mother had aired it out.

He walked into their bedroom. The door to the closet was closed, a benign-looking door, painted off-white, like every other wooden surface throughout the house. This was the plank of wood that protected him from a reality he didn't want to face. He dreaded opening it. When he did, the anguish of that moment did not disappoint.

He stood in front of the blouses and dresses, looking at the colors his wife had chosen for her own. Reaching out for her favorite blouse, a peach-colored silk tunic with three-quarter-length sleeves, he pressed its soft folds of cloth against his lips.

Later that day he wrote to Ruth:

There's nothing deader than the past of physical personality, only it so shocks and startles one to learn this. Today the familiar voice falls on our ear and we never think to look certainty in the face and recognize it for but heavily conditioned hope. Tomorrow we search all creation in vain for the same voice.

Edward was, at age forty, a widower, left alone to raise three young children. He had no idea how he was going to move forward from this point. He was grateful to count Ruth as his friend. He wrote in the same letter:

Death for myself does not seem such an evil, then why should it for Florence? Well, I suppose it is partly because I had always hoped the future would soften and reinterpret some grievous stretches of the past. That was a selfish motive, like absolution held in reserve. But there was also the feeling that Florence knew so well what to make of life, if only given her due chance.

In the days and weeks that followed, no matter how he tried, he was unable to move beyond the part he had played in his wife's death:

And the most terrible part of it all for me is the steady, grinding realization that these last terrible three years, link on link, are but the result of my own criminal wantonness that all the tragedy might so easily have been avoided.

THEY DANCE FOR RAIN

*And now the clouds have listened to the insistent mea-
sure of the song, to the rhythm of forty dancing feet, to the
beat of their turtle shell rattles.*

—RUTH BENEDICT

Summer 1924

Around the department it was known that after office hours, on
Tuesday and Thursday afternoons, good conversation and a cup
of strong tea could be had in Professor Boas's office. These gath-
erings were well attended by the clutch of female graduate students who
doted on "Papa Franz."

On this particular afternoon, the unspoken subtext was Ruth Benedict
and the abrupt change she had made in her travel plans to go to Zuñi. She
now planned to leave for the pueblo three weeks ahead of schedule.
When Dr. Boas had pointed out that by accelerating her departure she
would miss Sapir's conference in Toronto, she had met his inquiry with
a half smile.

Bunny Bunzel, secretary of the department, was tending the kettle.
Bunny was a short girl with dark brown hair, a sallow complexion, and
a hatchet-shaped profile. As usual she felt strangely diminished standing
next to the tall and elegant Mrs. Benedict, who in her mind resembled
a classical Greek statue.

As Bunny set out the cups, Ruth strained on her tiptoes to reach the
shelf where the tins of tea were stored. Suddenly one of the canisters
slipped from her hand, scattering tea leaves across the floor. When Bunny
looked she noticed that Ruth's hand was shaking.

Once the tea had steeped, Bunny poured some for Ruth and herself.
Standing next to Ruth, cradling the cup between her hands, she said,

"You know I've been thinking. I've saved a few dollars for a trip to Europe, but I don't really know if I want to go. It doesn't excite me."

Ruth was stirring sugar into her tea.

Bunny took a tentative sip of tea. "What if I went with you to New Mexico instead?"

Ruth looked at her. "Really?"

"I'm a good stenographer," said Bunny. "I can take down folktales and interviews in shorthand, and do all our typing."

"I think that would be completely wonderful," said Ruth. "Are you sure?"

"I think so," said Bunny, taking another sip. "I'll talk to Papa Franz."

When the room emptied out and Dr. Boas was putting on his jacket, Bunny approached him and suggested that perhaps she could accompany Ruth to Zuñi and work as her stenographer.

Dr. Boas heard her out before he snorted, "What are you going to do? Type? Don't waste your time."

Bunny was dismayed.

"Do a project of your own. You're interested in art?"

"Yes?"

"Well," he said, "they make pottery there. Go with her to the pueblo. Do a project on the relationship of the artist to her work."

Six weeks later, in the inky light of dawn, Ruth Benedict sat on the concrete steps of the one-room post office in Gallup, New Mexico. Next to her an excited Bunny Bunzel paced back and forth.

The train had delivered the two women to Gallup the night before. A coal-mining town that supplied the fuel for the transcontinental railroad, Gallup was considered the last civilized stop before Zuñi, which was some thirty-eight miles away, on the eastern border of Arizona.

Bunny had been told that soon the rainy season was going to start, but she didn't believe it. The air was bone-dry. Looking up the long dirt highway that stretched straight as a plank out of town, she could see, rising above the sagebrush, the sunbaked wooden sheds that housed the coal miners.

A boy led two horses to the front of the post office, to where an old mail wagon waited. The rig appeared to be something out of the previous century, consisting of a large rectangular box sitting atop four spindly wheels. Amid the general commotion of neighing and stomping, the horses were hitched, trunks lifted, and leather mail sacks heaved into the wagon. A few moments later the driver instructed the women to climb aboard, cracked his whip, and they were on their way.

Once outside Gallup they creaked along a dirt trail, rutted by furrows, potholes, and small gullies, ascending to a high broad plateau hemmed in by rugged mountains of red and white sandstone. The landscape, as they traveled through it, was cut by deep canyons and densely forested with thick conifers. As they moved west, the land began to open up, and before them stretched a wide plain, covered by low-lying sage, greasewood, yucca, and small cacti. Arroyos crisscrossed the landscape like seams on a sunbaked face.

Looking down from on high, Bunny could see a dry riverbed with a tiny thin trickle of water at its center. This, she presumed, was the Zuñi River. She searched for words that might trigger a conversation with her traveling companion, but the newness of their surroundings seemed to have rendered Ruth even less accessible than usual.

They rode in silence until they reached a vista.

"Look," said Bunny, "that must be the red terraced hillock of Zuñi."

Stretching out before them were the flat terra-cotta roofs of about thirty buildings, clustered around a plaza. Here and there the silhouette of a person could be seen, standing on a roof. The sight was peaceful, welcoming.

By the time the mail wagon reached the outskirts of the pueblo the sun had gone down. Coals glowed inside pits in the ground, sending swirls of white smoke into the air. Pervading the air was the unfamiliar and delicious aroma of roasting corn. Entering a small central plaza, Bunny and Ruth found themselves surrounded on all sides by the rough mud walls of houses, two stories high, with flat roofs covered with dirt. Ladders were propped against the side of nearly every building. The windows, such as they were, were small rectangular openings, so high in the walls that they seemed to be designed only for ventilation.

Climbing down from the wagon, the women began to walk through the plaza, looking for someone, anyone, to direct them to the home of Margaret Lewis, their Zuñi host.

Mrs. Lewis had been described to them as a former schoolteacher and "an extremely well-educated Cherokee" who had assisted Elsie Parsons on several of her excursions. Mrs. Lewis had promised to provide them with a clean place to stay and a list of potential informants. She was, in short, the linchpin of their fieldwork.

Seeing an open doorway, and what appeared to be a figure standing within its shadows, Ruth walked toward it. Bunny followed.

Suddenly Ruth was face-to-face with the gray-seamed face of an ancient soul who appeared to be neither male nor female.

Ruth asked in broken Spanish for directions to the home of Margaret Lewis.

The individual stared back impassively.

Ruth tried again.

The person said nothing.

Ruth turned around and went back outside.

Bunny said, "What was that?"

Ruth said, "I don't know."

A few other people had emerged from their doorways. Ruth approached one of the men, Bunny following a few steps behind. Ruth asked again for Mrs. Lewis, and the man shook his head. While Ruth was trying another way to ask for directions to the Lewis house, a young man approached her and gestured toward an adobe building. Leading them into a dark room, he pointed to a metal grate. On the other side of the grate sat a large wooden box. Ruth and Bunny crept forward to see what it contained.

The box held mail.

"All the letters in the box are unopened," said Ruth. "And there's one of mine. It's addressed to Margaret Lewis."

The enormity of their predicament was beginning to dawn on them.

Margaret Lewis was not picking up her mail. She had either left the pueblo, or she was dead. They no longer had a sympathetic local to oversee their stay in Zuñi, nor did they have a place to sleep.

Ruth addressed the man in Spanish, and he responded in Zuñi. Neither of them understood the other. His voice rose in volume, causing others to gather around. In the midst of the tumult a young woman stepped forward. She introduced herself as Flora Zuñi, a teacher at the government school. In broken Spanish she confirmed what they already had surmised. Margaret Lewis was no longer living in the town.

Flora invited them to come back with her to her family's home.

They walked through the dark lanes, their path lit by a crescent moon. By the time they reached the periphery of the pueblo there were only a few scattered houses. Flora led them into one. An old woman was tending something inside an open-faced oven. Flora introduced Ruth and Bunny to Catalina Zuñi, her mother.

A few days later Bunny sent Dr. Boas an account of their entry into the pueblo:

> *Well two days—or is it two years—ago we set up housekeeping a la Zuñi. Mrs. Lewis is no longer here so we have been thrown on our own resources. . . . It seems that Mrs. Lewis has gotten herself badly involved in the religious rumpus, and as a result did not get a school appointment for next year. Nevertheless, our hearts went down to our toes when we got here and found her gone, and our letters lying undelivered in the post office. We went to Flora as a next resort and were received like princes and rented from her a house on the edge of the village where we are more than comfortable.*

Within two weeks the women had settled into their routines.

Bunny spent several hours a day with Catalina, the undisputed master potter of the pueblo. Ruth liked to work with the old men, settling on Nick Tumaka as her primary informant. While Nick recited the sacred stories in a singsong voice, Ruth positioned herself so she could hear out of her good ear, taking notes "with flying pencil and aching arm." Despite Nick's high status within the community, it turned out he was something of an outsider, having once been tried for witchcraft and "hung by his thumbs" until he confessed. Ruth swore that Nick's information was reliable but Bunny wasn't so sure. Writing to Boas, Bunny called Nick "an old rascal who wants to see which way the cat jumps."

By late July of 1924, Ruth had discovered in herself a great fondness for Zuñi. It had come over her in a rush. The landscape, as she perceived it, was inspiring. She wrote:

> *Serpents lengthening themselves over the rock*
> *Indolently desirous, feel the sun*
> *Cover their flanks with sweetness . . .*

With great anticipation she waited for the Kachina ceremonies to begin. She'd heard it said, again and again, that the dances would bring on the torrential rain the community so needed.

Ruth was also waiting for a letter from Edward. Although he had warned her that corresponding with friends, while in the field, was trying, it had proved more difficult than she had imagined. She found herself watching for the mail wagon, day after day.

She knew that he was profoundly depressed. In a recent letter he'd said:

Most of my days and nights have been spent in numbness, articulated with regrets. If I had done so and so earlier or not have allowed the operation or not have allowed the extraction of the teeth, all might have been different. It is impossible to avoid this sickly reverie of what should or might have been. The last wasting days went by so unexpectedly and so stealthily that as I look back on them it seems hard to realize I was there at all.

Eventually, she knew, he would emerge from his numbness, and then what? Her relationship with Edward was changing and she wasn't sure what direction it was heading.

Ruth had become acquainted with Edward while he was married and inaccessible. She was married, too. She had been comfortable with the boundaries their other commitments enforced, content to let their feelings remain unspoken. Now Florence's death had tipped the balance by removing the center of the triangle. As one side of their special construct collapsed inward, pushing Edward toward Ruth, the space between them had shown itself to be in danger of disappearing. So disconcerting was this new dynamic, Ruth wasn't sure how to react.

When she'd informed Edward that her trip to Zuñi made it impossible to attend the conference in Toronto, he'd put up a protest, saying he was "sadly disappointed," and that he'd been "counting on seeing her." He'd gone so far to say that he'd lost his enthusiasm for the entire enterprise and, at this point, "would pay out cash not to have to go to Toronto."

For her part, Ruth believed it was far better to avoid a face-to-face encounter, at least for the time being. Distance and the passage of time would allow their emotions to find their natural level.

Edward loomed as large as he ever had. Only now it was no longer his marriage that held him at bay, it was Ruth herself.

On the morning of the Kachina dances Ruth found a seat along the perimeter of the plaza. When the masked and brightly costumed dancers appeared, they walked in two long double file rows. With their bodies bent a little forward, head and shoulders loose, their feet pounded the rhythm of the dance into the earth.

At some point during the ceremonies Ruth heard a deep rumble sounding from above. She looked up. Great black clouds were moving across the horizon, filling the sky to its zenith. Suddenly raindrops began falling, great translucent drops, splattering the red terra-cotta buildings, releasing a distinctly medicinal odor. She breathed in the scent, looking around. People were standing on the flat roofs of the buildings, their arms outstretched, their palms facing up to the sky. No one ran for shelter.

The Zuñis' petition to the gods had succeeded. Ruth wrote, "The song only rises a little louder, and a quiet happiness at heard and answered prayer moves the people of the pueblo."

By September the leaves began to change and the nights became cool. Ruth would be leaving Zuñi soon. It was during this time that she received a letter from Edward that contained a verse he'd written for her:

Through the dry glitter of the desert sea
And sharpness of the mesa keep the flowing
Of your spirit, in many branching ways,
Be running mirrors to the colored maze,
Not pool enchanted nor a water slowing.

She copied it out and tacked the copy onto the wall next to her bed. She was starting to feel less apprehensive about returning to New York.

One afternoon she walked out, past the gardens where melons were ripening on the vine, past the peach orchards where the full fruit was hanging in clusters. Coming toward her were groups of men, carrying their scythes up against their shoulders, their work done for the day. In the distance she could see the yellowish acres of wheat fields outlined by a darkening sky.

As Ruth neared the fields, she caught the smell of freshly cut wheat and damp earth. A roll of thunder echoed from above. Ruth held her face up and let the rain splash over her, cool and cleansing. She reached up her arms, spread them, opening herself to life.

HER HEAD WAS SPINNING

At present my soul won't stop. It's discovered perpetual motion in a circle.

—MARGARET MEAD

August 1924

A pot of water was boiling wildly on the stovetop. Margaret stood over it, feeling the steam rising around her face. Taking a spoon, she put a tomato on it, and lowered it into the water. When she lifted the tomato out, its loose and crinkled skin fell off. It had been Grandma who'd taught her this trick for peeling tomatoes.

She was thinking about what she wanted to say to Ruth.

Ruth was still on the mesa, not due to return to New York for a few weeks. It seemed like she'd been gone forever.

The letter was difficult to write. She'd been putting it off for days. Later that night she started.

I don't like to think of you there all alone—tho in many ways I suppose it will be less of a conversational strain at least. I wish we could go on a field trip together—only in my present state I'd talk you insane. I don't seem to be able to stop talking any more than I can stop thinking.

Margaret continued, "At present my soul won't stop. It's discovered perpetual motion in a circle."

The spinning in her head wasn't unpleasant. In fact she was thoroughly enjoying the sensation. She was brimful of energy with no idea what to do with it. She told Ruth that she had "a list in her pocketbook of stories to tell her," but they were "either too detailed or depended too much on intonation to be trusted to paper."

There was one story, however, that she had no plans to divulge. That story was hers alone to savor.

Margaret was just beginning to understand that for her, some people could be as intoxicating as that first taste of a fine wine.

It was one of those events that one plays out in one's head, over and over.

It had happened early in August, when Margaret had gone to the University of Toronto to attend the ninety-fourth annual meeting of the British Association for the Advancement of Science.

She'd arrived for the opening ceremonies on a hot and humid morning, stepping into the dank foyer of a nineteenth-century behemoth known on campus as the Anatomy Building. At the far end of the hallway she saw a line of people passing through the open doors of an auditorium. Her heels clicked as she crossed the marble floor.

It was her first experience on her own as a professional, presenting her work to a formidable group of academics, a coming-out before the scholars who would one day be her colleagues. They were, for the most part, at least two decades older than she, and soon she would be standing before them—these three dozen men and two women—delivering *her* paper, full of *her* ideas. She wasn't intimidated, in fact she wasn't even nervous. Dadda had made sure she had mastered the art of public speaking.

She was eager to see, with her own eyes, the men who were considered the most renowned anthropologists in the world: A. C. Haddon, an expert on the cultures of Melanesia and the author of *Head-hunters: Black, White and Brown*; and Charles Seligman, *the* Africa scholar, who used his knowledge of physiology to identify the Bushmen, Pygmies, Negroids, and Hamites, the four distinct races that inhabited the African continent.

She sat near the back of the auditorium so she could watch people enter. Many seemed to be old friends, calling out greetings to one another, clasping hands, embracing. She opened the program, scanning to see who was scheduled to speak over the next three days. Her eye caught "Rank in Polynesia," the paper she was going to deliver, and alongside it her name: Margaret Mead.

She was thrilled.

Suddenly the sound of a finger tapping on a live microphone drew her attention to the stage. Then a voice filled the room, calling notice to itself with an effortless command. The sound of the voice was deep, melodious and warm.

Margaret strained to see the speaker.

On the stage stood a dark-haired man dressed in a rumpled tweed jacket. He was pacing the floor as he talked, welcoming his "esteemed colleagues from across the Atlantic and south of the border to his adoptive country, the Dominion of Canada." He was gesticulating as he spoke, and his face, from what she could see, was animated.

This must be Edward Sapir—Ruth's Edward Sapir.

Flashes of the hours spent sitting in the seminar room with Ruth, telling each other "stories about people the other had never met, wondering and speculating why they had done or felt or thought what they seemed to have," all came back in a rush. And the individual upon whom Ruth had conferred a near mystical aura was this man, Edward Sapir, once the wunderkind of the New York City school system, the linguist who could speak over thirty-five languages and the chief of anthropology for all of Canada.

Ruth had even gone further, describing Sapir as a truly masculine man who wrote verse. A rogue poet.

Rising up in her seat, straightening her spectacles to get a better view, Margaret decided that he was even more attractive than Ruth had let on. And the timber of his voice was spellbinding.

No wonder people said Edward Sapir would be the man to succeed Dr. Boas.

It seemed all too soon when Sapir completed his introductions and turned the podium over to A. C. Haddon.

Haddon's paper was followed by three solid hours of mostly pedantic lectures on such subjects as "Diffusion as a Criteria of Age" and "An Analysis of the Ceremony of the First Salmon on the Pacific Coast." When an intermission was finally called, Margaret gratefully followed the crowd out of the auditorium and into the foyer.

People were milling about, chatting. Margaret met the unconventional Erna Gunther, who had made an avant-garde "contract marriage" with Leslie Spier and T. F. McIlwraith, who talked about his work reconstructing the old ceremonies of the Bella Bella. And Diamond Jenness, a New Zealander, who was every bit the maverick as his name implied, back from another expedition to the Arctic in which half the crew he had traveled with had perished in an ice-locked ship.

More and more, it was sinking in that each one of these anthropologists had a "people." Margaret, too, wanted to have a people on whom she could base her own intellectual life.

Then she spotted Goldie—the infamous Alexander Goldenweiser—a brilliant but risqué Jewish intellectual, another one of Dr. Boas's disciples, who had made a study of psychological factors common among tribal cultures. In spite of his "great big head and slight body," he was known to be quite the lady's man. There was even talk that he'd had an affair with one of his Iroquois informants.

Goldie was standing with a group of men; one of them was Edward Sapir.

Margaret moved closer.

"Your tales," a man with a French accent was saying, "contain words that are unreadable by the old schoolmarms. Daring, smutty words."

Sapir stuck his hands in his trousers. "You mean the words that they themselves used?"

"You know what I mean. Those items should have been removed."

"He's too candid to think of that," said Goldie.

"Nor do I agree with the principle of censorship," said Sapir.

"The two publications were denounced in Parliament by the members," said the man, who Margaret realized was Marius Barbeau, a French Canadian from Ottawa. "Later we heard that the king had given instructions to burn the editions."

"Actually," Sapir said laughing, "I've heard somehow they're still on the shelves."

At the luncheon Margaret made sure to sit at the same table with Goldie and Sapir. These two, like everyone else it seemed, were arguing over the merits of Freud's theories as compared to Jung's.

"Freud," Margaret heard Edward Sapir say, "is more interested in typical mechanisms of personality formation than in types."

"I tend to concur with Freud," said Goldie. "The individual is malleable."

"Malleable or not," said Sapir, "Jung proposes there are fundamental types over and above the mechanisms."

Goldie snorted.

Before he could elaborate, Margaret interrupted. "Not all people under the same circumstances will develop in the same way."

Sapir looked at her, his eyes happily dancing at the unexpected challenge. He turned back to Goldie. "If you doubt the usefulness of the classifications, consider what Seligman has to say." He then began to explain that Charles Seligman, that great dean of African ethnology, had suggested that Jung's typologies of extrovert and introvert could even be applied to tribal societies.

"The extrovert is greedy for experience," Sapir continued. "He tends to become greatly influenced by slight or fleeting stimuli. The extrovert is always asking, 'Where did he get it?' The introvert wonders, 'What will he do with it?'"

Margaret thought she saw Sapir glance in her direction, but then she really wasn't sure if that was just something she'd imagined.

The next afternoon, as the session was ending for the day, Margaret looked about for Sapir and saw him in the center of a group that included Goldie, Diamond Jenness, and several others.

She noticed he had a particular way of standing with his head cocked, his hands shoved in the pockets of his trousers, his legs spread, and his body tilted slightly backward. His jacket, once a presumably stylish cut, was now so frayed that the inside lining, torn and sagging, stuck out below the hemline.

Once again they were all talking about their fieldwork. McIlwraith had a story to tell about the Bella Bella, Buxton about the Navaho. Then Diamond Jenness, referring to his Eskimos as the "Twilight People," told a story about living among the Copper Inuit for a year.

The story involved an old woman who believed that Diamond, who had brought the remains of a human skull back to his tent, was responsible for causing a curse to descend on the village.

"She'd been sewing in her tent, she told me, when she saw my tent, a few paces away, begin to shake violently." "She ran in fear from what was happening."

He paused. They all waited.

"I'm a slow thinker. It never occurred to me she thought a ghost was in there. But her husband came to my rescue. 'Nail a lid on the box,' he said, giving me a sly wink behind her back. 'That will prevent it from doing us any harm.'"

"Like I've always said," Goldie said, "we all get the tribe we deserve."

Everyone laughed but Margaret, once again aware that she was the only one who had not experienced what Goldie was talking about. "Everyone has a field of his own," she thought, "each has a people to whom he can refer. Everyone but me."

As she turned away, she suddenly felt a hand touch her upper arm. Looking up she found herself face-to-face with Edward Sapir. "Oh," she said, feeling herself being gently guided away.

"I always enjoy spending time with Goldie," he said. "I like him tremendously, in spite of my periodic disgruntlements with him." Then, in an offhand manner, "What do you hear from our mutual friend, Mrs. Benedict?"

"Ruth?" She was surprised that Sapir knew about their friendship. "She's living in a house with Bunny Bunzel. Working eleven hours a day," said Margaret.

"A Puritan on the mesa," he said. "And what about you? Are you going to the Southwest, too?"

"No," she said, "certainly not. I intend to go someplace that hasn't been overrun by Americans. And anthropologists."

They were walking now, heading back to the auditorium for the day's final session.

"Be sure to give my regards to Mrs. Benedict," he said. "No doubt your letters will reach her before mine do." Then he stopped, for the first time looking directly into her eyes. "Have you ever thought how truly unfair it all is?"

"How unfair what is?"

"Here we are, dutifully waiting for another paper to be read to us, and there is Mrs. Benedict, in the thick of it, in Zuñi." His eyes, quite expressive, seemed to smile. "I'm sure she's enjoying herself hugely."

"Ruth tells me that you write serious verse," said Margaret.

"Is that what she said?"

He turned to go, then stopped and turned back. "I suppose she thinks I'm one of those dainty men who write poetry?" When Margaret didn't answer he added, "Lately my muse seems to have taken a holiday."

"Not a long one, one hopes," said Margaret.

"Who ever knows," he said, making a slight bow and walking away.

Watching him go, Margaret had much to ponder. Ruth had filled her mind with so many stories. She knew that he not only wrote verse, but also composed his own piano concertos. She knew that his wife had died, just a few months earlier. No wonder his muse had taken a holiday.

Margaret was a subscriber—as were others in her circle—to the

Jungian theory that a muse or "anima" existed within the unconscious of every man. There were times, during periods of great difficulty, or even for no apparent reason, that this anima was not accessible. After a long dry spell a man was only able to reawaken his inner anima when he recognized her in the external world, personified by a flesh-and-blood woman. Perhaps Sapir needed such a woman.

The hotel room was stifling and it wasn't just the lack of cross-ventilation. Margaret felt almost breathless. The feeling of being with him still lingered. He had constellated something within her.

She believed that just as a man possessed an anima within his unconscious, so did a woman possess an animus, or male figure within hers. And when the male side of a woman's nature was activated, it pushed her to achieve something in the outer world, something of meaning, something of worth.

This, above all, was what Margaret wanted for herself. She had, for a long time, been waiting for the maleness inside her to be given life. Somehow she felt that when it was, her animus would propel her to greatness.

She took off her dress and hung it in the closet. Wearing only a slip, she stood in front of the oval mirror that hung over the bureau. She looked at her reflection. Her arms were thin, her chest nearly flat. Her hair was cut in a short bob with unruly waves sticking out every-which-way.

Tomorrow she was going to read her paper to the professors.

Edward Sapir would be in the audience.

She pulled her slip over her head and, naked, climbed into bed.

She could almost hear his voice. It was almost as if he was there in the room with her. She lay on her back, imagining that he was next to her.

Sex with a man was not something Margaret had ever enjoyed. Although he'd tried, Luther had not aroused any real excitement in her. Often when they were lying awake at night in their bedroom, she in one of the single beds, he ten feet away in the other, she wondered if it was possible for her to ever be truly intimate with a man.

In fact, she'd had crushes on girls that had engendered more excitement than Luther ever had. For the most part these crushes had been fleeting and, in an era in which same-sex colleges were the rule, were not considered abnormal.

There had been one flirtation, while in college and before she married, that was different. At the end of her first year, Margaret had met a physics major named Lee Newton, the same Lee who had gone "hysterically blind" in the days before Marie Bloomfield killed herself. Margaret and Lee had created a fantasy life together based on their shared love of Shakespearean comedies like *As You Like it*, in which two of the female heroines hide their gender by dressing in male clothing. In their correspondence, Lee had assumed a character named Peter, while Margaret called herself Euphemia. Some of these letters were passionate.

For nearly a year, Margaret and Lee played out their flirtation in secret. While other coeds lingered with their beaus under an arbor at the center of the Barnard quad, Margaret and Lee had gone there as well, pinning notes for one another on a tree trunk. One of Lee's notes said:

> *The warmest glow just raced through me when I found your letter on the "tree" this morning. I seized it so hungrily that the 11-year old William inquired if I was a "feller." He couldn't understand about "a little wifelet."*

Margaret had been fiercely private about her attraction to Lee, aware that any hint that she might be romantically involved with another girl would be ruinous for her future.

In comparison to the fantasies that Lee had aroused, her experience with Luther seemed tepid. She loved him and she couldn't imagine life without him, so what was wrong?

Perhaps it was the pull of these other urges, tamped down and suppressed, that stopped her from being attracted to Luther. She wished she knew.

She rolled over on her side and wrapped her legs around a pillow. Then she thought about the things Ruth had said about Sapir. It was obvious that Ruth was in love with him. Her "vividly relayed conversations" had become a part of Margaret's thinking "long before she'd set eyes on him." All that talk, perversely, made Margaret want him, too.

And then it occurred to her that maybe Ruth had already slept with Sapir. It was strange to think of Ruth in that light. She'd always considered Ruth attractive, but not in an erotic sense. Ruth possessed a nature that was classical, orderly, and controlled, what Nietzsche had called the Apollonian form. The thought of a different Ruth, one who gave expression to her physical needs, was not anything Margaret had ever considered.

She stared into the darkness, wondering if she would be able to fall asleep.

Somehow she had to get to know Edward Sapir. He was, she thought, "the most brilliant person . . . the most satisfactory mind" she'd ever met.

How would she go about it? Would it even be possible? She tried again to re-create the touch of his hand on her arm. Had he even touched her arm?

In mid-September, while still on the mesa, Ruth received a letter from Edward. It was dated a few weeks earlier, on August 23, 1924:

> The meeting at Toronto was quite a success and there were a really large number of worthwhile papers. I think you would have enjoyed it but you did wiser, after all, to go to the Southwest, where you can see and feel it first hand. . . .

Edward told Ruth that what he "enjoyed particularly" was visiting with Goldie, and "getting to know Margaret Mead." He said of Margaret, "She is an astonishingly acute thinker and seems to be able to assimilate and invent ideas at breakneck speed."

"Getting to know Margaret," thought Ruth, "that was strange." She had received several letters from Margaret, all written since the conference, and there had been no mention of Edward.

In fact, it wasn't to be until two weeks later, in a letter dated September 8, that Edward Sapir's name appeared in one of Margaret's letters:

> This morning's mail brought your letter along, my paper and a letter from Sapir so I've had much food for thought all day. I suppose it's a very bad sign that Sapir has time to write letters but I do enjoy them. It's such a satisfactory friendship, defaced by no tiresome preliminaries (that's thanks to you) and founded on sure ground of like-mindedness.

"Like-mindedness?" wondered Ruth. Margaret had always gushed that it was *she* and Margaret who were like-minded, and now suddenly Edward had been made a member of their circle.

What Ruth couldn't possibly know was that for weeks Margaret had been careful *not* to discuss Edward, even though the desire to do so had been overwhelming. The fact that she indulged herself now was because, earlier in the day, Edward's letter had arrived, and she could no longer contain herself. Margaret felt compelled to tell *someone* about it and, when it came down to it, Ruth was her closest confidant.

GUARDIAN ANGEL

Dear George: I shall instruct all Navy personnel under my command in Samoa to do everything possible to facilitate the success of your daughter-in-law's project.
— REAR ADMIRAL EDWARD STITT

December 1924

A camel hair coat was slung over the back of the divan. It was the first thing Luther noticed when he entered his living room.

He moved to touch it. Perhaps it was the burnished ocher color, so rich and exotic, or the fur collar, a semicircle of genuine sable, haughty enough to frame a queen's face. Whatever it was, this insolent wrap dominated the room.

The coat was not Margaret's. It would be profoundly out of place in her closet.

It could only belong to one of two people—Pelham Kortheuer or Bunny McCall. They were the only girls swanky enough to wear it.

He stood stock-still, listening for a sound. The door to their bedroom was closed, and out of courtesy he did not go toward it. Obviously, Margaret had loaned out their bedroom for an afternoon tryst. She believed in supporting her friends in their attempts to find love, and Luther did, too.

He entered the kitchenette and contemplated the pile of last night's dishes waiting in the sink. Standing there, shirtsleeves rolled up to his elbows, he turned on the water and reached for a dirty dish. It made a clinking noise against the other plates. He winced. The impulse to tidy up was strong, but not as strong as his desire to be considerate of the lovers in the bedroom. He threw down the sponge and shut off the faucet. Putting his coat back on, he walked out the door and locked it behind him.

Once outside Luther walked along Broadway, peering in the shop windows. Shopkeepers were pulling down shades, turning off lights, locking up for the day. Only at the barbershop was there any activity.

When Luther reached the toy store he stopped. He always took pleasure in the miniature German soldiers. These perfect replicas of a 1914 infantry brigade made out of lead and painted with enamel were accurate in every detail.

Then his eye moved to a model of a schooner. It made him think again about Margaret. Now she was talking about doing fieldwork someplace in the South Seas. Ever since Margaret had done that paper comparing tattooing patterns from one island culture to the next, she'd been fixated on Polynesia.

A journey to the South Seas was the kind of adventure that Luther and every other boy of his generation had been raised on, thanks to writers like Herman Melville and Robert Louis Stevenson. It was Stevenson, sailing by schooner to Hawaii, the Marquesas, and far-off Samoa, who had best captured the allure of that unknown world:

> *I was now escaped out of the shadow of the Roman Empire, under whose toppling monuments we were all cradled, whose laws and letter are on every hand of us, constraining and preventing. . . . I was now to see what men might be whose fathers had never studied Virgil, had never been conquered by Caesar. . . .*

And now it was Margaret who might venture there, too.

She'd told Luther that Polynesia, meaning "many islands," was—according to the great British anthropologist A. C. Haddon—"probably the part of the world which most urgently needs ethnological investigation." It was one of "the primitive cultures that would soon become changed beyond recovery." Even so, Luther could hardly imagine her traveling alone to such a wild, far-off, and unexplored land.

Back at their apartment, before inserting his key into the lock, he caught the odor of onions cooking, then heard Margaret's voice coming loud and fast from within. He still thrilled at the sound of it.

He walked in. Margaret was standing over the stove, Pelham seated at their kitchen table. Pelham's eyes were swollen.

"You're much needed," said Margaret, shooting Luther a meaningful look.

Luther pulled up a chair.

Margaret had always taken pride in the way her friends opened up to him. She joked that Luther "liked women better than men, as people," and the truth was, he *was* completely comfortable listening to women. Louise Rosenblatt, who some time ago had nicknamed Luther "Margaret's guardian angel," had recently begun calling him "*their* guardian angel."

"He told me he needed breathing room," said Pelham, repositioning her chair.

"Here it is," thought Luther, "another one of these affairs, that start out like firecrackers on the Fourth of July and end with the hulls all burnt out and soggy on the wet ground." He reached across the table and pressed his hand over hers.

"He's got another think coming if he thinks I'm going to wait around for him to make up his mind," said Pelham.

Luther considered his own wife. She was purposeful, bossy at times, but always straightforward and generous. He was thankful that their life together was not fraught with false drama. Together they had pooled their energy so they could move forward in a productive and meaningful way. They were making life simpler for each other. It was the way marriage was supposed to be.

Margaret waited for Dr. Boas to answer.

They were the only two people there in the empty classroom, with its smell of chalk dust and radiator exhaust—the twenty-two-year-old student, and her sixty-six-year-old mentor.

From Margaret's perspective, Boas seemed ancient, almost decrepit. She rued the fact that, considering the very real possibility that his retirement was imminent, he was unable to give her opportunities for the kind of person-to-person contact she craved. It didn't make sense that, "as long as a student was doing well, he paid almost no attention to her," while the mediocre ones sucked up all of his time.

She watched him walk toward the front of the classroom. He moved gingerly, almost unsteadily. He seemed beaten, and with good reason. Just three months earlier, in October, his twenty-seven-year-old daughter Gertrud had been stricken with polio. She'd died at Montefiore Hospital in the Bronx where Dr. Ernst Boas, the professor's oldest son, was the medical director. Boas never mentioned his daughter's death, but his grief was palpable.

At the blackboard Boas pulled on a cord and unfurled an enormous map of the world. Moving closer to the map, squinting at it, he stood there for such a long time that Margaret found herself fidgeting.

She hated to waste the precious moments she had with him in silence. As one who was most comfortable in the midst of a high-spirited conversation, it never occurred to her that Dr. Boas enjoyed the silence, that he was satisfied just to gaze upon his map, taking in the names of far-off untraveled lands. She did not know that for Boas maps were as entrancing as great works of art, that he loved studying the topography of distant regions, the relationship of a people to their landscape, to the rivers and mountains that bounded them.

Nor did Margaret have any idea that her teacher was reliving that time in his *own* life when he had traveled to mysterious corners of the world, lands untouched by Western hands.

She could not possibly know that when Franz Boas was her age, with a graduate degree in physics from Heidelberg University, he had approached his own uncertain future with the same relentless determination with which she now confronted hers. He had felt then, as she did now, that by sheer willpower he could force the opportunities to materialize.

Always fascinated by the North Pole, Boas had devised a hair-raising scheme to bolster his credentials by becoming an Arctic explorer. Modeling himself after the heroes of his day, adventurers who had perished in their attempts to reach the North Pole, he had dreamed up his own expedition to the Arctic, and sold the story rights to a Berlin newspaper. With the advance he received on future articles, he financed his trip, sailing on a schooner to Baffin Island and spending the next twelve months among the Eskimo, traveling by dog sled to map their migration routes, sleeping in igloos, and surviving on raw seal liver.

And now Margaret was proposing her own far-fetched scheme—an expedition to a far-flung Polynesian island where ships docked only once or twice a year.

She watched him locate a cluster of tiny islands in a vast sea.

She held her breath.

Finally he turned back to her.

"No," he said, "Tuamotu is not possible."

"Oh, no," she thought, "he's going to insist I go to New Mexico."

"Tuamotu is too remote," he said, and he launched into a litany of the dangers she might encounter. Foremost on his list were the young men who had died while doing fieldwork outside the United States. His final example was William Jones, his own student, who'd earned his PhD from Columbia in 1904 and had gone to do research in the Philippines. Jones had been living in Dumobato, on the east side of Luzon, when he was assaulted and murdered by three members of the tribe he'd been studying.

Nodding her head, seemingly attentive, Margaret's mind was racing. If Boas were to refuse now he might never relent.

"There's enough to study here, with our own American Indians," he said.

"But I want to work on change," she insisted, "and the only way to do that is to work in an old and stable culture, one that has not been exposed to Western ways." Rushing headlong into a discussion of tattooing patterns in Polynesia, she began to spew out random facts about how the manufacture of pigments was changing.

Dr. Boas scowled. "Why don't you take on a study that you've lived through, that you can follow here, on our own continent?"

"I *do* know something about this, Dr. Boas, my dissertation—"

"No," he said, waving his hand to cut her off. "I mean adolescence. Why don't you do something on the adolescent girl?"

She paused.

"Put your tattooing aside," Boas said, "and take on a study that you've lived through."

Margaret felt her resistance rising like the rough on a dog's back.

"Adolescence is a phase most parents face with dread," said Boas, "but for all we know adolescence is a twentieth-century Western invention."

Margaret's mind leaped.

Here it was, the nature-nurture debate, the topic that was engaging the scientists of their time. Was it heredity or environment that determined the course of an individual's life? Margaret knew that Boas had recently published an article in *American Mercury* suggesting that the National Research Council—known as the NRC—underwrite a study to answer this fundamental question.

Maybe the NRC could be tapped to finance fieldwork in Polynesia.

"Some will claim," Boas was saying, "that adolescence is a universal phenomenon of human growth, that the difficulties of adolescence spring more from biology than from culture."

Margaret was well aware that Boas believed the *other* side of the argument, that early on he had come out heavily in favor of the environmentalists, who asserted that "in the great mass of a healthy population, the social stimulus is infinitely more potent than biological mechanism."

She studied him. Now adamant about making his point, he'd taken off his eyeglasses and was rubbing his eyes.

What she said now would determine whether or not he would let her go. She decided to try what she'd learned to do when she worked things out with her father—appeal to his vanity. She knew that there was one thing that mattered more to Boas than the direction she took in her own research and that was that "he should behave like a liberal, democratic, modern man, not like a Prussian autocrat." He would be unable to bear the implied accusation that he had bullied her into accepting a culture that didn't interest her. She'd never given any particular thought to adolescence, but she suspected that if she went along with his plan to study teenage girls, he might let her to go to Polynesia.

"We know how the young person experiences adolescence here, in our world," Boas was saying, "*Sturm und Drang and Weltschmerz.* But is this what we would find in other cultures that have no contact with our own?"

"It's a good idea," said Margaret. "It really is, but in order to do it justice I'll have to leave the continent."

Boas shook his head.

"North America has been overrun. If I stay here, we'll never know if it's biology or culture that determines behavior." She paused. "Tuamotu," she said . . .

"Tuamotu is far too remote," he said again.

Once again he turned back to the map. A long moment of silence hung between them while he let his finger trail across the small dots that comprised the islands of Polynesia. "What about American Samoa?" he said, his back still toward her. "There's a naval base there. You might be able to secure some support."

He turned to face her. "A boat must touch them every month, wouldn't you think?"

They all trooped up Broadway into the wind. They had been to a concert at Carnegie Hall and were on their way home. Luther was glad for the blustery weather. The general confusion made it less necessary for him to engage in conversation. Next to him Louise Bogan was talking in too loud a voice. "I'm reading Marcel Proust," she was saying. "I've given up Henry James as an old senile creature."

Margaret and her new friend Edward Sapir, an anthropology professor from Canada, were behind them. They were discussing the Finnish composer Jean Sibelius, whose orchestral work, *The Swan of Tuonela*, they just had heard performed.

Luther looked sideways at Louise, and saw her pull her coat close around her throat and happily toss her hair. He had always liked her, but now he was not so sure. Her conversation had suddenly become too highfalutin, no doubt because Sapir was with them.

Louise was moving to Boston to be with her fiancé, Raymond Holden, and about that, Luther was glad. At least that relationship seemed to be working out.

"My new address is rather a nice horse-hair-and-black-walnut kind of address, don't you think?" Louise was saying. "It's way down on the wrong side of the Hill, almost against the Charles Street jail."

Unfamiliar with Boston, Luther said, "I didn't know there was a wrong side of Beacon Hill."

"It's all I can afford," said Louise. "My entire exchequer is being ruined by visits to the dentist."

Louise had recently been elected acting editor of the poetry journal *The Measure*. Under her watch the journal had selected a group of Sapir's poems for publication. She admired Sapir's poetry and, Luther thought, tried too hard to impress him.

Just then Luther heard Sapir say, "Like a faint mist, the music seems to enter the body without passing through the central nervous system." Then Margaret said something that Luther couldn't quite catch.

Apparently, until just recently, Sapir had assumed that Margaret was an unmarried graduate student. There'd been some confusion over her last name. Sapir had only just found out that Luther and she were husband and wife.

Luther was suddenly aware that he was straining to hear what Sapir was going to say next, and he hated himself for it. He caught the words, ". . . like a vague dream that wanders irresponsibly, flowing, unbidden . . ." and thought, "What malarkey."

All night the three of them had tried to be polite, but really, Luther felt they had just been condescending.

Luther, Louise still at his side, reached the front steps of their building. He turned to look at Margaret.

He saw that her eyes were shining and happy.

Luther threw a football to his older brother, George. George took off at a full run. Visible behind him were the cold stark hills of French Creek.

Later, when they were coming back, George carrying the football, Luther sighed. "Women," he said, shaking his head.

George laughed.

Luther looked up at the gray clouds gathering overhead. "A storm is coming."

George laughed even louder.

"I don't know," said Luther. "Now she's talking about going someplace in the South Pacific."

"That little girl?" said George, looking at his brother with amusement. "And you're going to let her go?"

"Me?" said Luther. "I've got nothing to say about it."

He wanted to tell George about "the tensions, indefinite as to cause perhaps a feeling of not communicating, with not getting through to the other, that left a sense of uncertainty, ill-defined and meaning unclear." Of late, this sense of uneasiness had increased. He often joked that Margaret was so often absent he had to make appointments to see her.

"Worrying about it is a waste of time," George said. "People do what they want to do."

"That's not true," Luther said.

"Well, worry about it then," George said. "See if that will change anything."

"I knew you'd say something like that," Luther said.

It wasn't until later, when he was driving in the motor car accompanying his father while the doctor made house calls, that Luther found himself thinking about Margaret again.

Not looking in his father's direction he said, "Papa. Do you remember when Margaret was writing her paper on Polynesian tattoos? Well, she's stuck with it. She even has the idea she can do her fieldwork in the South Seas."

"My word," said Dr. Cressman, "she certainly does dream."

"The place she wants to go is called Tuamotu, a little dot somewhere in the South Pacific. Dr. Boas says it's too dangerous. He suggested American Samoa."

"American Samoa?"

"It's as safe place a place as any, if she can get some assistance. It's administered by the U.S. Navy."

His father grunted, then pointed to a small brick house set back from the road. "There," he said. "Pull over."

An hour later, when they were leaving the patient's house, walking up the lane to the car, Dr. Cressman said, "I've been thinking."

Luther turned to him.

His father had fished out his tobacco pouch and began to fill his pipe. He seemed to be dredging up some memory from the distant past. "I wonder if this would help Margaret."

Luther waited.

"Don't know if I ever told you the story, about how I stood in for Edward Stitt at his graduation from medical school?"

"Edward Stitt?" said Luther, racking his brain to remember why the name sounded familiar.

"I was a year behind Edward in medical school. Well, Edward was in the navy at the time. He was commissioned an assistant surgeon and ordered to his ship, just a week before graduation."

Luther was still baffled.

"That's when I stood in for him."

Luther opened the car door for his father, waited for him to climb in, and then went around and got in on the driver's side. Turning the key, the engine jumped to life.

"Could be time for me to write him now and collect on that promissory note," said Dr. Cressman. "Edward's now 'Rear Admiral Stitt,' surgeon general of the U.S. Navy. He might be able to provide the support Margaret needs."

Luther pulled away from the curb.

"If you think it would help," said George Cressman, "I'll write to him."

"If you do that, Papa," said Luther, "I think we have it made."

THE OLD KING MUST DIE

I am very eager not to take a false step. If it is possible for me to get started in New York, I feel that it's the proper place for me to be.

—Edward Sapir

January 1925

Edward pressed on with the letter that he was writing to his colleague Robert Lowie at U.C. Berkeley: "It is high time I got on to a university job if I am not to die without feeling that I spent my whole life as a square peg in a round hole," he said. "This place is getting confoundedly on my nerves."

Escape from Ottawa still continued to elude him. Months of searching for a university position had demonstrated that teaching jobs for linguists working with unwritten languages were practically nonexistent.

Berkeley, he already knew, was impossible. Alfred Kroeber, who professed to be his friend, had always been threatened by Edward's aptitude with languages. Harvard also seemed to be off the table. Roland Dixon—who was "sympathetic" to Edward's wish to devote himself to linguistics alone—had not been able to "cobble together" the funds to hire him there. And while a job offer seemed to be forthcoming from Fay-Cooper Cole, the head of Anthropology at the University of Chicago, there seemed to be little enthusiasm within that institution to combine the study of ethnology and linguistics.

For Edward, Columbia was still the most desirable location. After all, Boas was his mentor and New York City the hub of his intellectual universe.

Lately, Bill Ogburn, an ally who taught sociology and was privy to the inner workings of Columbia and its administration, had indicated there were rumblings of a sea change. The departments of Sociology and Anthropology might be combined, but only *after* Franz Boas retired.

Boas was sixty-six years old and looking frail.

In life, as in folktales, the old adage "the old king must die" still held. The question was when?

Although naive when it came to academic politics, Edward was wise enough to know that dancing on the grave of this hallowed patriarch would not only be unseemly, it would be profoundly counterproductive. In particular, caution was to be exercised among that clutch of female grad students who circled around Boas like mares in season. This especially meant treading carefully around Ruth. Although Edward considered her his closest confidant, her personal loyalty to Boas superseded even their friendship.

But Edward was in need of information.

There must be someone else within Columbia's inner circle, someone who did not perceive him as a rival, who could provide him with a glimpse of the future. Aside from his friend Bill Ogburn only one other individual came to mind—the archaeologist Nels Nelson.

For the last two decades Nelson had been associated with any number of thrilling expeditions launched by New York's Museum of Natural History. He'd surveyed the Upper Rio Grande Valley, excavated in Chaco Canyon, and had been part of the team that had discovered a Neolithic culture in the Qutang Gorge in China. Now he was preparing to go off with Roy Chapman Andrews on Andrews's third expedition to hunt for fossilized dinosaur eggs in Mongolia.

Nels Nelson was only too happy to keep Edward apprised of Boas and all his plans. And in early February, at the end of a chatty letter, in which Nelson detailed the full extent of his preparations for Mongolia, he dropped some news that caused Edward to stagger up from his chair.

The letter referenced a sudden tragedy that had befallen the Boas family.

Heinrich, Boas's youngest son, known to those in the department as Henry, had been killed in a freak accident

Nelson's tone had been sympathetic, but at the same time matter-of-fact. Only a man who had not yet taken on the responsibilities of fatherhood could so casually drop such a bombshell.

Edward paced the room for some time before he sat down to write to Ruth:

I have just received word from Nelson in which he states in a post-script: "we were all greatly shocked this morning to read of Boas' loss of his young son." Does this mean that Heine has died? That would be terrible. Please drop me a line at once.

The agony of waiting for word by return post was nearly intolerable. It took another ten days for Ruth's response to reach him. In it she described the freak accident that had killed Heinrich, age twenty-five, enclosing the obituary that had appeared in *The New York Times* on January 25, 1925:

TRAIN KILLS THREE IN MICHIGAN: Boas was taking the girls to Miss Bleasby's father's home at Pokagon . . . when the car was struck at a point where the view was obscured by trees. The bodies were found between the rails of the westbound track. The young man was a graduate of Storrs Agricultural College in Connecticut and had been at the Berrien County Farm about four months.

Edward visualized the bodies, lying on the rails, between the tracks. He was speechless. Within the space of three months, Franz Boas had lost two of his children, both in the prime of their lives.

Edward Sapir and Franz Boas sat in the study of the professor's home in Grantwood, New Jersey.

The old man had visibly aged. His right cheek appeared to be paralyzed, his eye hooded under a drooping lid.

Condolences had been expressed, and the room hung in quietude for a good long while. Edward knew that Boas understood that he, Edward, was no stranger to the waves of grief that come in the wake of a sudden and premature death. There were no words that could ease that kind of pain.

Nevertheless, it was time for Edward to elicit the old man's support in helping him escape from Ottawa.

Edward broke the silence, telling Boas that Fay-Cooper Cole at the University of Chicago had made him a serious offer. Perhaps Boas could use this information as a bargaining chip to leverage more interest out of Columbia's administration.

"If it is possible for me to get started in New York, I feel that it's the proper place for me to be," said Edward. "I would be willing to accept a more modest position just to be in New York."

"So you see teaching as the solution to your problems?" asked Boas.

As Boas was studying him, Marie Boas tiptoed in, carrying a tray with tea and an apple torte. She, too, looked worn and broken.

"What the hell do I care about exhibits?" said Edward, knowing that Boas was loath to see him give up control of Canada, which included a vast museum collection. "I should give so much to be in contact with people who are genuinely interested in linguistic research. It would give me the stimulus I so badly need."

"I can appreciate your feeling that you lack congenial people with whom you can talk over scientific interests," Boas answered, "but we all have to put up with that condition.

"However," he added, "I am able to offer you a summer school appointment, but that's all. You can teach two ethnology courses. There is some interest, which leads me to hope that in a few years a department of linguistics may be established. For that, we will have to wait." And then, standing up, he indicated that the conversation was at an end.

"This is much looked for news," Edward said. "Thank you."

A few days later Edward walked into the Stockton Tearoom where he'd arranged to meet Margaret Mead. He spotted her, seated in a corner booth. As he walked toward her he felt a twinge of remorse at how he'd handled their last exchange. She'd sent him one of her poems, which he thought was decidedly mediocre. Considering their developing friendship, he'd found himself in a predicament, and had said as much to Ruth:

> I wrote Margaret yesterday and decided to tell her gently but frankly how her verse affected me. She won't take offence, I am sure, especially as I make the positive point she should go in for simple narrative verse, and I don't think it would have been really frank or friendly of me to have passed over her verse in utter silence. That kind of charity would have seemed an insult to me if I had been she.

From the look of her now, she didn't seem upset. Reaching the booth, he slid in across from her and said, "I am glad to see you looking as buoyant and as industrious as ever."

Margaret smiled and pushed a package wrapped in brown newsprint across the table.

"What have we here?" he said, lifting the package.

"Don't worry," she said with a laugh, "it isn't any more of my poetry."

He undid the string and ripped open the paper. Inside was a book entitled *The Growth of the Mind* by Kurt Koffka.

Edward turned the book over in his hand. "I've heard of him."

"He's a professor of experimental psychology," said Margaret.

"I see that."

Edward opened the book to a page at random and read several paragraphs. He was aware that she was watching him closely.

"He probes some of the questions that you've been working on," she said. "What forces shape personality, what forces determine behavior."

He continued to read.

"For example, what would have been the fate of people we know," said Margaret, "like Louise Bogan, Léonie Adams, or Ruth, if they had been born into another culture, like the Zuñi?"

"Ruth as a Zuñi." He laughed. "Can you imagine that?"

Edward then said that he was going to teach two classes at the Columbia summer session. He planned to structure his ethnology course around topics of interdisciplinary theory. "I want to overhaul some of the fundamental concepts in a way that might be of interest to students of psychology, sociology and history."

Margaret was listening to him with rapt attention.

The waitress appeared at their table, and he ordered for the two of them.

Margaret began to unbutton her sweater.

As Edward was talking, telling her that the manners and morals of tribes, as well as those of their own culture, were not piecemeal examples of behavior, but part of an overall pattern, he noticed her blouse. The pale ivory chiffon was nearly translucent. He could actually see the outline of her nipples pushing against the cloth.

He looked away, embarrassed. A moment later, in mid-sentence, his eyes returned to her blouse and he stared again.

He raised his eyes to hers.

Her face was tilted upward, her eyes looking straight into his. He reasoned to himself that a young lady would consider it unseemly to go around without a brassiere. He knew, however, that Margaret had some unconventional ideas.

"When one works with a living culture," he continued, "this wholeness is a part of everyday experience."

"That's why I think you'll really enjoy the book," Margaret said. "Like you, Koffka interprets human activity as a pattern that unfolds in a series of actions, each one triggering the next."

He was surprised at the sophistication of her thinking.

"You might be able to use him in your classes," she said.

"Thank you," he said, patting the book. "I look forward to reading this."

Back in Ottawa, Edward Sapir was restive. As usual, he blamed the weather. It was supposedly spring, and yet the sky still persisted in dropping pellets of frozen rain. On April 15, 1925, he wrote the following to Ruth:

> I've been reading Koffka's "Growth of the Mind" (Margaret's copy) and it's like some echo telling me what my intuition never quite had the courage to say out loud. It's the real book for background for a philosophy of culture, (your, my philosophy), and I see the most fascinating and alarming possibilities of application of its principles, expressed and implied, mostly implied, to all behavior, art, music and culture, personality and everything else.

He looked up from writing the letter. It didn't occur to him that perhaps his enthusiasm for the book was, in part, an enthusiasm for the person who had introduced him to it.

Since his lunch with Margaret he'd found himself thinking about her more and more. He found it perplexing that she was a married woman. That boy Luther, her husband, was a strange sort of fellow. Obviously he had sanctioned her decision to be called by her maiden name.

When Edward had commented on what he found to be a bewildering marital arrangement, Margaret had retorted with the rejoinder that he, Edward, was of a different generation than she, and perhaps this was the reason he didn't understand.

Edward continued his letter to Ruth:

> If somebody with an icy grin doesn't come around to temper my low fever, I'll soon be studying geometry again in order to discover what

really happens when a poem takes your breath away or you're at log-
gerheads with somebody. Nay more—unless a humanist like your-
self stops me, I'll be drawing up plans for a generalized geometry of
experience, in which each theorem will be casually illustrated from
ordinary behavior, music, culture and language.

He thought again about the way Margaret carried herself, with a step so light it was as if she was walking on air. She'd told him that she was trying to persuade Dr. Boas to let her go to an island in Polynesia. She said if she was able to secure backing from the U.S. Navy, he might actually let her do it. That was a foolhardy idea. He and everyone else knew her to be a person who was high-strung. How could a girl like her even consider going to the tropics?

But that would never come to pass, he was sure of it. Boas wouldn't let it happen.

He ended his letter to Ruth, "How is Margaret? It's too bad she has such a frightful time with the neuritis. Can't something be done?" Then he shifted gears. "And how are you? And what news about the place? Here spring holds back. Hail today. Is this a place to live?"

With summer school just a few weeks away, Edward was busy making arrangements. He planned to leave the children in Ottawa, under the care of his mother, and come down to New York on his own.

He gave little thought to Chicago. When Ruth queried him on the possibility of a job there, he replied, "Until I actually get a black and white offer, I shall not count the cup as having attained the lip, nor shall I have the family's pictures taken for the use of the immigration authorities."

In truth, his hopes were still pinned on Columbia. Once he was ensconced in the department, perhaps Boas would be loath to let him go.

Most of all he kept thinking about Margaret Mead. While in New York he intended to spend as much time with her as possible. He gave little thought to her threat to go to the South Seas, nor to the fact that she was married.

A SECOND HONEYMOON

All competing affairs had been laid aside; and without in-
trusion, we were 'living together in marriage,' a kind of
second and true honeymoon.

—LUTHER CRESSMAN

June 1925

Spools of light flared out from their moving car, illuminating hairpin turns. Margaret gripped the sides of her seat and stared ahead.
North woods such as these were loaded with deer. Earlier, at
twilight, she'd already seen a herd bounding through the trees.

Ruth had tried to warn her that the cottage was deep in the forest,
that reaching it wouldn't be easy.

Margaret glanced over at Luther. He seemed unperturbed.

"Please slow down," she said.

"Relax," he said as he negotiated another turn.

Luther was a good driver, but whenever he got behind the wheel of
Charlie Cressman's red Buick roadster, he took too many chances. She
prayed they wouldn't hit anything.

They were returning from a holiday on Narragansett Bay.

Fannie McMaster, Margaret's aunt, had generously lent them a quaint
vacation cottage on a grassy field, just a couple hundred yards in from a
muddy tidal flat. Considering that Margaret's departure for Samoa was
only four weeks away and she'd be gone for almost a year, Aunt Fannie
thought they needed some special time together.

Margaret and Luther decided that the Rhode Island shore wasn't any
good for bathing but they both enjoyed the isolation. On the first night
they'd laughed when they noticed, on the floor by Luther's side of the
bed, a carpenter's hatchet, positioned at the ready, just in case danger

threatened. A nearby restaurant served swordfish steaks and strawberry shortcake, and after their first meal they returned there for every dinner. The six nights in the cottage had done much to shore up Luther's flagging confidence. He'd even told Margaret that for him the week was the happiest of their marriage. He called it a "second and true honeymoon."

Luther didn't want the honeymoon to end, so on the way back, when Margaret suggested taking a detour to visit the Benedicts' cottage in West Alton, New Hampshire, he readily agreed.

They had both heard so much from Ruth about the north woods. She had made the "dark, dark blue" Lake Winnipesaukee and the surrounding countryside sound irresistible:

One of these clear northwest wind days we drove up through the White Mountains, up one and down the other—a beautiful old stand-by of a ride. We found a hidden little lake on a back road— green as beryl, and set in pinewoods against a bare cliff.

Besides, Ruth would be leaving soon on her own trip; she was going again to do fieldwork in Zuñi. Margaret wanted a proper good-bye and finally, a chance to get to know the elusive Stanley Benedict.

Margaret found it exceedingly strange that Ruth kept Stanley so hidden. Obviously he was a challenging personality. Ruth had told her he barely tolerated Ruth's passion for anthropology and poetry, shunning social encounters with any of her colleagues. She'd cautioned that because he was preparing for his own trip, a solo hiking trek across Alaska, he might be even touchier now, saying "he always needs much waiting on when he's packing up for the summer."

All of this had done little to dampen Margaret's enthusiasm for a visit. She felt it was well worth the 370-mile detour to fill in this missing piece of Ruth's life. Who could say when she'd get another opportunity?

Ruth had warned that West Alton was "isolated." She'd said that getting a letter there "might be a precarious matter," and that even telegrams were not delivered "unless they contain the words death or died." With this in mind, Ruth had left her with a set of directions that one might use to locate buried treasure:

You can put away your Blue Book when you strike the New Hampshire line and keep your eyes on the green posts. Manchester is the

*only bad town to get through and it's well posted. I take it that it will
be after dark by the time you reach these parts. Therefore watch the
left side of the road well ten miles below Lakeport—somewhere
between ten and twelve miles you'll see the "Woodlane" sign. Turn
the hairpin turn into our wood road.*

"It's supposed to be on the left," said Margaret, "about ten miles past
Lakeport."

"We've gone at least ten miles," said Luther.

Suddenly they saw a road, so narrow it could be a footpath, and Luther made a sharp turn into it.

"There's where we're supposed to leave the car," said Margaret, pointing to a stone garage at the top of the hill.

Luther pulled over and parked. They both got out of the car and stood
for a moment, stretching, breathing in the balmy night air. Margaret
could hear the soft gurgle of a brook someplace in the darkness.

Down by the cottage the earth was rich and fecund. An old stone
path led to the porch. They climbed the stairs. Pushing open the door
they tiptoed through a dark front room. Ruth and Stanley had obviously
already gone to sleep. A door was ajar, a flickering light and a double
bed beckoned from within.

Margaret undressed and slipped into her nightgown. She climbed
into bed next to Luther. She'd been looking forward to this visit and she
knew Ruth had, too. When Margaret had told her that they planned to
visit, Ruth had said, "I'd have been more lonely than you'd have guessed
if you'd decided against coming. I count the days."

Margaret had been counting the days, too.

Margaret watched Stanley's large pale hands crack eggs on the side of
the bowl. He was making his acclaimed French toast to be served with
the local maple syrup. His movements were economical, precise, and
certain. "This is how he must be in his laboratory," thought Margaret.
When she finished her piece she was still hungry, but when Stanley made
no motion to make more, good manners prevented her from asking for
a second helping.

They'd woken up to a clear cloudless sky. It was a perfect day for a
hike out to the lake but Margaret assumed their excursion would not
include Stanley.

"Stanley has been immersed in Canadian Pacific literature," Ruth was saying. "He plans to start for Alaska a week after I leave, going through Banff and Lake Louise."

"I've mapped the route to take me past eight glaciers," said Stanley.

"He'd never have started," said Ruth, "if I'd been here to stay on with all summer."

Inevitably the discussion switched to the Zuñi and Ruth's travel plans.

Ruth planned to take the train to New Mexico in late July, at approximately the same time Margaret would be leaving for San Francisco, to catch the steamer that would take her to the South Seas.

It turned out that Stanley had been giving the whole situation some serious thought. He'd decided that Ruth and Margaret should travel together.

Stanley proceeded to lay out the plan: The two of them could ride together as far as New Mexico. At the Gallup station, Ruth could get off to catch her mail wagon for Zuñi. Margaret could continue on to the West Coast.

Luther agreed it was a wonderful idea.

Ruth, who had already heard all of this, caught Margaret's eye before turning back to Stanley. "But I've already made plans to go with Goddard," she said, referring to a long-standing arrangement she'd had with Pliny Goddard, the director of the Museum of Natural History. "I'm to meet him in Cincinnati and travel with him across country. I can't possibly change that now, can I?"

"You know what I think about that," snorted Stanley. "Why you have to ruin a good trip by traveling with Goddard, I can't for the life of me understand."

Ruth's smile showed great forbearance. She explained to Margaret and Luther that as she had plans to visit a relative in Cincinnati, and Goddard was picking up his train in St. Louis, traveling together had made logistical sense.

"Logistical sense isn't always good sense," said Stanley. "I have a different idea."

"It's his contribution," said Ruth, nodding toward her husband, "that in due time I write Goddard that there's a chance I may not have to stay in Cincinnati, and ask for his train reservations out of St. Louis so I can go with him if I find it will be possible."

"*If* it will be possible," said Stanley, "and of course it won't."

"A nefarious plan," said Ruth, winking at Margaret.

Later, when Stanley had taken up his camera and disappeared into his darkroom, Ruth took Margaret and Luther on what she described as her "favorite short walk."

Ruth's stride was long and both Luther and Margaret struggled to keep up.

"Isn't this day priceless?" said Ruth. "We've had storms and two days of wind from the northwest."

As they neared the lake, Ruth stopped and pointed to the gray mountain that rose behind it. "Look how it throws its shadow on the lake."

Its stately presence, so quiet, solid, and commanding, was much like Ruth herself.

For a while they walked single file. After a bit Ruth dropped back and said, "How is Elizabeth? My mind has been so full of her lately."

Margaret's face darkened. "We all consult each other in corners and tell lies to her," said Margaret. "It's hateful."

For weeks Margaret's younger sister Elizabeth had been running a steady fever and coughing. In an attempt to enforce inactivity, the family had confined her to the garden. No one was uttering the dreaded word "tuberculosis," but of course it weighed heavily on everyone's minds. For Margaret, the mere possibility raised enough concern to undermine her determination to go to Samoa.

"They've consulted a specialist near Pittsfield," said Luther, referring to a doctor who ran a sanitarium in Massachusetts.

"I wonder when you'll have any conclusive word," said Ruth.

"Dadda says no matter the outcome, I'm to go. He says I won't do anyone any good by staying back."

By the time the three returned to the cottage the sun was high above them. Luther picked up his *Audubon Guide* and ventured out again. Margaret said she was tired. Following Ruth into the kitchen, she saw that vegetables from the garden were resting on the counter.

Ruth laughed. "Lunch," she said. "Another one of Stanley's nefarious schemes with me having to do the dirty work." She started busying herself, washing and chopping.

Margaret hoisted herself up on the counter.

"Stanley is inspired," said Ruth, a note of giddy excitement rising in her voice. "His scheme is unequaled in the annals of Italian poisoning diplomats."

"Stanley," said Margaret, "is a born crook politician."

"Isn't he, though," said Ruth. As she chopped, an untidy strand of hair fell over her face.

Margaret watched her purse her lips and blow it aside.

"It's an excellent scheme to get Goddard's plans," said Margaret. "But I'm afraid Stanley is terribly right. Better tell Goddard, *after* he's bought his tickets, that you can't travel with him at all."

After a few minutes Ruth said, "Darling," and then, lowering her voice, "Luther seems better. Much better. Or am I wrong?"

"No, he is better," said Margaret. "He wants to be sure I need him. He's been doubting that all spring. And, of course, the verse is a symbol of it with him," referring to the poems she'd been writing since her friendship with Edward Sapir had blossomed. "I've been awfully involved in it—and awfully remote. This trip has helped with him, but . . ."

Then, beginning to pace the room, "I find myself trying to break all the threads that bind me to this life as quickly and painlessly as possible."

"You poor dear," said Ruth.

Margaret walked to her, laying her hand on Ruth's forearm. "I don't know why, but you always seem to sympathize with my obscure vagaries."

What Margaret didn't say was that lately her feeling of self-sufficiency had gone to pieces. The reason was that her feelings for Edward Sapir had begun to undermine her commitment to her marriage. Luther had sensed her confusion, but had construed it for something else, reassuring her, again and again, that it was natural for her to have a case of the jitters before leaving for the South Seas.

Ironically, her show of vulnerability had given Luther the first confirmation that she needed him. He'd even told her so.

The truth was that lately Edward had been so much on Margaret's mind that he intruded himself into nearly every situation. She found herself fantasizing about him, even when she was in bed with Luther. During their "second honeymoon," Edward's unspoken presence, constantly hovering over her, enveloping her in a mist of desire, was a lubricant in her lovemaking with Luther.

But Margaret knew that any talk about Edward with Ruth often ended in driving a wedge between them. The fact was he also loomed large in Ruth's fantasy life. Ruth had told her so, saying that her unresolved feelings for Edward were so strong that even Stanley had noticed and admitted some jealousy. Some months ago she'd confided to Margaret that Edward had become "a convenient personification of all my interests apart from him, anthropology, poetry and the rest."

Possibly Stanley was still brooding over Edward.

Margaret looked at Ruth. Her face was serene.

"How is Stanley's state of mind?" said Margaret. "I can't tell."

"Well," Ruth said, "he always believes that whenever we're separated awhile, that something could come between."

Margaret watched Ruth at the cutting board. She'd come to realize that Ruth's placid features, so elegant and outwardly calm, often masked tumultuous emotions.

Margaret liked it when those feelings came to the surface.

Sensing a current running between them, Margaret moved closer. Ruth turned to her and their eyes locked. Margaret did not look away and neither did Ruth. After a few moments Ruth bent down and kissed the top of Margaret's head.

That night, slowly rocking back and forth, Ruth sat with Margaret on the swinging bench on the front porch. Their husbands had gone to visit the frog pond down by the lake.

Fireflies darted past them. A faint odor of burning logs emanated from another house, somewhere in the darkness.

"Of course it was all right to tell Sapir I was coming here," Margaret said, turning to Ruth.

Ruth drew her long legs up under her and pulled her shawl around her shoulders. Margaret, she thought, looked especially beautiful tonight.

Ruth was aware their arms were touching.

"It seems absurd to keep secrets from him anyway," said Margaret. "Our three doings and conversations and obsessions have been correspondence material for so long."

Ruth felt Margaret lean into her. In response Ruth gently ran her hand down Margaret's bare arm. "Darling girl," she said. "I worry so about you. Do the arms still shriek?"

Margaret cast her eyes down. As her trip approached her neuritis had increased. She'd told Ruth that often her arms hurt so much she couldn't fall asleep.

Ruth took Margaret's hand in hers, and with her strong fingers firmly began to massage it, working her way up the forearm. Even in the darkness she could see the relaxation spreading over Margaret's face.

Ruth felt Margaret nestle in, closer. As she sank into Ruth's side, she threw her head back and sighed a long, deep sigh.

Ruth looked down at her.

"Can I tell you something I've been thinking about?" Margaret asked, looking up at her.

"Of course," said Ruth.

"It's my curse, I suppose, but to me it seems perfectly natural to love two people at the same time."

Ruth's hands slowed and then stopped moving on Margaret's arm. For a moment neither woman spoke. The faraway cry of a loon echoed across the lake.

"It's a lovely sound," said Margaret.

"Isn't it," said Ruth.

"I'm beginning to think that I'm incapable of meeting the demand of a single-hearted devotion," said Margaret.

Ruth began massaging Margaret's arm again, trying to work the pain out of it. It seemed to her that Margaret might start crying.

"Marriage," said Ruth, "is a marvelous institution."

Margaret pulled back to look at her.

"I know I complain about Stanley, but really he and I are like-minded."

"I know you are," said Margaret.

"And for you," said Ruth, "Luther is a *perfect* husband."

"How so?"

"He, like Stanley, provides comfortable companionship. Except that Luther is even *less* demanding than Stanley. And if a woman has a mate like Luther, one who is mild-mannered, undemanding, and supportive, he gives one a great deal of freedom."

Ruth thought that somehow she *had* to make Margaret realize that having Luther was critical to her happiness. For when she thought of Margaret—and she was *always* considering what was best for Margaret—she realized that in order for her to be happy, she would have to find a way to satisfy her ambition. Ambition was Margaret's strongest impulse, the motivating force in her life. If Margaret were not to reach for her dreams, she would never, could never be happy.

And it was essential that Margaret craft an image of herself that was appropriate to that of a professional woman. Margaret, Ruth knew, must appear conventional. Any deviation from the socially accepted model would threaten her success.

"The love one has for a man," said Ruth, "is not the same as the love one has for a woman. They move on separate tracks. They don't intersect."

Still resting against Ruth, Margaret closed her eyes.

"You must realize," said Ruth, "that you're fortunate to have a husband like Luther."

"I do," said Margaret. "At least I think I do."

Ruth wanted Margaret to truly understand this. She bent and gently kissed Margaret's hair, then tilting her face up, brushed her lips with her own, feeling Margaret's lips slightly parting.

"Ruth," murmured Margaret, "you give me such strength."

Suddenly Ruth heard the men's voices, coming up from down below. They were back from the lily pond. Margaret heard them, too, and straightened up and pulled away.

"Be true to your instincts, dear, and drink sharply from them," said Ruth.

Luther appeared first, his face shining with happiness. "A thousand tiny frogs," he said, "all chirping in their miniature voices. As soon as they sensed our approach they fell silent."

"Magical," said Stanley. "They're always magical."

Ruth looked at Stanley, then glanced back at Margaret. Margaret's face was flushed.

It was important for Margaret to understand that in the coming months she could feed on Ruth's strength, whenever she needed her.

Ruth reached out and squeezed her arm.

On the night of July 5, 1925, Margaret was at the family farm, sitting in Dadda's office. Luther had left for a few days to stay with his own parents in Pughtown. The rest of the family had gone to bed, but Margaret was up late writing to Ruth.

She reported, "Elizabeth's a little better and the Doctor says there are no 'positive sounds' in her chest and that she can cure here this summer."

She knew Ruth's concern for Elizabeth was genuine, not only for Elizabeth's sake but also for her own. Ruth desired to see Margaret make the trip to the South Seas free of unnecessary anxiety. Not a day went by without Margaret giving silent thanks to Ruth for her unconditional love and support:

. . . all this should be hearty prelude to a proper expression of our gratitude for your hospitality. All thanks to Stanley for host-like qualities by day and hermit proclivities at night. I can write quite properly about your bread and butter and strawberries—But when the bread of heaven is still sweet on my lips, it is not so easy to say "thank you."

Now for the challenging job. All afternoon Margaret had been trying to make heads or tails out of the transcontinental rail timetables. At her side was a pile of dog-eared, annotated brochures. She needed to relay this information to Ruth.

Positioning a piece of carbon paper between two sheets of Dadda's stationery, she fed them into the typewriter. A typed timetable would be so much easier to deal with than one she could produce by hand:

Enclosed you will find the result of several hours intensive examination of all known time tables. This is the best we can do. It's a day in New York versus a day at the Grand Canyon and you will have to decide how you want it to be. The waits between trains and the number of nights and days are equal.

Margaret and Ruth were now fully committed to making the three-day train trip together and alone, without Goddard. But the situation was delicate. As director of the Museum of Natural History, not only was Goddard Ruth's senior colleague, but he was also Margaret's potential boss.

Recently a position had opened at the museum for an assistant curator to take charge of the African, Malaysian, and South Sea exhibits. The job was subject to the passage of the budget, but if approved it would start in the fall of '26, after Margaret's return from Samoa. It would be the perfect fit for her.

As exciting as the prospect of spending three days and nights alone together was, they both knew they had to be extremely careful not to offend Goddard.

She presented the comparison between the two routes, leaving the final decision to Ruth. "Will you check your preference and send it back so I can put it through, please."

A few days later Ruth's reply arrived: "Does it mean we go all the way together? That's an excellent hope—I promise not to count on it too much till I know. By all means I vote for the day at the Grand Canyon."

Then in a rush, Ruth explained how she'd already set in motion the first phase of their plan to jettison Goddard. She'd told him that she was unable to leave with him from New York because of an obligation to care for one of Stanley's relatives who was sick and on her way to a sanitarium.

The next phase of the deception was to occur when it was too late for Goddard to change his tickets:

> . . . then I'll telegraph him after we're started . . . telling him "she" is suffering from melancholia and has gone from Cincinnati to a relative's where I must follow her.—What a masterpiece! Art for art's sake!—the only problem is, who will telegraph for me after we're well on our way?

Margaret slipped Ruth's letter into the pocket of her sundress and walked to the back door. Three days and nights alone with Ruth; there was much to contemplate. From where she was standing she could see her sister stretched out on a rattan lounge, on the lawn. Elizabeth seemed a little better; her temperature had returned to normal and she was more animated.

Margaret crossed the lawn and sat down at Elizabeth's feet.

Elizabeth repositioned herself on the chaise. Turning to look at Margaret she said, "You see how I'm taking care of myself?"

"You're an angel," Margaret said with a smile, thinking that it had been smart of Dadda to promise Elizabeth a year abroad if she behaved herself. Leaning back, looking up into the clouds, she realized that now she was free to start her own adventure without gnawing guilt. The prospect left her both thrilled and terrified.

ARIEL

Of the heedless sun you are an Ariel,
Rising through cloud to a discovered blue . . .
—EDWARD SAPIR

July 1925

We call this Rabbit Run," said Margaret.

"I can see why," said Edward. He looked down at Margaret. Somehow she seemed different in this rustic environment. It suited her. When he'd received her letter inviting him to come to the farm for the weekend, he'd been surprised. She'd told him, quite directly, that Luther would not be present. He'd come without any preconceptions. Now that he was there, amidst her family, the experience was turning out to be more enjoyable than he expected.

They were walking away from the house down a winding, tree-lined road. The lane was so narrow that every few feet Edward's arm brushed against her shoulder. In the distance he could see a meadow carpeted with wild blue hyacinths that rolled down to the edge of a stream.

"I mapped out my courses and sent them off to Cole for announcement," he said, making reference to Fay-Cooper Cole, the head of the Anthropology Department at the University of Chicago and his new boss.

"Oh, my," she said. "It's really happening."

"I'm not buoyantly pleased about it, yet not depressed—quietly expectant about expresses it."

"Maybe it'll be the change you wanted."

"Maybe," he said. "For years I'd been placing my hopes in Columbia and Boas, but it seems fated not to be. Boas said he wanted me. Obviously he didn't want me keenly enough to really wrestle."

Margaret was looking up at him, listening.

"I suspect Boas merely goes through a few innocent motions and comes away thinking he's moved heaven and earth," he said, warning himself to be careful. Boas was always more receptive to his female students. The girls—both Margaret and Ruth—worshipped him. It would be a mistake to heap too much criticism on the old man. "I decided there was no use waiting any longer and that I must take what I could get," he said. "I shall miss you and Ruth very much."

They walked on in silence.

"You and Ruth would have been my chief reason for preferring New York, aside from the obvious advantages of New York as New York, but perhaps you girls can come to Chicago yet, or maybe I won't stay there very long."

He looked at her face. Usually so zestful and garrulous, today her mood seemed almost dreamy.

"Once this farm had over a hundred acres planted in wheat and rye and oats," Margaret was saying, "and two fields of maize."

Edward realized he felt more comfortable in her presence than he ever had before. Breathing in the sweet hot air, he said, "This looks like it was once a real working farm."

In the distance she pointed out an old threshing machine now collapsed in a rusting pile. She told him how, when she was young, more than a dozen men worked there to thresh the wheat. Sometimes her mother brought her down to the lunch table so they could serve them their midday meal.

An old windmill stood by the stream. All around them, it seemed, were the relics of the farm that used to be.

Edward wondered how Sherwood Mead, a man seemingly so urbane and out-of-touch with his physicality, had ever managed to run this place. Perhaps he'd left it to his wife.

As they neared the ravine, Margaret surprised Edward by taking his hand. It was totally unexpected. Whatever happens today, he told himself, he wasn't going to let himself feel guilty about it.

Margaret led him off the path and they passed under a little bridge. Suddenly the earth crumpled inward, slanting down precipitously toward the stream. Letting go of his hand, she picked her way through the mud and stones. He followed closely behind. The late afternoon sun glinted off the gold in her hair.

They walked along the banks of the brook. Every so often Margaret bent down to pick a wildflower.

"Oh, look," she said, "there's the barn."

She led him toward it. It was a three-storied structure, the wood bleached and dilapidated. Obviously it hadn't been used in quite some time.

"Up there," she pointed, "are the old pigeon lofts." She was straining up on her toes to see into the lofts. Standing so close to her he could feel the heat coming off her body.

She guided him into the old barn, taking his hand again. Shafts of sunlight pushed through the rafters.

"This haymow floor was just the right height for giving plays," she said. "See those chutes—that's where we used to play hide-and-go-seek."

He looked down at her. "Sometimes you're like a child," he said, laughing, "an absurd little girl."

"Well," she said, as if considering that idea, "I am virginal."

"What does that mean?" he asked. "You've been married for how many years? Two? Three?"

"I don't mean it in a literal sense."

"No?" said Edward. He couldn't for the life of him penetrate to the heart of her relationship with Luther.

He hesitated, then pulled her to him and took her up into his arms. She met his kiss with an open mouth.

He thought her body might be childlike, but she felt like a full woman.

"I've wanted to do this for a long time," he said.

"Whatever was stopping you?"

"Come here," he said, pulling her down on the hay.

She was under him, the contours of her body fitting so perfectly with his. He felt her reposition herself and hike up her dress.

He was conscious that her hands were at his belt, undoing it.

It was happening so fast that he couldn't stop himself.

Later he said, "What are we going to do about Luther?"

She ran her fingers through his hair. "Luther won't mind," she said. "He's not jealous. He believes that I should be free to do what I want."

"Am I supposed to believe that?" said Edward.

She just looked at him.

"I hardly think that's possible," he said.

"No, really. We made a vow, before we got married, that neither should try to control the other."

They were lying side by side, facing each other. "With all my heart, I love you," she said, snuggling into his body. He pulled her closer. As they were kissing Edward became conscious of a voice calling out Margaret's name. He pulled back. The voice was right outside the barn.

"Oh, my God," Margaret said, "it's my mother!"

Edward jumped up and grabbed for his trousers. As he thrust one leg into the pants he nearly lost his balance before he managed to get them up.

Margaret was already up on her feet, smoothing down her dress.

"Margaret," said Mrs. Mead.

Edward turned. The woman was standing in the doorway. "There you are," she said, her eyes taking in the scene, glancing at Edward's shoes on the ground. "Dinner is ready."

That night sleep proved to be elusive. Edward was in a state of excitation. He knew Margaret was somewhere down the hall. His mind replayed every detail of their lovemaking in the barn. All he could think about was when he'd be with her again.

There were so many questions he wanted to ask her. Their future together was so fraught with challenges he couldn't imagine how they were going to work things out. Luther, her "childhood friend," as she referred to him, was the least of their difficulties.

The next morning, at breakfast, he noticed that Margaret was subdued.

He returned to his room to pack his bag and gather his thoughts. As he was carrying his suitcase down the stairs he found her waiting in the foyer.

"Come outside with me," he said.

She followed him out the door.

"Find a reason to come into the city for a day. And a night. I'll get a hotel room."

She looked at him like he was crazy.

"Why not? We deserve to be happy."

"It's impossible."

"Impossible?" He searched her eyes. They were clear and true. "What do you mean? Impossible? Do you love me?"

"I love you beyond words," she said. "You *know* how much I love you."

"Then you want to be with me."

She flushed.

"You do."

Then, squaring off her body to his, as if to underscore the point, she glanced back at the house and said, "You know I can't."

His eyes searched her eyes again. "How am I supposed to believe you love me?"

"You have to believe me."

Ruth was troubled. It had been five days since Edward's weekend at the Meads' farm and Margaret had not yet said a word about it. Later that day she wrote to Margaret, doing her best to sound nonchalant.

> *Perhaps I'll hear today about the weekend you had with Sapir. He congratulated me on my trip with Goddard—no other comment;— he shall not be forgiven for that! Is he really as ebullient as his letters have sounded?*

The next day the hoped-for letter from Margaret finally arrived. It had been written a few days earlier:

> *Sapir's visit was most delightful. He is, as was reported to you, in a happier mood and quite encouraged about Summer School. . . . We talked amicably of all sorts of patterns; they are the order of the day— the* raison d'etre *and the "open sesame"; Jung to the reference shelf, and less amicably, we argued about Boas. It is so easy to involve sex differences as explanation. "You girls are humanizing him, etc."*

According to Margaret's telling, the visit had been quite innocent. But Margaret could be a dissembler. Edward was more trustworthy. Ruth would have to talk to him to find out what had *really* happened on the farm.

As soon as he returned to the city Edward sank into a depression. He couldn't believe that he might not see Margaret again before she departed for Samoa. The strange thing was that he had not sensed, in any of their murmured discussions, any disposition on her part to allow the world of practical affairs to have a place in shaping their love.

He'd written a verse about her. He called it "Ariel," a reference to the androgynous sprite in Shakespeare's *The Tempest*, who—held captive at the beginning of the play—yearns to break free. Edward considered it one of his best efforts:

> *Of the heedless sun you are an Ariel,*
> *Rising through cloud to a discovered blue . . .*
> *Reckless, be safe. The little wise feet know*
> *Sun-ways and clouds and earthen aim,*
> *And steps of beauty quicken into flame*
> *Wherein you burn up wholly in arrest.*

Two days later he received a note from her. She announced that since he seemed to "doubt her love," she had decided to meet him in the city after all. Besides, as luck would have it, she'd been given the perfect pretext for a visit—Pliny Goddard had written, asking her to come in for a job interview.

Margaret said she'd be arriving by train Thursday morning, July 23. She told him to book a hotel room for that night.

He wrote back, naming the Pennsylvania Hotel, right across the street from Penn Station, as the site for their assignation. He had six days to wait. It felt like an eternity.

Edward went over and over the events of the weekend. He could hear the lilt of her voice when she said his name and the pleasure in her laugh when he made a joke. Then, of course, there had been the electric touches from her hands moving over his body. All this had "reawakened his capacity to love which he thought had died for all time."

Margaret, his Ariel with "little wise feet," was so much on his mind that he wanted nothing more than to talk to someone about her. Just the mere thought of saying her name was as tempting as red meat to a dog.

He fought the impulse and the following day, after teaching his morning class, was finally able to resume some of his own work. After all, he told himself, he would be seeing Margaret by week's end and there was nothing to do in the meantime.

As Edward was leaving his office, he encountered Dr. Boas in the hallway.

Boas was moving purposely toward his own office and seemed disinclined to stop.

Suddenly Edward was reminded of the recent conversation he'd had with Margaret, the one in which she'd told him how solicitous Boas was of her health and well-being. Edward had responded by saying that with men Boas was aloof, formal, and superior. Margaret had laughed and said, "It's easy to blame everything on sex differences."

Seeing Boas now, stooped over yet still energetic, Edward's anger increased. How many years had he waited for a permanent position at Columbia, all the while believing the old man's assurances that it would happen? And when Boas had finally thrown him a crumb—two summer school classes—he'd been fool enough to feel encouraged. The end result? Now he was going to the University of Chicago.

Well aware that if he'd been able to remain in New York, *with* Margaret, many of their challenges would have disappeared, he pounced. "Dr. Boas," he said. "How are you?"

"Ah, Dr. Sapir," came the thick German accent. Boas reached out and shook his hand. Then, fishing out a handkerchief from his pocket and removing his spectacles, he began to clean the lenses. "How do you find your students?" he said, looking down at the glasses in his hand. "Are there any we should be following?"

"What? You mean in my summer classes?" said Edward.

"We like to know if any have a special inclination towards the science," said Boas.

"Well, there is a situation I'd like to speak to you about, if I may."

"Yes?"

"It's the Mead girl."

"Margaret Mead?" said Boas, putting his glasses back on.

"Yes, Margaret Mead. I am worried about her. Distinctly so."

"In what regard?" said Boas, his brows knitting.

"She's going to Samoa, right? What for?"

Boas froze, as if finally aware that the conversation might turn unpleasant.

"Do you really believe she's up to it?"

"Well," said Boas, "her health is frail, that's true."

"It's more than that," said Edward.

Boas waited, dabbing at his palsied lip with his handkerchief.

"It's the latent neurotic situation. I know for a fact she has had suicidal daydreams. When we spoke she told me she might not ever return."

The old man's face darkened.

"Don't you think you should do something to stop this whole infernal business, before it's too late?"

Leaving Schermerhorn Hall, Edward headed for Amsterdam Avenue. Pedestrians filled the sidewalk, moving with the slow rhythm of a late summer afternoon. Edward was annoyed. As usual, his discussion with Boas had left him feeling dissatisfied. The old man, although concerned, seemed unwilling to take action.

Upon returning to his room Edward wrote to Ruth, sounding another alarm:

> I communicated my uneasiness to Boas today but he thought it would be a distinct mistake to interfere. He is still a little nervous about her going but seems inclined to minimize the danger. Apparently he considers the main thing to fear is her frail health, but I fear the latent neurotic situation which I feel to be rather grave. Please don't let anyone know I spoke to Boas. I have thought of writing to Mrs. Mead but probably it would not be wise. And I have tried to dissuade Margaret again by letter. I hope I'm unnecessarily jumpy. Tell me what to do, Ruth.

Ruth contemplated the two letters that lay on her desk.

Edward's scrawled missive was on a sheet of what looked to be scrap paper, a hurried and frantic outpouring of genuine anxiety. It told of Margaret's "suicidal day-dreams," and the threat that after Samoa Margaret might not return to New York.

Dr. Boas's typewritten letter was on Columbia letterhead, its neat precision marking the occasion of his writing as official business.

As she read the Boas letter, she could see the old man's face, alarmed yet self-possessed:

> Sapir had a long talk with me about Margaret Mead. You know that I myself am not very much pleased with this idea of her going to the

tropics for a long stay. It seems to my mind, however, and it has seemed to my mind ever since I prevented her from going to Tua-motu, that it would be much worse to put obstacles in her way that prevented her from doing a piece of work on which she had set her heart, than to let her run a certain amount of risk. In my opin-ion Sapir has read too many books on psychiatry . . . to trust his judgment; he does not really know the subject and therefore sees abnormal things in the most disastrous forms. Of course I know that Margaret is high strung and emotional, but I also believe that nothing would depress her more than inability on account of her physical makeup and her mental characteristics to do the work she wants to do.

Ruth rose from her chair and paced the room. If only she were back in New York and could deal with this face-to-face. Sadly she wasn't. She walked out to the front porch and read to the end of Boas's letter:

In my opinion an attempt to compel her to give up the trip—and that is all Sapir has in mind—would be disastrous. Besides it is en-tirely against my point of view to interfere in such a radical way with the future of a person for his or her own sake,—unless there is actual disease that needs control. Of course, Sapir takes that point of view, but if he were right, then who should not be restrained? I should like to hear from you, if possible, at once.

It was clear that Boas was after something from her, but what? He seemed to already have made up his mind to let Margaret go to Samoa. Obviously he wanted something else.

Ruth knew that Boas trusted her judgment, that her opinion carried weight. Reading between the lines, she felt—in the event something went wrong—that Boas didn't want to take full responsibility for Margaret. He seemed to be asking Ruth to assume some of the burden.

If this were the case it meant that Boas feared there *was* some truth to Edward's analysis of Margaret's state of mind.

And if Ruth were to be honest, she did, too.

Margaret's physical ailments–particularly the complaints about the "shrieking pain" in her arms—came too often. Perhaps Margaret's com-plaints *were* emblematic of a deep-seated psychic pathology.

In fact, just five days earlier, Ruth had arrived at this very same concern all on her own. Adopting a playful tone, she'd written to Margaret:

I shall kidnap you some day and subject you to full TB regimen. I'd give a lot to see what seven months of it would do for you. May I be jailer? Sweetheart, do be good and rest best you can.

The fact was that Ruth really could no longer afford to take Margaret's complaints lightly. Edward might just be right. Boas knew it and so did she. Margaret was "high strung and emotional," maybe even unstable.

Ruth returned to her desk and fed some paper into the carriage of her typewriter. Best to answer an official letter with an official-looking response. To Boas she wrote:

All these things that have alarmed Sapir I have known for a long time and tried to take into account. Last spring I sent her to two doctors of the highest standing, one a neurologist, and they could find nothing organically wrong. The diagnosis is nervous fatigue and they prescribe rest. It seems to me that it is perfectly possible that the natural relaxation of a tropical climate, and the necessarily rather haphazard character of the work she will be doing, far away from the strenuous setting she is used to, may be the best possible change for her.

Having evaluated Margaret's "mental condition" as workable, Ruth moved on to another situation—Margaret's employment at the museum the following fall.

Of all the alarms Edward had sounded, the one that bothered Ruth the most was the possibility that Margaret might not return to New York City. Having had her deepest feelings stirred, Ruth didn't know how she could bear life without Margaret. Boas was in a position to ensure Margaret's appointment. If he did, Margaret's future would be tied to New York:

She has written me about the offer of the museum for next year, and I think that, coming at just this time, nothing better could happen to allay the attitude Sapir is worried about. She is most enthusiastic.

Ruth then concluded her letter with an argument she knew would carry much weight with Papa Franz:

*I credit her with a great deal of common sense and I know she can
carry out any precautions she agrees to, as far as humanly possible.*

The next morning, her mind full of Margaret, Ruth stood over the bed
methodically folding Stanley's shirts, stacking them in a neat pile so they
would be ready to place in his suitcase.

Upon her return to New York she would finally see Edward. In his
last letter he'd joked about her upcoming transcontinental train ride saying, "I'm sorry you're going with Goddard. He's more greasy and las-
civiously smiling than ever. Why don't they chloroform him?" And then
he'd signed off with, "Precisely what dates are you in town?"

The truth was Ruth was worn out by Edward's histrionics. Worse,
she sensed he was still holding back information. In all that he'd written, and there had been a lot, there had been no hint of what had *really*
happened on the farm. Nevertheless, something in his description had
elicited in her a feeling of disquiet:

*Of course Elizabeth is wonderful. A regular Saint of the Primitives.
But Margaret is still more wonderful. She is ever so much bigger
than I had imagined her. I had misjudged her. In that beautiful rustic atmosphere she comes into her own.*

Whatever did he mean, by saying "in that beautiful rustic atmosphere
she comes into her own"?

Ruth looked down and saw that her hands were trembling. Then she
saw she'd made a mess of Stanley's dress shirt. Grabbing it, she shook it
out, then set about to fold it again.

She was relieved that soon she'd be seeing Edward. Obviously he was
looking forward to seeing her, too. He'd ended his last letter by saying,
"I am reserving Tuesday, the 28th, for you. You have a standing invitation
to come to all my classes, university regulations not withstanding."

Placing Stanley's shirts on top of the other clothes in the valise, she
dropped the lid and secured the latch.

18

HOTEL PENNSYLVANIA

Margaret, we must have a little child together someday.
In or out of wedlock. I just feel the mystical necessity.
—EDWARD SAPIR

July 1925

While they were at dinner they discussed the offer she'd received to work as an assistant curator at the museum.

"Goddard says it's mine," said Margaret. "It would start in the fall, after I get back from Samoa."

"Somehow," said Edward, "I feel it in my bones that you should refuse that offer."

"You would be opposed to *anything* Goddard had to say. For my part, I can't see how I could do much better for the next two or three years."

Edward shook his head. "I say it on perfectly compelling, intuitive grounds." Reaching out, he took her hand. "But I can see you have no intention of refusing it."

They traveled up in the elevator, standing apart, as though they did not know each other.

When they'd entered the room and closed the door, she fell into his arms.

She didn't know she could feel like this with a man.

The next morning he was in the bathroom shaving, a towel wrapped around his waist. Sunlight came in through the blinds. On the bedside table was a little box that held the ring he had given her the night before. The ring had been Florence's wedding ring. Lying on her side, watching him, with the sheet pulled up over her chest, she started to laugh. "I think you left your razor strap at my parents' house."

"That's where it is!"

"My mother told me 'Dr. Sapir' left something here."

"Dr. Sapir?" He laughed. "You think it's funny, don't you?" Walking back to the bed, letting the towel drop, he pulled back the sheet and climbed in next to her. "You thought it was funny when she found us in the barn."

"That's not true."

She rolled toward him, grabbing his arms and pinning him down. He tried to push back but she wouldn't let him. They wrestled for a minute but he still couldn't break free.

"You're so strong," he said. "Where does that come from?"

"I love you," she said, still not letting him break free. "I love you."

Afterward, while they were lying side by side, he said to her, "Margaret, we must have a little child together someday."

She didn't answer.

"In or out of wedlock. I just feel the mystical necessity."

She looked up at the ceiling, studying a crack that ran across the white plaster.

"Do you agree?" he asked.

"Yes."

They were in each other's arms, her head on his chest. "My beloved," she said.

When she was dressing he came up behind her and stood looking at their reflection in the mirror. "Are you happy? Is the nervous tension lessened?"

"Yes," she said laughing.

"What are we going to do about Luther?"

"Luther?" She turned to look at him. "Why do we have to do anything about Luther?"

Ruth sat at the back of the small auditorium, listening to Edward's lecture on patterns in language. He certainly had no trouble commanding the room. Many of his students were enthralled, especially the young women. No doubt they'd heard that his wife had passed away.

When Ruth walked up to him at the end of class he reached out to clasp her hand. "Just the person I most want to see," he said, leading her outside.

For old times' sake they went to the Stockton Tearoom.

As soon as they were seated, Edward brought up Margaret.

"You may think I'm exaggerating the danger," he said, "but what could be worse than not airing my fears now?"

"The work will help carry her through," said Ruth.

"Work has a way of doing that," said Edward. "Listen. I'm very glad Margaret has obtained her desire. Chances are she will enjoy the year in the South Seas hugely and will profit greatly by it." He paused. "She lives intensely in the outer world and it will all mean a great deal to her."

"What a dear girl," said Ruth. "She has such determination."

The waitress appeared with a pot of tea and a chocolate cream soda.

"You never told me about your visit to the farm," said Ruth.

"Margaret's younger sister Elizabeth is wonderful."

"She's been ill, you know," said Ruth. "I gather there's been a tuberculosis scare." She took a sip of her tea. "Whatever did you mean, Margaret seemed 'so much bigger' there?"

"A feeling," he said, smiling. "She overpowered me."

"My goodness," said Ruth.

"I wonder," he said, "what exactly is Margaret's attitude toward Luther?"

"What do you mean?"

"I mean," said Edward, "does she love him?"

"He was her childhood sweetheart. Of course she loves him."

"I'm afraid I'm confused," said Edward.

Ruth sat waiting, her face immobile.

"Margaret and I are lovers," he said. "No doubt she will tell you. She tells you everything."

"Lovers?"

"She gave herself completely. She was completely happy."

Ruth stared at him.

"I even called her 'little wife,' once or twice. She rejoiced when I said it."

When Ruth still didn't say anything, Edward said, "I don't understand, though. Just what is her relationship with Luther?"

"Luther?" Ruth paused. "She loves Luther."

"With you I can be utterly frank," Edward said. "I do not believe in the love of Luther and Margaret, nor do I think that most observers who know them sincerely believe in it."

"Dear boy," said Ruth, "I don't know what to say."

"She's on my mind and in my heart night and day," Edward continued. "I'm afraid my bewilderment, fear for her, and aching desire for her presence make me of little use for anything just now."

Ruth drew her napkin up to her lips and patted them dry.

Edward reached out across the table and, taking Ruth's hand, covered it with his own. "Tell me what to do, Ruth."

"The worst day of my life," cried Ruth as she marched down the sidewalk, not caring who heard her, "the very worst day of my life." Tears streamed down her cheeks.

Edward's talk of making love to Margaret was unbearable. Where had it happened, surely not within earshot of Margaret's parents?

Not that long ago she—Ruth—had loved Edward, wanted him for *herself*. Margaret *knew* that. But that's not what hurt. What hurt was that Edward had experienced the erotic side of Margaret that she, Ruth, had only fantasized about, and lately, at night, those fantasies had come unbidden.

Before, when Ruth had been in love with Edward, she had never thought about being intimate with him. That side of their relationship was so unimportant she hadn't even realized it was absent.

Now she did visualize Edward in the act of sex, not with her, but with *Margaret*. And the images of Margaret together with Edward stimulated her erotic imagination. She yearned to experience with Margaret a physical love and its climax.

Ruth reached into her pocketbook. Her hand closed over the railway pass, a crisp voucher for a sleeping compartment on the B&O, traveling from Manhattan to Williams, Arizona, on July 27, 1925. Ruth looked at it. The ticket represented three days and nights alone with Margaret. She reinserted it into its envelope and placed it carefully back into her handbag.

Now that trip was ruined.

She thought about Edward at the Tearoom, sitting next to her, drinking a soda, letting her know that he had been intimate with Margaret.

Now he wanted to stop Margaret from going to Samoa. He wanted to take Margaret away from Luther. He even wanted to persuade Margaret to leave New York City.

He'd said that Margaret had called him "my beloved."

Somehow she *had* to make Margaret realize that Edward's plans for her were wrong, all wrong.

On July 25, Ruth wrote to Margaret, "I thought of you Thursday. How did the job come out? . . . I'm hoping you can take it if it's something actually to count on. You'd enjoy it and the job would be in reserve afterwards."

She ended her letter on a practical note. "Believe me I shall be well-informed about the exact moment when I can hope to be hitched up to the train you are on."

She stood at the Western Union window, setting into motion their scheme to trick Goddard. Margaret had arranged with a friend in Cincinnati to send him a telegram in Ruth's name, as though it was Ruth sending it from Cincinnati:

HAVE CANCELLED SANTA FE RESERVATIONS MUST REMOVE COUSIN FROM HOME (!!) WILL FOLLOW SOON AS POSSIBLE DESOLATED RUTH

That should take care of the Goddard problem.

As she walked home she thought about Margaret and their future.

Ruth remembered what Margaret had said—that the love in one's heart need not be restricted to one person. Love was as full and limitless as the air one breathes. Why couldn't it extend to two?

In this regard, Luther as a loving support system was indispensable. Not every man would be willing to play this part.

Edward, for instance, would reject that idea. He would demand exclusivity.

Surely Margaret could see that Edward, with his possessiveness, would put restrictions on her, restrictions that would make her very unhappy.

He would kill what she and Margaret had together. Ruth knew this, and knew she must help Margaret realize it, too.

————

Good-byes were being said and the entire Mead family—Margaret's parents, grandmother, and three siblings—had moved off to the side to give Luther a last moment alone with his wife.

The vast station—dark, steamy, and brooding—rose around them. Luther stood with Margaret, holding both her hands in his.

"Good luck," he said, pressing her hands and looking deeply into her eyes. "I'll see you in Marseilles next spring."

Over and over, he had told her that he would never stand in her way. Letting her go off on her own for ten months was the ultimate proof.

"You're hitching your wagon to a star," he said.

"What star is that?" She laughed.

He was conscious that her hands were clammy, a sign, no doubt, that she was nervous.

At the porter's last call Margaret climbed aboard the Pullman. Luther watched from the concrete platform. A moment later he saw her turn and wave. The porter closed the door. With a great clanking and belching, the train lurched forward. A moment later she was gone. Luther and Emily Mead waited on the platform until the last car cleared and then suddenly a yawning emptiness enveloped them.

Luther took Margaret's mother's arm. They walked slowly and thoughtfully toward the Meads' car where the others were already waiting.

In a voice that indicated she was looking for reassurance, Emily Mead said, "You will meet her in Marseilles next spring, Luther?"

"That is our present plan, and I don't anticipate any change," he said, wondering what they both would be like after a year apart.

That afternoon Luther returned to his own parents' house. He wrote a note to his mother-in-law:

> *You made my visit so pleasant with all the somberness that over-hung. Thank you so much. I don't know about coming down again. I could not come for quite awhile. I have never known the valley or your home without Margaret and I'm sure I should find myself wandering about expecting to see her. So if I hesitate about coming please understand and don't think me ungracious.*

Margaret sank into her seat, looking out at the line of concrete block factories and tenements that stretched endlessly along the tracks.

Edward Sapir, with his ardent lovemaking, had done his most to hold her back.

When they had left the hotel room that morning, he had gone up to the concierge to return their key. She'd waited next to him. A moment later he'd turned to her and whispered, "For God's sake, do you remember what name I used to check us in?"

"No," she said, reflexively moving away so as not to be associated with this embarrassment. "I wasn't there when you checked us in." On quiet feet she headed across the lobby, then to the street.

When he caught up with her, his face was still red.

"What did you say?"

"What *could* I say? He just had to look me up by our room number."

She laughed thinking about it. At least that had added some levity to a morning that had ended on a difficult note.

The night before he'd shocked her by taking her hand and slipping Florence's wedding ring on her finger.

"I can't take this," she'd said, pulling her hand back. "It would be disloyal."

"Margaret," he'd said, "don't think of it as a *cultural* symbol. Those symbols are meaningless to me."

She looked down, twisting the ring on her finger.

"It's meant to say that I'm giving you all the love that had once been Florence's."

This had been alarming. She'd yearned for him, dreamed of being with him, and now the intensity of his feelings frightened her.

The rhythm of the train moving forward was a relief, and later, when she had tired of blaming herself for the emotions she'd unleashed in Edward, she went to find her carry case. Inside was the letter Dr. Boas had sent, just last week:

> *Another interesting problem is that of crushes among girls. For the older ones you might give special attention to the occurrence of romantic love which is not by any means absent as far as I have been able to observe, and which, of course, appears most strongly where the parents or society impose marriages which the girls may not want.*

How, Margaret wondered, would she ever learn enough of the Samoan language to converse freely with teenage girls? Her first task, once she reached Pago Pago, the U.S. naval port, was to find someone to give her lessons.

Edward had stressed the importance of mastering the language before she ventured into the field. But she was no Edward Sapir, a man who could immerse himself in a foreign language and become fluent within weeks. Learning Samoan could eat up months of precious time and prevent her from doing any work at all.

She wanted to talk to Ruth. Ruth would know what she should do—how long she should work at the language, how long she should remain in Pago Pago. Blessedly, soon Ruth would be with her, to talk to her, to give her strength, because that's what Ruth did. And Ruth made her feel so good inside.

Beautiful, beautiful Ruth.

A NEED FOR SECRECY

*Ruth . . . was the most impressed by the effort of the river
to hide, a torturing need for secrecy which had made it dig
its way, century by century, deeper into the face of the
earth.*

—MARGARET MEAD

August 1925

They sat across from each other, both leaning forward, their elbows resting on the white linen tablecloth. The place settings
before them gleamed, fine white porcelain and silver-plated flat-
ware. In the center of the table was a small crystal vase filled with roses.
Quiet waiters circulated among the tables, taking orders for dinner.

The train was moving, moving with a rhythm and a sway, like some
living being with a heartbeat. The light from the setting sun coming in
the windows reflected off the glass of the vase.

"Darling," Margaret said, "I was so afraid you'd mind."

Margaret's eyes were still red from crying.

She'd been caught in a deception and was ashamed.

Ruth's legs moved to touch hers under the table, a gentle nudge as if
to say all was right between them again.

Earlier that afternoon, the trains had made their connection in
St. Louis and Ruth's car had been hitched to the train that Margaret
was traveling on.

Margaret had walked from one car to the next until she'd seen Ruth
coming toward her.

Waving, Ruth had said, "I knew the exact moment our trains were hitched." She'd sounded happy, but when they embraced, her touch was stiff.

It was clear that she already suspected something had happened with Edward.

For days Margaret had known she was going to have to confess it all to Ruth. She'd fully expected there to be a scene. She had assured herself she didn't care, that she'd reached a point where she could no longer hide what had happened with Edward. She wanted to make love to him, and she'd gone after him.

Once they had reached their compartment and had a moment of privacy, Margaret had blurted it out. "I wanted him," she told Ruth. "Without the moves I made, he never would have realized my existence."

Ruth's face sagged. She sank down on one of the bunks and pulled off her sweater, throwing it aside.

"It's too hot in here," she said. Finally she looked up. "I can see your eyes are dizzied with this other love. I'm happy for you."

"No," Margaret said, "that's *not* how it is."

Ruth was quiet.

"Don't you see?" said Margaret. "It's the association with you. Maybe it's symbolic, but so much of it has to do with *you*."

Ruth shook her head. As she turned away, Margaret sat down next to her and reached for her hand, sliding in closer.

Now, sitting in the dining car, waiting to be served, they were past the confession, searching for ways to again reconnect with each other. As they had on so many other occasions, they discussed the death of Edward's wife, a loss that had left him so vulnerable. Margaret was insistent that she didn't want to cause him any more pain.

Ruth turned to catch their waiter's attention. She motioned for him to refill her water glass. Repositioning herself to face Margaret, she said, "Trust love to be sheer gain."

Margaret looked into her eyes, perplexed. Ruth went on, "Whatever happens, it can only mean gain for you, gain for him.

"He wants me to leave Luther."

"Don't you see?" said Ruth. "That's part of the warping."

The crease between Margaret's eyebrows deepened.

"The warping goes deep, deep, deep," Ruth said. "The thing you must never do is to imagine that by any utmost giving of yourself you could disperse his obsessions."

"He says it's not possible for me to love him, really love him, and stay married to Luther."

"Of course he does. He will say many things that sound plausible. You must not let your brain shrink from understanding which wells in him they spring from."

Margaret looked down at her hands, folded in her lap.

"There will be letters from him, words fused by his love into a shape you hadn't reckoned possible," said Ruth. "He will say many things. You must keep your head."

Margaret glanced away.

"Sweetness," said Ruth, "it's the one thing I know out of the extra years—this return of the spirit of life when it all seemed impossible."

Ruth's feelings and her need for physical contact, were palpable.

"Didn't you come to me?" asked Ruth.

Margaret nodded.

"Well, you came to Edward, too," said Ruth. "You've done more for him than you imagine. No matter what happens."

While they had been at dinner, their porter had made up their adjoining berths, turning down their beds. Wall sconces threw a pale golden light on the narrow bunks.

Margaret slipped into the toilet to undress and brush her teeth. When she returned to the berth, Ruth was already seated on one of the beds, her simple white cotton nightgown revealing her shapely shoulders and arms.

Margaret went over to Ruth's bed, climbed past her so she could position herself against the wall. Lying on her back she said, "It's a shame really, that we had to buy tickets for two berths."

"Precious," said Ruth, spreading herself out, and rolling toward Margaret, her long legs entwining themselves through Margaret's shorter ones.

Margaret leaned in to Ruth, opening her mouth, pressing her lips to Ruth's, enjoying the sweetness of the kiss.

They kissed for a long time.

Then Ruth said, "Come closer." Repositioning herself and raising her arms to pull off her nightgown, she pulled back the sheet. Margaret sat up, unbuttoned her own nightgown and slipped it off. Naked, she slid in next to Ruth.

Once under the sheets together they began to explore each other's bodies, Ruth stroking every part of Margaret, and Margaret quivering with pleasure under the touch.

Ruth seemed to understand just how to excite her.

Afterward, lying peacefully side by side, Ruth said, "Now you know everything I could ever say to you."

Margaret took her finger and traced the line of Ruth's lips. Then letting her hand fall, she lay back and sighed.

"Darling," said Ruth, "we might have loved each other with all our hearts and not had this, too."

"When I'm earthborn this year," said Margaret, "I will draw my strength from you." She paused. "And this night."

"Take the days as they come," said Ruth, pulling Margaret's face a little closer, "and trust that there's something worth the learning in the blackest living."

"Dearest," said Margaret, "I do, I really love you."

The next morning they sat in the dining car, once again across from each other.

In the early light the landscape of Kansas was flying by, flat and dreary, stretching on seemingly forever. Every so often an unpainted house, weathered and forlorn, appeared then disappeared.

"If I was less selfish I'd have denied myself the privilege of burdening you with my bewilderments all across the continent," said Margaret.

Ruth looked at her. She knew she had to help Margaret "develop all the expedients she could against weeping." One such way was to remember that living alone in Samoa would not last forever.

"Around the time you plan to meet Luther in Marseilles, next spring," said Ruth, "I will be traveling to Europe myself."

Margaret was surprised.

Ruth explained that Stanley had been invited to deliver a paper at a scientific conference in Sweden, that he imagined they'd go over the first of June. When he returned to the States, Ruth would stay on in Europe with the idea of attending the Congress of Americanists, scheduled to take place in Rome in September of 1926.

She knew that Margaret was also hoping to attend the congress.

"Come stay with me in Rome," said Ruth.

"It's always been one of my dreams to see Italy with you," said Margaret. "I never reckoned it in the world of possibilities."

"What have the meetings to do with it really?" said Ruth. "They're admissible for public use. We must stay a teeny while in Rome. I have a towering affection for Rome—and Florence."

An hour later they were still seated in the dining car, a sheet of paper on the table between them. This sheet, which contained two long columns consisting of letters of the alphabet, was of great interest to both Margaret and Ruth. This was the key for a code that would enable them to communicate with each other by cable.

For one as dependent as Margaret on daily and close contact with family and friends, having access to some form of rapid communication was essential. After all, it would take more than three weeks for a letter from the United States to reach Samoa, and at least as long for the answer to get back. A telegram, while providing nearly instantaneous communication, would be wildly expensive, its cost calculated by the number of characters in the text. Consequently, Margaret had devised a way to truncate the already abbreviated form of a telegram. She planned to distribute a copy of this key to her family and friends.

Naturally there would be some messages that were private, meant for only a special few. It was in regard to these secretive exchanges that Margaret and Ruth now turned their attention.

"There must be a letter that stands for Edward," said Ruth, "and one that stands for 'I had a letter from Edward and it was everything you could have wished. He was happy and on your terms.'"

Margaret jotted down combinations of the letters, "Ex" and "Exx."

"And another," said Ruth, "that means he writes happily having worked past the words you'll probably get for the next three weeks."

Margaret toyed with her pen. "I don't as yet know his cabling habits," she said. "Perhaps he will tell me that himself."

"And there must be one that means, 'I'm sending this just because all day I've been unbearably lonely without you—in a *very particular* way,'" said Ruth, fixing her with a look. "It will mean I can't go to bed without sending you this, just for the sake of love."

Sunrise over the Arizona desert covered the whole bowl of the sky.

"The desert has charms of its own," said Ruth, looking out at the bright sandy surface of the clay-colored terrain, which was spotted with sagebrush and cut into deep temporary channels by the rain. The pueblos they passed here were sand-colored, too, the adobe houses so flat that they receded into the landscape.

At the stop in in the town of Williams they changed trains to travel the last sixty-fives miles on the Grand Canyon Railroad. As their train approached the southern rim of the Grand Canyon, Ruth became agitated. She had only twelve hours to show Margaret the land she had developed such a fondness for.

Along the way they saw many Indians baling alfalfa into square blocks.

"It's still green," marveled Margaret. Pointing to some gaunt and gray cattle grazing close by she said, "Those poor creatures, they look so lost."

As they passed some juniper trees, Margaret opened a window. "They smell like evergreens," she said. Then she noticed some delicate scarlet-colored flowers, growing here and there. "Amazing that they bloom in this wasteland."

Ruth was gratified that Margaret took notice of many of the things that she, too, loved about the desert.

But it was at the Grand Canyon that Ruth realized how different she was from this girl she considered so "like-minded" in all the important ways.

Looking out at the miles of pinnacled clay, red and white, and fantastic, changing their aspect under each new shadowing cloud, Margaret sighed and said, "The part I love the best are the endless possibilities."

Ruth's eyes scanned the view.

"Look," Margaret said, pointing at a far-off canyon wall, "there's a castle, with a great white horse of mythical stature, tethered by the gate."

Ruth looked, but did not see it.

"And there," said Margaret, pointing farther over, "that's a great Roman wall."

In the afternoon the rain did not stop the sun from shining until a dark blue cloud moved over them. It was then that Ruth told Margaret what the canyon always made *her* think about.

"The river," she said, "and its torturing need for secrecy."

Margaret was silent.

"The river had to hide," said Ruth, "that's what made it dig its way, century by century, deeper into the face of the earth."

Margaret looked down, toward the deep crevice with all its dark shadows that wound through the canyon, many hundreds of feet below.

Ruth felt Margaret's hand reach around her waist.

In the late afternoon, as they turned to head back to the train depot, Margaret said, "We had everything except the canyon by moonlight."

That evening they said good-bye at the depot in Williams, Arizona. They were bound for different destinations, in distant corners of the globe.

Ruth's journey was short. She was headed back to Gallup to catch a mail wagon that would take her to the Zuñi pueblo.

Margaret was riding the train to Los Angeles, then up to San Francisco, where she would catch a steamer bound for Honolulu.

Waiting, next to the platform, were two trains, their engines humming.

Once she'd boarded her train, Margaret went to her seat, but after a few minutes she stood, anxious and uncertain. She began making her way down the aisle. In a moment she was rushing, moving from car to car, looking out at the platform, hunting out Ruth, who she knew to be somewhere on the other train.

Later, her train speeding through the desert, Margaret took a sheet of paper out of her case and began a letter:

> *And then I get no further for my tears. . . . O Ruth seeing you, even thru a heavy screen where you couldn't hear me and I couldn't see you was far, far too precious to surrender a moment of.*

Margaret stopped, thinking about that last glimpse she'd had of Ruth, while both their trains were pulling out of the station. This was the image she'd carry with her to Samoa:

> *. . . you and I were both moving, both moving fast—and as my train seemed to be rushing thru space you were always just opposite my window, a lovely wind blown figure.*

Ruth, on her own train, was also writing of their parting:

> *I got on the train at eight o'clock and found the berth all made up— only this time I went to bed alone and lay awake for hours and hours. But darling, for all my loneliness I had the comfort of those very nights. I could have wept for joy—the precious thing in life. I kiss you Darling.*

QUICKSILVER LOVE

Now the theory of polygamy that Margaret evolved (she uses the term herself) is a mere rationalization. . . . It had to be a "quicksilver love," a modernly beautiful and noble and unfaithful "free" love to be truly love!

—EDWARD SAPIR

September 1925

L uther walked along the narrow streets of Halifax, Nova Scotia. Once a charming town, the Halifax docks had been blown to smithereens during the war when a French munitions ship exploded in the harbor. Now, eight years later, the docks were still heaped with rubble and much of the charred waterfront remained boarded up.

The sight was emblematic of how Luther himself was feeling.

A week earlier Luther had begun his own adventure, setting sail for England, steerage class. The ship had stopped in Halifax to pick up freight.

Luther was thinking about the last letter he'd received from Margaret. She had said, "I'll not leave you unless I find someone I love more." It was the first real suggestion that she might be considering such a step.

To make matters worse, Luther had lost his sense of direction. Ostensibly, he was going to England to make a study of how social institutions disseminate information about birth control to the urban poor, but really, he had only a lukewarm interest in this project. He'd confessed to friends that going to Europe was "far more a device to facilitate M's Samoan plans than a carefully thought out educational program." In a more fundamental sense, he no longer aspired to be a parish priest. Although he hadn't yet acknowledged it, he was deeply depressed. Later he was to say, "It seemed to me sometimes that one of the options was suicide, and while it was more than a passing thought I was not at ease with it as a solution."

Summer school was still in session but Edward's enthusiasm for teaching had petered out. He freely admitted, both to himself and to Ruth, that he was "useless."

On August 5 he wrote to Ruth:

> I'm so sorry our visit together was so fleeting. You were gone by the time I turned to say, "How do you do?" And I know I wasn't a bit polite—I was all involved in Margaret. Forgive me.

When last they'd met, Ruth had demonstrated an agreeable willingness to discuss any and all matters that pertained to Margaret. In Edward's current state, there was nothing more he wanted than to unburden himself to a receptive and sympathetic listener:

> I don't understand Margaret's point of view at all. It's all words, arrangements, escapes, curiously involved relationships, elaborate duplicities, half gifts, and, if I mistake not, unconscious demands for dominance.

He kept coming back to the question that bothered him the most:

> She seems to me to expect the impossible. She wants the very highest type of love relationship but that is not to affect her relationship to Luther one iota! The more she loves me, the more she loves Luther apparently. That's glorious mysticism but I'm too weak to follow.

And now, with Ruth back on the mesa, he'd have to wait at least three weeks to get an answer from her.

When last he'd seen Margaret, she'd explained her theory of love, as she thought it should be lived. She called it "polygamy." According to her, a "polygamous love," unlike the more conventional "romantic love," was not bound up with ideas of monogamy, exclusiveness, jealousy, and undeviating fidelity.

The very notion that any personal conduct that valued monogamy should be construed as a negative left Edward bewildered. He had his own name for Margaret's kind of love; he called it a "quicksilver love." He told Ruth:

Now the theory of polygamy that Margaret evolved (she uses the term herself) is a mere rationalization. Having made of her erotic life a mere tentacle of the ego, she could not possibly allow herself to pay the price of love. It had to be a "quicksilver love," a modernly beautiful and noble and unfaithful "free" love to be truly love!

What really galled Edward was that Margaret's theory was based on lived experience. He simply couldn't expunge from his mind the very graphic images of Margaret rolling around in bed with another man— with Luther:

She cannot give her body to another at the same time without defiling the love relationship. That is cardinal. I stand helpless before the intuitive certainty of it.

"Who the hell was Luther Cressman, anyway?" wondered Edward. A divinity student, an earnest young man, decent but dull. Based on his few brief encounters with him, Edward could tell that the man had no real sense of humor. What good was a man who did not make Margaret laugh?

When he'd written back to Margaret, vehemently objecting to her notion of simultaneous love relationships, and suggesting that they find a compromise, she dug in her heels, insinuating that their difference of opinion boiled down to a "generation gap," that he simply didn't understand the "New Woman."

He was grateful that he could confide in Ruth, that she was willing to take on the role of go-between. He and Margaret had a strong passionate love and he was certain that would win out, that is, if he didn't let his temper run away with him. On August 8 he wrote to Ruth:

Your letter from Williams Arizona cut me to the heart. It is not you who are cruel, it is I. I have been so inconsiderate, even brutal, in the things I have said to poor Margaret. Your letter disturbed me so much that I sent a wireless to the Matsonia to assure her that I loved her and that I needed her love.

He ended by saying,

> *You must stand by us both, dear Ruth. Each of us is both strong and weak, each has tangled psychic problems that are not clear to the other. Do all you can to assure Margaret of my love. Tell her to attach more importance to that than to anything I say in a moment of anger or in a helpless burst of jealousy. Will you do that? You are our well-beloved friend and we are brought nearer to each other by your love.*

In 1925, Margaret Mead, at the age of twenty-three, still had strong ties with her immediate family. Prior to her departure for Samoa, she'd been in the habit of communicating with her parents and grandmother on a regular basis. She also had her hand in managing the many friends she'd collected while at Columbia. She was determined to keep on top of all these relationships.

Once the SS *Matsonia* was under way for Honolulu, Margaret decided that the most sensible way to handle much of her correspondence was to write group "bulletins." These were generated by placing carbon paper between sheets of paper so that Margaret could make a half-dozen copies at one time. This meant that a half-dozen people would receive her news firsthand. These recipients, in turn, could distribute the bulletins to others.

From the very first these public dispatches sounded a note that was both upbeat and conspiratorial, as Margaret tried to take her audience along with her on the journey. Regaling them all with descriptions of personalities that were idiosyncratic, and encounters that could only be had on a transpacific steamer, her letters displayed a sense of humor her friends had rarely glimpsed:

> *My table has been fun. At first I sat with the three priests and a gay and pious Catholic lady. The conversation turned on various and minor ecclesiastical dispensations and her 21 Catholic first cousins . . . I play bridge with them [the priests] in the morning and I made a grand slam. . . . Tonight is the Captain's dinner, balloons and full dress, I have been incredibly lazy for the whole trip, and this is a poor account but mine own, Sir.*

On the morning the *Matsonia* was scheduled to arrive in Hawaii, Margaret woke at five to find that land was in sight. She stood on the prow as the ship rounded point after point of rugged clay-colored mountains. The landscape was blanched of color, with only occasional patches of green showing as gray. At first glance, the city of Honolulu seemed to be resting somewhere on the cliffs, while the wandering mists, which seemed extensions of the clouds themselves, covered the tops of the mountains, hiding all signs of industrial civilization.

After landing, Margaret was taken in hand by staff from the Bishop Museum. Among them was Dr. Herbert Gregory, the museum's director, who showered her with hospitality, treating her to a daylong tour of the island in his open roadster.

Following along narrow winding roads for forty miles, they passed long stretches of green transparent rice fields interlaced with thick tangles of jungle foliage. Around each turn they encountered unexpected botanical enchantments, sometimes a banana grove, or a sugarcane plantation, or a pineapple plot. Margaret remarked, "The principle of this country is endless folds, folds of rock and folds of red soil, and perpendicular mountains that look like stiffly folded green velvet."

But while the public persona Margaret was presenting in her bulletins was chatty and upbeat, her letters to Ruth were not:

> Edward's long letter . . . still is too much to read peacefully. Just reiteration of course, he will share me with no one, I would love too lightly, I am dominating and egotistical and selfish. One thing I know I can never bring thru this year, and that is self-confidence and self-respect. They will be riddled into net worth before it is over. He can think of so many terrible things to say, and I shall believe them, all of them. And how to live, accounted a parasite on love, and too ill to do decent or consecutive work?

After two pleasant weeks socializing with the staff of the Bishop Museum, Margaret left Honolulu, "weighed down with flower leis," which she tossed from the stern of the SS *Sonoma* into the sea, as she watched Hawaii recede into the distance. The voyage crossed the equator. On the fifth day at sea she wrote in her bulletin, "It's no use, dear friends, I just can't write you a nice long descriptive letter on the ship; the darn thing rolls too much." She was impatient to reach her destination: Pago Pago—a port on the island of Tutuila, the largest of the five islands that comprise American Samoa. Surely this harbor, which had been a coaling and repair station for the U.S. Navy since the turn of the century, would offer an exciting introduction to the primitive landscape into which she was about to set foot.

The ship arrived at dawn on a cloudy morning on August 31. The sun appeared sullenly for only a moment before it disappeared again, while the heavy surf showed white then green then white again against the sides of steep black cliffs. Dense woods spilled down to the sea, and the narrow beach was ringed with palm trees. Margaret noted that the navy, in deference to the native style, had constructed their buildings to look like the Samoans' own green-roofed houses, many of which were clustered under the trees.

No one was waiting at the dock to meet her. As she walked along the crowded wharf looking for a welcoming face, what she saw was totally unexpected:

> The presence of the fleet today skews the whole picture badly. There are numerous battleships in the harbor and on all sides of the island. . . . Airplane's scream overhead; the band of some ship is constantly playing ragtime.

Finally she made herself known to a Mr. Walters, an official with the Bank of American Samoa, who offered to escort her to the one hotel in town.

On the way to the hotel, Walters told Margaret about life in Pago Pago. The station was primarily a supply base, which included coal sheds with a capacity of 4,500 tons and two fuel oil storage tanks of 55,000 barrels each, for vessels of the U.S. Navy. The station had sixteen officers and an enlisted complement of 147 men. It had a radio station that maintained "direct schedule" with Honolulu, San Francisco, and Washington, D.C. All government quarters had sewerage, running water, and electric power from 6:00 a.m. until midnight. Provisions of all kinds, including meat and other cold storage supplies, could be purchased from the commissary. Motion pictures were screened several times a week, and there was even a "four-hole, five-green golf course on which nine holes were played." What Walters did not say was that recently the island had entered a "period of unrest," stirred up by the Mau, a Samoan opposition movement. Only the year before, this protest movement had reached the breaking point when a group of visiting New Zealand policemen opened fire on a procession of Samoans, killing a high chief.

In American diplomatic circles, Samoa was now recognized as a thorny problem. The question that circulated among officials was, "Do we navalize or civilize it?"

Mr. Walters deposited Margaret at her lodgings, a ramshackle two-story structure that sagged under a roof of corrugated iron. She was excited to hear that six years earlier Somerset Maugham had stayed in this same hotel, and had used it as the setting for his story "Rain." As she was checking in the clerk told her that a Miss Hodgson, the head of the navy's training school for nurses, had been there, looking for her. The news gave Margaret a moment's pause as she thought wistfully of how Luther's father had intervened on her behalf, contacting his old friend Admiral Stitt at a critical time, making sure that she could bring her dream to fruition.

While Margaret was unpacking she received a visit from the governor's aide-de-camp who had come to deliver an invitation to that night's dance on U.S.S. *Seattle*, which had recently arrived in port carrying Admiral Robert E. Coontz, commander in chief of the U.S. Pacific Fleet.

That evening Margaret was thrilled to step out on the dance floor with Admiral Coontz himself. Later she made the acquaintance of Ellen Hodgson, who had heard all about her:

> *Surgeon General Stitt had the Superintendent of Nurses write Miss Hodgson asking her to help me. She's going to let me put my evening dresses in her dry closet, which is the greatest help of all; otherwise they rot or get rust stains from cockroach bites.*

As it happened, Ellen Hodgson, at the behest of Admiral Stitt, was working on accomplishing something even more important—language lessons. Having learned that the young anthropologist intended to stay in port until she had a rudimentary mastery of Samoan, Miss Hodgson was doing her utmost to secure a good tutor.

The next day, Margaret visited the parade grounds of the naval station, where she attended a celebration in honor of Admiral Coontz and the fleet. Here Margaret got her first glimpse of the people she'd come to study. Sami, the high priest's daughter, was presented wearing a *tuiga* (headdress) that was made from human hair bleached a russet color. Sami danced a *siva* (ceremonial dance) accompanied by her retinue, all of whom were bedecked with flowers. Margaret found them "magnificent" but "too muscular to be pretty." Then Tufele, the district governor of the Manu'a group, made a "glorious speech" in broken English. He was "gorgeous in full regalia, a high grass headdress and elaborate grass skirt and naked above the waist with his body oiled till the skin glowed." With his retainers behind him, all seated under black umbrellas, Tufele presented Admiral Coontz with an array of Samoan valuables, including a finely woven mat and freshly husked coconuts. Margaret learned that Tufele had been educated in Honolulu and that the Manu'a group consisted of a trio of tiny islands, sixty-eight miles away, all part of the territory administered by the U.S. Navy.

Margaret quickly understood that the Samoans gauged "a visitor's importance by the rank of the naval officers with whom he or she associated." She was, right from the start—thanks to her turn on the dance floor with Admiral Coontz and her indirect association with the surgeon general—conferred a high status. This she felt was fortunate. Certainly there was "nothing to be gained in Samoa by working in independence of the naval authorities."

As for mixing with the local population, it was clear that in Pago Pago this was not to be part of the experience. Samoans were everywhere, but as far as the naval officers and their wives were concerned, they were to be treated as part of the servant class, or as exotic creatures to be held at arm's length.

It was after two weeks in Pago Pago that Margaret heard that the mail ship was due to arrive. Writing to Ruth, she confided, "This last night of waiting for mail is dreadful. I can't read, I can't write coherently. I can't sit still."

On the expected day, after word of the ship's approach circulated, Margaret and throngs of others walked to the dock to wait:

> It is difficult to exaggerate the importance of "Steamer Day" in these parts. Everything stops, that is, everything which ordinarily happens. Cook boys disappear, unless forcibly detained by their lavalavas and meals are most uncertain quantities.

The distribution of mail took place in a warehouse on the dock. Names were called and Margaret went up to receive her letters. Stuffing the bundle into a cloth bag, she departed, feeling much like she was carting off a treasure.

Once alone in her hotel room, she dumped the letters on her bed. There were seventy to eighty of them. "The emotional effect," she said, "of having all one's news spread out on the bed . . . was very curious."

The manner in which she absorbed the tidings from home soon developed into a ritual. She read the letters that weren't important to her first, saving the ones she cared most about for last.

At some point she realized that the sequence never varied.

Among those closest to her, her mother's letters came first. They usually centered on practical considerations, from matters of wardrobe to steamer schedules.

Luther's were next.

Invariably his letters contained reports of his tentative forays into London's cultural life and planned sightseeing tours of the continent. Only occasionally would he permit himself to express his gnawing doubts about the future.

Then Ruth's letters, which were a soothing balm.

They reflected an awareness of how isolated one could feel, working in the field. Ruth had concocted a scheme to help Margaret—and herself—withstand these bouts of loneliness. The idea was that their separation, while painfully real, was physical and not mental. Distance could be bridged by a leap of the imagination:

> Today was one of the days when I took the next boat from San Francisco to satisfy myself that you were all right. Nothing would do but to overtake you. Sweetheart, if I did, I know you wouldn't know any more than you know now the love that folds you round always— but it would be a comfort to look upon you.

And then there was the way Ruth dealt with sexual desire. Letters were, at the moment, the only way she had to make love to Margaret, but letters could fall into the wrong hands. Anything that bordered on the erotic had to be communicated in code, their own special code. Images that would seem innocuous to one pair of eyes held a secret meaning for Margaret, like when Ruth referred to having "my fingers tangling in your hair."

At other times Ruth found the urge to communicate her longings was too powerful to mask and she dispensed with the code:

> I've been lying awake making love to you and I've turned on the light so that I can satisfy my foolish senses which think that you

*know better when what I write is for you than when I love you all
to myself.*

Then there were Edward's letters.

His were the ones Margaret designated for last, the ones left to savor—and sometimes to fear. She hadn't consciously planned it that way, it was just something that happened on the first Steamer Day, when she saw the slant of his handwriting across an envelope.

He wrote as if he were having a conversation with her.

"Margaret," he'd say, "if you were here, your eyes and hands would tell me much." And in another, "Margaret, don't you think we should have a child together?"

She could hear his voice, gently mocking her, or himself. He'd have her laughing out loud. At times like these, the seventeen years that separated them seemed inconsequential. Then at other times, when his mood darkened, the distance between them was vast. His maturity, the years he'd spent watching Florence die, the children who were "growing up like weeds without a mother," all this put him on a different trajectory than the one she was on. At these times he'd turn against her, consumed with jealousy, demanding obedience. In one rant he suggested that she'd devised a "water-tight system of rationalizations that only succeeded in hemming her spirit in and giving her chronic fatigue," and in another he told her she had a "prostitution complex," which stemmed from "a compulsive desire to make others happy by way of sacrifice of self." After she soaked up his criticism she was so shaken she told Ruth that she felt "cowardly and contemptible," and could get "no stronger in dealing with it."

She found she was only able to recover her self-confidence by revisiting Ruth's letters.

Ruth's words spread over her like a "benediction." Margaret told her, "The gifts you bring me are too heavy for my hands, some fall out and I have the added joy of stooping to pick them up, kiss them tenderly all over again."

A few weeks after her arrival in Pago Pago, Margaret received a much coveted invitation to attend a Saturday night dinner party at the home of Commander and Mrs. Mink. Dr. Owen Mink was the station's chief medical officer and the most powerful government official living permanently in Pago Pago.

Margaret wore a pale blue crêpe de chine gown with three-quarterlength sleeves. When a horn beeped outside her window, she pulled on her gloves and descended the stairs. Miss Hodgson was waiting for her in the backseat of an old rusted black Ford.

The Minks' house was one of only a handful of two-story structures on the base. Inside it was filled with polished mahogany furnishings and porcelain bric-a-brac. A large metal fan hung from the ceiling, turning slowly through the heavy air.

As soon as Margaret and Miss Hodgson were inside, Mrs. Mink assailed them. "Dinner is delayed," she cried, taking Margaret's arm. "Jopani, our cook boy, had to leave. He ran home to provide for his pig, which was shot at for invading the fita plantation."

"Jopani, that scoundrel," said Dr. Mink, "has got my wife wrapped around his little finger."

During dinner Margaret found herself subjected to endless comments about the price of embroidery, where to buy the best rugs, and, of course, servant troubles. By the end of the evening she felt that if the boredom didn't kill her, the catty looks would.

She told Ruth,

This sweet little group of gossips are just seething with speculation as to why I "left my husband." Of course they are sure I have. And I know I oughtn't to mind, but it's so depressing to be greeted with suspicious unfriendly glances. . . . It's curious how this remote insular living develops as much rigidity of social standards among the whites as among the natives.

As much as Margaret wanted to distance herself from the navy people, she had the good sense to understand that the success of her project might just depend on how well she was able to negotiate the shoals of station etiquette. Toward this end, she was prepared to demonstrate that she was a lady who was very much at home in upper-class company. Judging others by their social rank was what made these officers and their wives tick and, if truth be told, class was important to Margaret, too. Writing home, she said, "I've learned that if people lack both personality and brains it's a comfort to have them well-bred."

———

A few days later, on the morning of September 24, Margaret waited with Dr. Charles Lane and his wife under the awning that extended over the porch of the Officers' Club. She'd already concluded that most of the "ladies of the station" were empty-headed. They knew just enough to put "rose petals in their finger bowls and complain that their nurse girls were not respectful." The only exception was Mrs. Lane, "who although mightily spoiled and childless," had a certain "savoir faire and magnetism that was a life saver."

Their destination that morning was the Atauloma Boarding School for Girls of the London Missionary Society. The school was one of many run by evangelical Protestants who had come to Samoa in the mid-nineteenth century and were now "heavily entrenched" all over the islands. It would be Margaret's first *malaga* (ceremonial visit) beyond the confines of the naval station.

When they arrived at Atauloma, Margaret found that an elaborate feast had been prepared. She and the others were enjoined to sit at a table that had been erected beneath a narrow arbor "heavily freighted with strings of flowers."

Their hosts brought out platters consisting of baked taro, "almost raw pork," and "boiled bananas." Then the entertainment began. The girls of Atauloma sang and danced the *siva* in their "neat, ill-tailored white muslins, which hit their knees in just the wrong place," followed by three of the school's teachers, who made seemingly endless speeches full of Christian platitudes.

Margaret fought to stay awake. It was clear that these teenagers were being inculcated with the same values as any good Christian girl. It seemed that physical chastity for an unmarried young woman was the unquestioned and sole requirement of an education. By the end of the performance she was relieved to say good-bye and slog back to the car.

Back in her hotel room she wrote to Ruth, saying she felt "boxed up beside a sullen sea." She was feeling sorry for herself:

> This is a lonely job and I do value having a decent meal occasionally and talking something—not much, it's true, but <u>something</u>. I'm too weak minded to face real dislike in the eyes of a pussycat. But

where there isn't a living soul who'd give a pewter platter whether
you live or die at least friendliness is welcome.

The next morning—as she did every day—Margaret's tutor, G. F. Pepe, arrived to give Margaret a language lesson before she continued on to her job as a nurse at the naval hospital. Twenty-nine years old, "of chiefly family and a cousin of Tufele's," Pepe had graduated from the Atauloma Boarding School and was one of only a handful of Samoans who had learned to read and write in her native language.

Margaret described their routine in a bulletin: "She dictates to me in Samoan and then I try to give it back to her with the correct pronunciation, phrasing and cadence." The work was tedious and progressed slowly. Margaret complained, "It is remarkable how difficult it is to accomplish anything here." And it wasn't just the language instruction she found frustrating. Pago Pago had been "overrun with missionaries, stores and various intrusive influences"; it hardly offered an unspoiled environment in which to study adolescent girls. There was little doubt that she was going to have to distance herself from this naval enclave, which meant leaving the island of Tutuila. Only in an isolated location could she effectively investigate the subject Boas had sent her to study: How did teenage girls mature into women? In Samoa, as in Western cultures, was this transition a time of conflict?

The success of this investigation depended on Margaret's ability to establish an intimacy with her informants and this required a fluency in their language. Just thinking of this left her seething with envy at Edward Sapir. If he were here, he'd already be fluent in Samoan.

That night she told Ruth: "I'm in a state of despair at present. There is a limit to the time one can spend on the language per day without useless satiety."

She looked at a map that showed her location in Pago Pago in relation to the other neighboring islands that constituted American Samoa. There was a myriad of possibilities, but as she contemplated spending the next few months going native in an isolated setting, the potential problems seemed to multiply. She dreaded "the nerve wracking conditions of living with a half-dozen people in a house without walls." She was only half joking when she told Ruth, "Next week I'm going to start sleeping on the floor for practice." Even worse was the thought of eating the food. Boiled taro, "a putty-tasting, soap textured" glob of gray, was "too starchy" to live on.

She rubbed her arms. They hurt "frightfully":

At present this whole task seems utterly fantastic and impossible. How in Heaven's name am I to learn the language and the psychology of a people in a year. Not even a year—9 months. It suddenly seems completely absurd. . . . What mind folly ever made me want to pick something as difficult as this?

THE TELEGRAM

Margaret is a far more typical woman than either she or you know. And there is no shadow of doubt that Margaret loves me—why God only knows.

—EDWARD SAPIR

October 1925

Margaret was aware she'd reached a pivotal moment in her fieldwork, though she hadn't even started it. What she would decide now would determine the rest of her time in Samoa.

Her new friend Miss Hodgson had suggested an approach to her research, one that she had not considered. It involved leaving the naval base in Pago Pago and relocating to a small medical compound on one of the more remote islands.

Miss Hodgson told her that Ruth Holt—Mrs. Ruth Holt—currently residing in the maternity ward of the Pago Pago naval hospital, was waiting to give birth to her second baby.

"Her husband is Edward Holt. The pharmacist's mate at the dispensary on Ta'u," said Miss Hodgson, referring to one of the three islands in the Manu'a group, over sixty miles away. "She'll be returning there after the baby's born, in about three weeks. If you are ready to travel you could go with her."

If she went to Ta'u, Margaret could live in the naval dispensary with the Holts, within immediate proximity to the village of Luma. This would give her access to 251 natives in an unspoiled setting.

However, in order to effectuate this plan, Margaret would have to set the wheels in motion immediately. In order to relocate to Ta'u, she needed Dr. Owen Mink's consent.

But Margaret was uncertain. Maybe such a move was premature or, worse, wrongheaded. After all, she hadn't yet grasped the most rudimentary language skills. Nor was she persuaded that living with an American family rather than a Samoan one was the right way to approach her fieldwork.

If only she could ask Boas for his opinion, or at the very least, confer with Ruth. Even though her letter would not reach the United States for another month and there was no hope of receiving a timely response, that night she wrote to Ruth:

> Oh how terribly I need your loving arms! How used I am to turning to you in every emergency in every need—Sweetheart! Sweetheart! And so much has happened even in this interval of muddleheadedness. . . . I don't see how I can manage.

Confused as she was, something was telling her that living with Americans—while it would never win a "purist's" approval—was the most efficient way for her to accomplish her goals.

At the beginning of October, Margaret pushed forward with the idea of relocating to Ta'u. She made the acquaintance of Mrs. Holt, who agreed, pending Dr. Mink's approval, that Margaret could return with her when she caught the boat back to the medical dispensary.

Knowing that Dr. Mink had received orders to "do everything possible to facilitate the success" of her project, Margaret was optimistic. She reported to Ruth, "having just told you I could *never* learn the language I suddenly decided that I knew quite enough of it to go out into the country at once. And I've decided on Manu'a because it's not difficult to get to."

Her change of heart had been so sudden she felt she needed to justify it, even to Ruth.

> It's also optimum from an ethnological standpoint for we have no information from there at all. It's practically unspoiled by such things as mores. . . . There are 3 little islands, 2 connected at low tide and about 2,000 people in the three islands. I'm going to the disconnected one, Ta'u. A boat comes over from there about once a month. There are three white people on the island. The navy dispensary man, his wife and a corps man.

Heartened that her stay in Pago Pago would soon be at an end, Margaret pressed forward with renewed energy. She arranged to interview Mrs. Helen Ripley Wilson, a "half-caste" woman educated in Honolulu, and a special friend of G. F. Pepe, her language instructor.

On October 10, Margaret traveled to Mrs. Wilson's house in the village of Leone, riding in a "rattletrap" of a bus that was packed with the locals, carrying "baskets of food, ice, pigs and chickens in sacks." Margaret's chief purpose in making the acquaintance of Mrs. Wilson was to learn more about the upbringing of teenage girls.

For the interview, Margaret took with her a list of twenty-five typewritten questions. As she worked her way down the list she heard, once again, how much value the Samoans placed on physical chastity. Throughout the islands the Samoans practiced a custom that underscored its importance. In each village the *ali'i* (titular chief of high rank) had the right to confer on one of the sexually mature virginal girls of his family the rank of *taupou* (ceremonial virgin). Usually the girl chosen would be one of the chief's own daughters. As a *taupou* the girl belonged to the whole village and was required to travel in the company of an older woman wherever she went. Margaret learned that, in fact, even "girls of common families" were never sent from village to village without a chaperone, as this was considered a necessary safeguard of their virginity.

By the time that Margaret finished her interview with Helen Wilson, she understood that, for unmarried females, virginity was an absolute requirement.

This attitude toward chastity was not so different from the way Margaret herself had been brought up.

Edward Sapir sat at the desk in his Ottawa office, barely conscious of the men in overalls who were labeling his boxes of books and stacking them on a dolly. His focus was on a letter to Ruth:

Ever since Margaret and I found ourselves, nothing else has seemed capable of entering into my head and heart. Summer school, museum, Chicago, all pass by on the merest periphery of my consciousness. My office looks very bare. My books and papers have all been packed and they're marking the Chicago address on them. I am hoping to sell all the furniture.

Two weeks earlier Edward had wrapped up his summer courses at Columbia and returned home. Now he was closing out the Ottawa chapter of his life—his marriage, the birth of his three children, and the prime of his manhood. It had lasted thirteen years. He looked around. Dull yellow rectangular stains showed on the walls, marking the place where framed pictures of his family once hung.

Yesterday he'd taken the children and his mother to the Immigration Office to have photos taken for their passports. His mother, while well-intentioned, was of little help; with her health failing, she had turned into yet another problem.

He continued with his letter, making reference to his new boss, Fay-Cooper Cole:

> *Cole has taken an apartment for me and I have already paid the October rent. Are these details interesting? But they show that I am soon to be a Chicagoan. But then how am I ever to see Margaret? A permanently absent love is too cruel. I could never bear it.*

The future loomed before him as an empty expanse. The university with its oodles of Rockefeller money and its community of engaged intellectuals meant nothing to him. All he could think about was that he would arrive in a place where there would be no Margaret. When she returned from Samoa it would be to New York City, not to Chicago. Somehow he had to convince her to join him. As soon as he was settled he would talk to Cole.

At the moment what he wanted was to see Ruth. He urged her to route her return trip through Chicago:

> *There's no one on God's earth (of those residing on this continent) I'd sooner see there or anywhere. . . . And do stay in Chicago as long as you possibly can, for I want you to at least glimpse the children, if that is possible. And I want to talk to you. Perhaps you can help me buy furniture!*

On a Friday afternoon Edward stood under the massive portico of Union Station, outside the Western Union office. Looking in, he could see that a line of customers had formed in front of the counter. When he stepped inside he smelled the familiar odor of ink and heard the rapid click of a teletype machine.

The tone and content of Margaret's last letter had alarmed him. She had complained about feeling lonely and, of course, about her arms. Granted, his letters to her had been harsh, impulsive, and self-centered. Perhaps he was responsible for making her feel worse.

To make amends he had decided to send a cable.

His hand closed around a scrap of paper covered with letter combinations. He'd written out a message in code, the code *she'd* devised for just these kinds of situations. It said that he loved her, only her, and was anxious to know that she was all right.

He looked at his watch and calculated the time difference. Right now it was dawn in Samoa. When Margaret woke, she would find his cable waiting for her. Filling out a form, sliding it through to the clerk, he waited for the clack of the teletype. Once he was sure of the cable's transmission he felt better.

The next morning he woke up early and found that his mother was already awake, busy in the kitchen, making the children their breakfast.

"Has there been a cable?" he asked, his voice booming out too loudly.

"A cable?" she said, looking up, startled by his tone.

"I'm expecting one. Please let me know when it gets here."

That day he stayed at home all morning and afternoon, trying to read, waiting for Margaret's reply. By the day's end he was becoming alarmed.

He thought how, in a number of Margaret's letters, she'd referred to the pain in her arms. She refused to take the neuritis seriously. If one knew anything about her complexes, one would simply be forced to assume, on general principle, that she was exhibiting some sort of hysterical symptom. He hoped she was not at the beginning of a physical breakdown. All the signs indicated that it was due.

As the night wore on he became even more convinced that something must be seriously wrong. He had to find out if she was all right.

She was staying in that hotel alone; he had to locate someone who could go to her room and check on her. Suddenly a name came to mind. Margaret had mentioned a Dr. Owen Mink, the chief medical officer. He was the navy man who'd been instructed to look after her.

By the time Edward reached Western Union he'd composed his message. Entering the office he was relieved to see there was no line. He wrote out the cablegram and had it sent it to Dr. Owen Mink, Tutuila.

Margaret, always one to be industrious, was pleased with herself for identifying a place in the station where there was daily interaction between people speaking both Samoan and English so she could "practice hearing translation." That setting was the High Court. When Margaret eased herself into a seat in the courtroom, a case was in progress. A fifteen-year-old girl had been accused of biting off the ear of a rival. The presiding judge was an American lawyer from Los Angeles. After two hours, he sentenced the defendant to three months in jail. Margaret left the courtroom with the feeling that the judge "believes with all Americans here that the Samoans are a suggestible lot of children."

As Margaret was walking down the courthouse steps she heard someone call her name. She looked and saw Dr. Mink walking toward her, in his hand a piece of paper.

"Miss Mead," said Dr. Mink. He waved the paper. "Miss Mead, your father cabled."

Hearing this, she was worried.

Rushing toward him she grabbed the cable out of his hand. Seeing it had been sent from Ottawa she felt the heat starting to spread over her cheeks.

Dr. Mink said, "I thought you said your father was at the University of Pennsylvania?"

"He must be doing some work in Ottawa," said Margaret.

When she showed no inclination to discuss the matter further, Dr. Mink said, "Well, all right then, I hope everything is as it should be," and walked away.

Later in the day, Margaret encountered Mrs. Mink and three other ladies as they were heading to the Officers' Club for a game of bridge. She didn't know if she was imagining it, but they all seemed to look at her with disapproval. If she wasn't so much at the mercy of Dr. Mink, she'd find it amusing.

She wrote to Ruth:

> . . . and then to cap the climax Edward cabled me Saturday and I couldn't answer until Monday, and so he cables Dr. Mink. Heard now on every side, "Who do I know in Ottawa?" They thought my father was at the U of P, etc. I've written him very wrathfully, but

please reiterate when you write to him. It just needs about a feather's weight to have these people shut their doors and not only not cooperate but actually hinder my work."

"It's more than generous of you to take up my letters with such beautiful interest," said Edward, pulling out a chair from behind the desk, turning it around, and straddling it. "You are no doubt shocked by my last letters."

"Why?" Ruth asked.

"I am thoroughly ashamed of them."

Edward and Ruth were together in Ruth's hotel room. Ruth was perched on the edge of the bed, holding a cup of tea in her hands, Edward facing her. Neither was paying any attention to their surroundings.

"What exactly did you say to her?" asked Ruth.

"At the moment I don't know," he said, running a hand over his eyes. "When I get into certain moods, I go completely off the handle."

They had eaten dinner in a restaurant close to the hotel, on Chicago's South Side. Edward had brought the children there so Ruth could see how much they'd grown. After dinner, he'd taken the children in a taxi back to his temporary lodgings and left them with his mother, before hurrying back to Ruth's hotel.

Now finally, he and Ruth were free to talk.

"Margaret is a girl of extraordinary power and insight," said Edward. "She's whittled down Luther's personality to the point where, apparently, the only claim he has on her is to accept what gifts she wife-mothers him."

"I don't know that I'd characterize it like that," said Ruth.

"Leaving him no choice but to declare that he's happy with that."

"I think you have to take him at his word."

"And Margaret?"

"She loves you both."

"Loves? Loves us *both* you say?" Edward struggled to his feet and started to pace. "Forgive me. But I still belong to the ninety-nine percent statistics who believe that a woman's love cannot be shared by two men."

"I'm just expressing for Margaret what she can't at the moment say for herself."

"Am I to accept Margret's philosophy of love without a wink, though the mere contemplation of it causes me untold misery?"

Ruth said nothing.

"I can see by your silence that you think I should," said Edward.

"Even with Luther in the picture, there must be some way for you to hold on to the beauty of the experience," said Ruth.

He held up his hand. "Please, Ruth, try to see things a little my way as well as Margaret's. I can't eat, can't sleep, can't get my heart into work or planning. I feel absolutely lost. The image of little Margaret actually *loving,* with what all the word means, two men at once just sets me crazy."

Ruth gave no indication of what she was thinking.

"Now I realize the hopelessness of moving such cultivated girls as you and Margaret to recognize the claims of the misguided majority which, by the way, is likely to be more nearly ninety-nine and nine-tenths percent."

"Really, Edward, when you say such things, it sounds like your possessive panic is taking over."

"Does it not occur to you that possibly there is something Margaret might reasonably sacrifice?"

Ruth seemed to shake her head.

Edward laughed. "You know, Ruth, there is a real element of comedy in the whole situation. Someday I may discover that a woman can love, truly love, two men at the same time, giving her body to each, but I haven't discovered it yet."

He walked to the window, undid the latch, and lifted it up. Leaning on the sill, his back to Ruth, he looked down on the street. The street lamps were glittering and car headlights illuminated the road.

"She is so much younger," said Edward, almost to himself. "I mustn't tie her down. So I sacrifice the home, if need be. I don't demand wedlock. Nor do I, for a single moment, expect her to trim her scientific career for my sake."

He turned, looking straight into Ruth's face. "Margaret is a far more typical woman than either she or you know. And there is no shadow of doubt that Margaret loves me—why God only knows. And there is as little doubt that I love her."

"I know you do," said Ruth.

"Conflict or no conflict," said Edward, thinking back on his last night with Margaret. "There's dynamite latent in it all. Time and love will have to work out our solution, and there's no forcing we can do."

Ruth sat in the B&O's dining car, looking out the window into the darkness. The train was rumbling through the farmland of western Pennsylvania. Sometime in the night they'd be passing through Philadelphia, Margaret's hometown.

The night before, after Edward had left, Ruth had had a fitful night, her sleep broken by one bad dream after another. In one of them she and Margaret had adjoining rooms. She'd gone into Margaret's room. Margaret was in bed, but she made no sign for Ruth to come to her, so Ruth went out.

Ruth woke up feeling miserable.

She could not deny that she was sick with worry. Edward wanted to bring Margaret to Chicago. If Margaret's love for him was strong enough, he might succeed. If he succeeded, Margaret would disappear from her life. Truthfully, she told herself, the odds that this might happen were impossible to gauge.

She looked down at the stationery before her.

Darling, everything is a nice dark conspiracy to make me lonely for you—going back to New York; riding on the B & O; talking all last night with Edward. It was rather a joke on both of us—how we both talked of you and wished the other could be metamorphosed one precious moment into you.

She sat for a long time, ruminating. She knew that she had to tread carefully. Margaret's love for Edward seemed to wax and wane; from what Margaret had been telling her in her most recent letters, that love was making a resurgence. It was best not to overreact.

Much might depend on Goddard's job offer.

Ruth understood that Margaret's ambition was unremitting. If the museum appointment came through, Margaret would be hard-pressed to turn it down. If she were working at the Museum of Natural History, she'd be anchored to New York City.

Ruth decided she must have a talk with Goddard. She'd make sure that Boas spoke to him, too.

She continued her letter to Margaret, mustering as much dignity as she could. About Edward she said,

> *But don't think we didn't enjoy each other too. He is looking a little thin, but alert and well. He's very curious to know how he'll like Chicago. All together I've never seen him when I'd more trust him to meet his problems as they could best be met.*

Having shown self-restraint throughout, only at the end of her letter did she let some of her anxiety leak out, writing, "Dear love, write me that you love me. I treasure it so much it is hard for me to believe in it."

A CEREMONIAL VIRGIN

*In my three months down here I don't think I've made a
single friend except the Samoans in Vaitogi. Probably it's
because I'm so wrapped up in my own silly little woes.*
—MARGARET MEAD

November 1925

Margaret had ten days to wait before she could leave with Ruth
Holt and her newborn baby girl on the gunboat that was to
sail for Manu'a. In the meantime, she was determined to get
away from the naval station and out into the bush where she would be
forced to talk Samoan. She'd heard about an out-of-the-way spot called
Vaitogi that was twelve miles from the station and three miles from the
last bus line. From time to time navy personnel visited there, and some
had reported it was so pleasant they cried when they had to leave. With
a letter of introduction from the Secretary of Native Affairs to Ufuti, the
chief who was to be her host, she set off, ignoring the warning that she
would return "covered with lice, fleas and boils."

Vaitogi, known in American Samoa as the Village of the Turtle and
the Shark, was on what was called "the iron bound coast" because it
overlooked a shoreline edged with recently cooled lava, where the wild
surf crashed to heights of fifteen-feet plus.

The villagers welcomed Margaret as if she were a goddess. Some of
them had never seen a woman with golden hair and blue eyes. Many simply wanted to touch her white skin. Ufuti showed himself to be "keenly
intelligent and surpassingly kind and gentle." His wife Savai'i and his
daughter Fa'amotu, immediately set to work making Margaret comfortable, spreading out a bed with "some twenty fine mats, mats which it takes
a woman a year or more to make." Moreover, when Margaret made the

effort to converse with her hosts in Samoan, Ufuti and the other chiefs were so "tickled" they ordered "two young chickens a day" to be killed and prepared, and heaped her plate with mangoes, limes, and papayas.

Then Ufiti conferred on Margaret the highest honor possible, naming her *taupou* of the village. Margaret was not a virgin, and she certainly wasn't unmarried, but she did not try to disabuse her host of his mistake. After all, there were to be many special *fiafias* (entertainments with singing and dancing) with her at the center, and the experience of participating in those would be invaluable.

Justifying her deception as necessary for the advancement of her ethnological research, Margaret passed herself off as chaste. For the days she spent in Vaitogi she reigned as the community's ceremonial virgin alongside the chief's own daughter Fa'amotu.

At the end of a delightful ten-day stay Margaret presented Ufuti with a hanging lantern as a *tofa* (good-bye gift). She composed a farewell speech in English, and asked Ufuti's nineteen-year-old son to translate it into Samoan so she could recite it from memory:

> *America excels in the making of machinery. France excels in the making of clothes. From Italy comes the greatest singers. But the Samoan people excel the whole world in hospitality.*

When she was done the whole family cried, and so did Margaret. The people of Vaitogi really had made her feel like she was one of them. Writing home, Margaret said: "I never spent a more peacefully happy and comfortable ten days in my life."

The islands of the Manu'a group were three tiny specks in the South Pacific, a day's journey by boat from the naval base in Pago Pago. Ta'u, the largest of the three, was eight miles wide, eleven miles long, and thirty-two miles in circumference. Approximately nine hundred to a thousand people lived on Ta'u, spread between four villages on the west coast, all connected by a steep, often muddy trail. The U.S. Naval dispensary—Margaret's new home—was situated in the village of Luma, facing west and overlooking a lagoon and coral reef. The dispensary was the only *papalagi* (foreign house) on the island, built of weatherboard with a corrugated iron roof. It was at the center of a small medical compound that provided supplies and nursing care to the native population.

Margaret joined a household that consisted of the Chief Pharmacist Mate Edward R. Holt, his wife Ruth, their two-year-old son Arthur, and new baby girl, Moana. Mr. Holt was tall and fair. In appearance he reminded Margaret of her brother Dick. Also living at the dispensary was Sparks, ". . . a young sailor whose chief preoccupation was the fact that he had only a third grade education." Sparks spent his days "fooling with new types of radio apparatus and reading radio magazines," and only appeared when he sat down to the table for a meal.

Margaret's room took up half of the back porch and was next to the area where provisions were stored. A loosely woven bamboo screen divided where she slept from the metal cabinets that held all the sundry medical supplies.

For much of the day the sticky tropical heat made work of any kind impossible. Margaret wrote home, "there is the most peculiar sensation one gets . . . a feeling as if one's skin were going to fly off in thin gossamer layers and a curious buzzing inside one's head." It didn't take her long to realize that the pleasantest time of day was at sunset and she soon made it her habit, at the end of each day, to stroll out to the shore.

On an afternoon in late November, accompanied by a dozen girls and a handful of children, she walked to the outskirts of the village of Siufaga. There they stood on an ironbound point, with the waves lapping around their feet, watching as the sun dropped behind the coconut tree-covered hills, throwing the village and part of the beach into shadow.

Most of the adults were already there, clad in *lavalavas* and carrying buckets for water borne along on shoulder poles.

On one side of the beach all of the heads of families were seated in the *fatetele* (roundhouse) grinding *kava* (drink made from the kava root). Not far off a group of women were filling a small canoe with a solution of the native starch—arrowroot.

Only when the sun had disappeared into the sea did Margaret start back for home. The soft footsteps of the half-dozen children who were following close behind was a comforting sound. They had all nearly reached the store when the curfew-angelus began to sound, a wooden bell that sent a mellow clang through the village. Suddenly the children scurried for cover, scuttling under the store's wooden landing. There they waited, until another bell sounded, signaling that the Lord's Prayer was over.

Since she'd arrived in Luma, three weeks earlier, Margaret had let life unfold with the predictable rhythm of the village. She'd finally begun to think about how to tackle her fieldwork or, as Boas liked to call it, the "problem" she'd been sent to investigate. She'd managed to identify sixty-five teenage informants but had not yet interviewed any of them. At the moment, the scope of the undertaking felt overwhelming. She complained to Ruth:

> *I am furious that I didn't come sooner. Why did I feel I needed six weeks to learn the language? But I was simply in a hurt daze. All the echoes of Edward's inducements still sounded in my heart— everything seemed too hopeless to think about and I was an inert lifeless machine . . . if I'd been a quarter of myself I would have had sense enough to come out into the villages sooner.*

"Thanksgiving was a turkey-cranberry celery-mince pie sort of a day," wrote Ruth, making sure to keep her tone lighthearted. "May and Agnes came out and the dinner was really all that could be desired."

With the meal at an end, and Stanley in bed, she could finally relax. She was in no hurry to join him. She took her time undressing, slowly folding her good cashmere sweater set and putting it away in a garment bag. Standing in front of the mirror she looked at herself. The lines in her forehead were more noticeable, the silver in her hair more pronounced. No wonder. These last few months had been stressful.

In her last letter to Margaret she'd mused, "I do wonder what living with the Holts will be like. It would be wonderful luck if you could like them." But the fact was Ruth was not thinking about Samoa. She was worrying about Chicago—and Edward.

In a recent letter Margaret had reported, "His present point is that I must come to Chicago—on any terms. I see no clear path." To Ruth it sounded like relocating to Chicago was actually under consideration.

Even Edward—although still pessimistic about being able to bring Margaret to Chicago—was now starting to address some of the practical considerations:

> *The bittersweet fact remains that I love Margaret and cannot bear the thought of indefinite separation. Now I am not in the least sanguine about being able to get her to come here. Quite aside from her own attitude in the matter, I don't see clearly how people here can be induced to take on a girl so little known as yet.*

But what if Edward *did* succeed?

Ruth wanted to be kept apprised of his every move, but the problem was that he was withdrawing. Letters from him had become less frequent. It was as though he viewed her as "an interloper," and "grudged her knowledge" of the affair.

Picking up her hairbrush, Ruth began to brush, sweeping her hair back from her widow's peak in hard, unforgiving strokes.

There were times when she felt it was a mistake to continue in the role of Cupid's messenger. Not only was it duplicitous but it was dangerous. She'd told Margaret, "Sometimes I have a nightmare that I'm risking your love in this same role, and I wonder if I could take courage to go on." But she knew if she didn't intervene, Edward might succeed, and that would be devastating.

The next morning Ruth woke up thinking that she had to muster some self-respect. If Margaret chose to be with Edward, it was incumbent on her to get out of the way. She began her letter, "I pray that you may draw every drop of sweet the gods will allow out of your love for each other. . . ."

However, she couldn't stop herself from sounding a warning: ". . . there is no way but to love Edward on his own terms. Do not even believe him if he protests differently."

And then she passed on some choice gossip she'd heard from their colleague Paul Radin, who loved to talk about Edward. The story dated back to the early years of Edward's marriage:

> . . . *he was so jealous he couldn't bear to have Florence talk with the postman . . . he used to storm publically if Goldie telephoned his house, or if Radin sat beside her at a dinner.*

It seemed that Edward had no control over his jealousy. Ruth went on:

> *Darling, by all the rules I should not be writing you in this fashion, and yet you know . . . it's with eyes open wide—and still loving him—that you'll be able to give him the most happiness.*

Edward, she wanted Margaret to know, was powerless to understand the "cruel warping" of his psyche.

No sooner had she dropped the letter in the mailbox than she regretted it.

The next Monday, after returning to the city, Ruth went straight to the Museum of Natural History to speak to Pliny Goddard. The door to his office was closed, but she could see a light on inside. She knocked.

Goddard opened the door and greeted her with a wry smile. "Don't tell me," he said. "You're here to talk about Margaret Mead."

Self-conscious, but not enough to stop herself, Ruth asked Goddard when the board was scheduled to meet.

"What if I told you we've already had our meeting," he said, his smile broadening. "We should be hearing something soon."

Later that day Ruth wrote Margaret that she'd found Goddard cautiously optimistic, saying, "I hold that knowledge close."

Edward was seated at his desk when the young woman first appeared. She was wearing a dark coat, navy skirt, and black boots. She stood in his doorway and addressed him as Dr. Sapir.

She knew who he was although she didn't identify herself as his student.

Edward rose to his feet.

Her hand was small, her handshake firm. She seemed to take possession of him before the conversation had even begun.

Her name was Jean McClenaghan, "*Miss* Jean McClenaghan." She said she'd heard him speak in Ottawa when he'd given a lecture on the connection between psychology and the formation of language.

"Ottawa?" He laughed out loud. "What were you doing in Ottawa?"

"That's where I'm from." She smiled.

"You have my condolences," he said.

"Now I'm working here, at the Chicago Institute for Juvenile Research," she said.

He noticed now that her eyes were striking, a pale green, like the color of crystals.

So far for Edward, coming to Chicago had been a blessing; this was yet another example of the surprising things that seemed to be happening to him.

His main problem, if he had to name one, was that he was forced to juggle too many social engagements. After Miss McClenaghan made a deliberate effort to contact him again, many of these engagements turned out to be with her. He learned that she was of Scottish Irish descent and was twenty-five years old. Her sudden inclusion in his life was met with resistance from some of his students, many of whom were the same age. In the end, he didn't care that they disapproved and had to admit that he was terrible at managing his time.

Now, when Edward sat down to correspond with Ruth, he found that writing to her no longer felt like a release. On the contrary. He resented the fact that he was forced to defend his position in regard to Margaret:

> *Ruth, dear, I may be horribly unjust in all this. The truth is that Margaret and my values are too dangerously far from each other to make it humanly possible for my love to thrive. Assume if you like, that Margaret's views are not only sincere but possible and even ideal, still I cannot accept them. Call me weak and conventional and anything you like. All I know is that I don't feel at home in Margaret's world.*

For the first time it seemed possible that he might be facing a future that did not include Margaret:

> *Margaret has given me more than any woman has given me, which is precisely why she must give all or have her gift fade into meaninglessness. Is that so very hard to understand?*

The fact was, this new woman, Miss Jean McClenaghan, had more than piqued his interest.

"Only life and years can teach Margaret," he said, "certainly not I. And when she *has* finally learned, I shall be much too old to interest her."

Margaret woke up feeling sick. She supposed it was the stress of the work she'd not yet started. After gargling a glass of warm saltwater she went to the Holts' door and knocked. Ruth Holt, still in a nightgown, opened the door. Margaret could tell she wasn't happy to see her standing there. Margaret asked to have her temperature taken.

"My word," Mrs. Holt said, "you're so full of complaints. I'm beginning to wonder if you're not a hypochondriac." She put her hand to Margaret's forehead and said, "You're not even hot."

Margaret returned to her room still wondering if she had a fever. Strange how Ruth Holt's condemnation cut her to the quick. Describing her state of mind as "a borderline delirium," she told Ruth:

> I got into a terrific mood—which fortunately I spared you. I decided I'd lost my drive, that I didn't give a damn about the problem or any other problem, etc. You've heard it all . . . and I've been in bed ever since with a sort of flu or tonsillitis or something.

She even thought to herself how "very comfortable it would be to die." To make matters worse, it was only a few days until her birthday.

As a girl Margaret had always demanded that her parents and siblings make a fuss over her birthday. At college, she'd expected her roommates to do the same. So it was on December 14, two days before she was to turn twenty-four, that she found the distance that separated her from everyone else especially hard to endure.

While in this mood she wrote to Ruth:

> In my three months down here I don't think I've made a single friend except the Samoans in Vaitogi. Probably it's because I'm so wrapped up in my own silly little woes.

So far it had only been in Vaitogi that Margaret had felt appreciated. She certainly didn't among her own people, the whites who resided in the naval compound. While not so long ago she had rejected the idea of immersing herself in a native household, saying, "I couldn't live like that and do my problem," she was now beginning to think that she'd made a mistake.

Then the situation with the Holts deteriorated even further, turning into "a lovely fiasco."

Margaret had been in her room, working at her desk, going through her index cards, making a list of the adolescents she intended to contact. She had the list open so she could check off the names of any girls who came in to see her that evening, some of whom were already sitting in a circle at her feet.

Just then "a sweet little thing named Filialosa," around twelve years old, came through the screen door and approached Margaret. Filialosa said that Tapuni, her older sister, was outside and wanted to come in, too.

Tapuni sauntered into the room. She was "a coarse slovenly creature" and looked to be about twenty-five to thirty years of age. Margaret recognized her as the village prostitute.

Standing in the center of the room, singing in a loud voice and rotating her hips, Tapuni urged the younger girls to stand up and dance. Raising her voice, she shouted at them to go faster and faster.

The performance was "pretty awful," but Margaret decided that as long as it had started, she had better let it finish. Before she knew it, the noise was deafening.

Suddenly Edward Holt pushed aside the curtain and stood in the doorway. "Go a little slow on the racket, Miss Mead," he said. "That wasn't in the bargain when you came here."

The noise of Tapuni's dance had disturbed Mrs. Holt and awakened the baby but as far as Mr. Holt was concerned, what was really inexcusable was that Margaret had permitted the village prostitute to enter his home:

> He's a frightful prude, the psychology of his simper was simple enough—and tho he's very nice he's thin skinned and by no manner of means a gentleman. Just a silly little row. But they've refused to let me send any cables until I file my code.

The cable code was Margaret's safety net. Being told that she couldn't use it until she "registered" it with the naval administration was infuriating:

> Oh Ruth, I am so damnably lonely—as long as everything goes like a song—comparatively—I manage reasonably well. I remember that I mustn't cry—my eyes are sore enough as it is. . . . But just let some little thing go wrong and the whole superficial structure of efficiency goes under.

Once Margaret started to feel sorry for herself, there seemingly was no end to it:

> And it's the eve of my birthday. Usually I fall down stairs or break my best tea set or get into a fight on my birthday and I suppose I just started betimes. But oh, how spoiled, how terribly, terribly coddled I've always been—with one person and usually many more around who cared whether I lived or died. And now, when I cry Arthur [the

Holt's two year-old son] puts his arms around my neck and that's all. And there's five more months! I'm getting perfectly pathological about my time, my thoughts, everything being mortgaged to the NRC.

It had been thanks to Professor Boas that the National Research Council had agreed to finance her fieldwork in Samoa, and now Margaret was determined to accomplish what she'd been sent to do, not only because the men on NRC's Board were expecting it, but also because Boas had gone out on a limb on her behalf. The possibility of failure kept her up at night worrying.

It also caused her to wonder if there was some truth to what Edward had said when he accused her of rating "love lower than external accomplishment." In his last letter he'd complained that although her letters had many loving passages, they were "so riddled with . . . shoddy values," their love was doomed. He seemed to be warning that he was going to end their affair. Was this an empty threat, or were his feelings changing?

She wished she knew.

On December 24, Sparks was sitting inside the radio room when the teletype machine hummed to life, signaling an incoming cable. The message was addressed to Margaret Mead. It stated that her appointment as assistant curator of ethnology on the scientific staff of the Museum of Natural History, beginning in October of 1926, had been formally approved.

Later that afternoon, with the cable tucked in her pocket, Margaret "walked along the beach alone," reveling in the knowledge that her senior colleagues recognized her worth.

It was a marvelous sensation. The following year she would be returning to New York City with a prestigious job, earning an annual salary of $2,000. She no longer had to apply for another grant from the NRC to extend her time in Samoa.

She was, as she wrote to Ruth, "counting and weighing the minutes of the days" that were left in Samoa.

A BONFIRE ON THE BEACH

*You see I've never stopped loving anyone whom I really
loved greatly.*

—MARGARET MEAD

January 1926

On the island of Ta'u, the celebration of the New Year began
early in the day, in church. That morning Margaret watched as
women wearing their finest fringed *tapa* (bark cloth) dresses
walked past. She had decided not to join the partygoers because she'd
resolved to start work on her "plan of research" for the NRC, the report
she'd been putting off for weeks.

She sat on the dispensary steps, looking out at the sea. Dark, low-lying
clouds were moving in fast and the day promised to be "wet and ominous." A storm was coming. Teenage girls skipped by, unconcerned and
carefree, colorful paper necklaces draped around their necks.

Margaret had compiled a list that included these girls and approximately fifty others who could be loosely classified as adolescents. They
were to be her informants, but the prospect of interviewing them about
their sexual conduct was daunting. All these girls had been indoctrinated
with the values of Protestantism and the London Missionary Society.
The primary emphasis of their education had been on tamping down
their sexuality. How, with only a rudimentary command of the language,
could she probe so sensitive a subject?

Margaret looked down at her hands now poised over the keys of the
typewriter. The young professors back in Washington, D.C., the men
who sat on the NRC, had made it clear they wanted to hear details about
when and how the girls first started to have sex. Margaret had nothing

to tell them but, conditioned to be a conscientious student and to do the very best job possible on any and all assignments, she was determined somehow to meet their expectations. She began to type.

Two hours later the sound of laughter broke Margaret's concentration. Looking up she saw some of the high-spirited churchgoers trooping back through the rain, "their paper necklaces already drooping pathetically." She turned back to her draft, but a few minutes later she was interrupted again, this time by revelers from Faleasao who carried gifts and an invitation to return with them to their village. Sensing that it might be unwise to be out on the road, Margaret wrapped up tobacco and a few tins of salmon and sent her regrets.

The storm was getting too noisy for "consecutive work." Wind whipped the palms and lashed the roof of the engine shed, sending pieces of tin flying. From where she was sitting Margaret could see Sparks and Mr. Holt in the front yard, looking toward the sea. Rising, she folded up her unfinished report and put it away, and stashed her typewriter on a high shelf.

Dinner was planned for four o'clock but soon enough rain was coming through the kitchen roof to fill several buckets. Using "butter that hadn't seen ice for weeks," Margaret made the hard sauce for a fruitcake while Ruth Holt "anxiously lit and relit the flames of the oil stove."

The Holts' long dining table was set for eight. By the time they sat down, the racket outside made it too noisy for conversation. "Pieces of tin banged on the roof and the palm over the engine shed lashed its tin roof in a perfect fury of chastisement."

They all went out on the front porch to eye the storm. Margaret noticed that Mr. Holt was chewing on a matchstick, a sure sign that he was worried.

The wind was coming from behind them where a huge hill broke its force. Even so, at the other end of town, the buildings were kneeling down in "a long thatched line. A minute later the schoolhouse and the singing houses went down."

Suddenly the storm's fury seemed to abate. The calm lasted less than a minute, and while it did the air seemed "choked full of coconut leaves so stiff they might have been wired." Even the blowing sand seemed suspended in the embrace of that calm.

And then the other edge of the storm, charging straight over the sea from Ofu, hit us, tearing that little calm into a thousand pieces.

After that, it was just a question of how long before the house went. The two-months-old baby was the main point. One would be safe enough out in the open spaces between the houses. But it was pouring rain and the air was full of flying sand, coconuts, parts of tin roofs and so on.

Mr. Holt made the decision that they were all to shelter inside the concrete water tank. Handing Sparks a hatchet, he gave the order to start hacking a hole to let the water out.

Margaret was told to go in first so she could receive the baby. She went up the side and over the edge, stepping down into the pitch-black tank filled with several inches of water. Mrs. Holt followed.

Mr. Holt called, "Here comes the baby and she's upside down." A large blanketed bundle was put into Margaret's hands. Righting the baby, she heard Mr. Holt's voice call again, "Here comes Arthur," as he helped his two-year-old over the edge and into his wife's arms.

It was hours before the lashing rain and roaring surf subsided. When they crept out to survey the damage, only one room of the house had been spared. They crawled in between wet blankets and slept until morning.

The next day Margaret and the Holts picked their way through piles of sodden palm fronds, woven mats, and hunks of twisted metal. The village had been completely decimated. By Margaret's count, only five of the natives' homes had been left standing.

One week later the United States Navy dispatched Chaplain William Edel with a tugboat full of emergency goods. Edel had been chosen because he was acknowledged to have as good a command of Samoan as any officer on the base. Quickly proving himself a stickler for naval etiquette, Edel ordered Lieutenant Holt and Sparks to don their dress whites for a formal salute. Once he'd established his authority, he went to work "putting the place back on its feet."

For Margaret the days and weeks following the hurricane proved to be enormously frustrating. The interviews she'd intended to conduct had to be postponed because "the whole village was busy building itself new houses, or weaving itself new walls or floors." Informants, she complained, "were not to be had for love or money." She spent most of her time wandering about, "sometimes engaging in useful activity and some-times merely sitting on the floor and looking on."

On January 5 she wrote to Dr. Boas to let him know that she was sending a preliminary report to the NRC that covered a period of field-work "too short to justify even tentative conclusions." Even this was a stretch. She had yet to begin sustained research on the adolescent girls she had selected for her study. With only four months remaining to her on Ta'u, this was a matter of serious concern. She also confessed that she was "very much at sea" about how to present her results, once she had them.

Should she organize the material in a "semi-statistical fashion," which might be misleading, or would it be preferable to write up her conclusions in the form of "illustrative case histories"? While she herself favored the latter approach, she made it clear that she would accede to his judgment. She took the unusual step of sending her letter by airmail post with the request that Boas "dash off an airmail answer" as soon as possible.

In mid-January she wrote to Boas again:

> It is very sad that anyone as willing to take advice as I am should be so far beyond the reach of it. Life here is one long battle with my conscience as to whether I am working correctly and whether I'm working hard enough. I remember your saying to me, "You will have to waste a great deal of time," but I wonder if you guessed how much.

The good news, she told herself, was that her future no longer depended on the success of her project. She didn't need any more grant money. In fact, she didn't intend to stay in Samoa any longer than she had to.

But while Margaret railed against her enforced idleness, beating herself up for the wasted time and unmet obligations, she failed to recognize that a remarkable transformation was taking place.

As the days passed she was actually practicing and improving upon a new and invaluable skill. Even though she wasn't doing any sustained work on her "problem," she was writing her bulletins, and they were turning out to be enormously entertaining. She was making the South Seas come alive for a rapt, if tiny, audience of family and friends.

The impact of this style of correspondence had not been anticipated. When she had begun the first of the bulletins, Margaret had done so for ease and practicality. "There was no way of knowing what lay ahead in the many months that I would spend on those far Pacific islands, but I wanted to share what happened so that, when I came home, they would know me better, not as a stranger but as myself." She had no idea that the accumulated bulletins would form a written record of "her evolving consciousness."

Nor did she know that these observations and her way of expressing them would be pivotal to her own coming of age.

Margaret had always wanted to be a *writer*—had tried her hand at different forms of written expression, from the rhetoric of debate, to short fiction, to verse—but she'd never really succeeded at any of them. To her great consternation there had always been someone who was better than she—like her close friend Léonie Adams, now a recognized poet. But the desire to write had never left her. If anything, her ambition had become even more consuming.

The genre she was now working in had been mined by many famous male writers, including Herman Melville, Robert Louis Stevenson, and Jack London. Theirs was the adventure literature she'd grown up with.

Now she was venturing into that same genre, but as a woman.

By exploring an exotic setting and recording her reactions to the landscape and the people who inhabited it, she was breaking new ground. She was creating a persona that—for a woman—had rarely been seen.

Frustrated in her attempts to get her research done, Margaret turned her attention to making plans for the steamer journey back to Europe.

"Mother Dear," she typed, "This letter is about clothes." Her typing had always been fast and accurate, and now that she had instructions to impart, her fingers flew over the keys. She consulted her calendar, comparing it to the steamer schedule she had copied out. Her letter wouldn't leave for the United States until February 16. She needed to make Mother understand that the instructions she was sending were time-sensitive.

I've no mind to land in Sydney in the middle of winter in dotted Swiss. The reason I want dark clothes is because I have so many light ones. Didn't that occur to you? For long trips light clothes are a terrific bother.

She wondered about the latest styles and what her friends were wearing these days. Not Ruth, who dressed with a studied indifference, but the ladies who had a sense of style, like Pelham Kortheuer or Louise Bogan.

Margaret was explicit about the various ensembles she needed for the ship. "I would like Mrs. Stengel to get me a smart silk traveling suit or dress," she began, "but if a suit, one piece, not requiring a blouse."

She described in detail how she envisioned it:

> I would like it to be either black or dark blue or dark green (not brown). Something on the order of that little white and gold suit she got me, with at least three quarter sleeves. Something smart enough to wear right up till dinnertime, on ship board.

Whatever the color, she needed gloves to match, size 6.

She then went on to ask for another informal dinner dress. "Crêpe de chine would be nice and it's not too expensive." She also needed a dress to go with her big lace collar, a new slip for her peacock evening dress, and "a pongee blouse . . . or a tricolette one, something that doesn't have to be washed all the time."

Now that she knew she'd be returning to New York and starting the museum job, there was lots to do. In one letter to Luther she told him to find them an apartment. In another to her mother she instructed her to "scrounge around" the local antique stores and buy them some good used furniture.

But her thoughts were constantly drifting back to the date of her departure from Samoa, which would fall somewhere around the end of May or beginning of June. When she sailed, she intended to travel in style. In her next letter to Luther she asked him to research sailing schedules and the cost of a first-class cabin from Sydney to Marseilles.

Life was different now, and it all had to do with Edward Sapir.

Edward's letter was in her hands, one sheet of paper containing four short paragraphs. It had been written four weeks earlier, sometime around New Year's. In it Edward said that he didn't want to hurt her, but he'd fallen in love with another woman.

The letter wounded like a knife in the heart.

She was, she admitted, "hysterical enough to conjure up any demon." Was this a defensive move on his part? Or a sadistic urge to give her a taste of her own medicine?

Her eyes searched the page, trying to read between the lines.

He explained that his values had not changed by "a millimeter," that they were "emphatically more real to him than ever."

"No doubt I'm being unjust," he wrote, "but I seem to feel little necessity to do otherwise."

He went on to explain that as his love for this new woman had grown, and "it had grown fast and strong," his passion for Margaret had waned.

She looked again at the letter's date. It was written a few days after Christmas. That was before he and Ruth spent time together in the city. She wondered when, exactly, had Ruth found out about his new love interest? Feeling her cheeks grow hot, she began to look through the letters she'd received from Ruth, searching for clues. Unable to find any she dashed off an angry letter accusing Ruth of keeping the news from her.

The minerals in the driftwood sizzled and popped, sending sparkles of blues and reds and yellows up in the flames. Margaret watched as the colors of the bonfire danced. There was no moon. Fog blanketed the sky. The multitude of stars that she knew to be above were not visible. The velvety darkness merged with an endless sea, a pounding surf that softly echoed all around her.

As she sat cross-legged on the damp sand, staring into the fire, there was no possibility of peace. Pulling the burlap sack toward her, reaching inside, she grabbed the first letter she touched, crumpled it in her hand, and threw it into the flames.

She watched its corners curl, then fully ignite.

She wanted the letters gone. She wanted Edward gone. Pulling others from the sack, hurling them, one after the other, into the fire, she sat riveted by the conflagration.

They were all burning fast now, and the tears were running down her cheeks.

Not so very long ago Edward had told her that she had reawakened his "capacity to love," which he thought had died for all time. Now, it seemed, that capacity to love could be easily shifted from one person to another:

When circumstances and the clash of our temperaments and ideas made the continuance of my love for you a sheer impossibility, I found, paradoxically enough, that I had to love another. . . . I did not find, as you claim that you have found, that a simultaneous love of two is possible.

Who was this girl he had fallen in love with? What was her name? What did Ruth know about her?

As Margaret stared into the fire, and its fury began to abate, a different feeling came over her. She found herself wanting to *save* the letters, or what was left of them. If ever a group of words and thoughts should be saved, these were the ones.

But it was too late.

Edward's words, his magical words, were gone.

Leaving the empty sack where it lay, she started back.

As she tramped across the sand, her tears continued to fall freely. Her eyes, still sore from an attack of conjunctivitis, burned.

When she finally was calm enough she wrote one more time to Edward. She thought she was being magnanimous by telling him that she hoped he would be happy and asked him to write her, "to assure her that he was."

Above all, she wanted to know who this girl was he was falling in love with now.

A PRACTICAL JOKE

Doing straight ethnology is just fun and so easy once the people love you.

—Margaret Mead

February 1926

It was one of those sleeting rainy Sundays when no one was about and there was no question of going out. Stanley was in bed with a cold, and when Ruth brought him in some tea she found that he'd dozed off. Sitting back down on the couch, she tucked her legs under her, and looked out on the peaked roofs of Bedford Hills and the swirls of smoke curling up from the chimneys.

Gone was the specter of Edward Sapir. Soon he would be faded into memory, like the wisps of smoke outside her window. It was unsettling that even the most intense love could be so transitory.

By all rights Ruth should have been relieved that he had backed away from Margaret, and yet she experienced his change of heart as a defection. Worse, as a form of treason.

The girl was Jean McClenaghan, a graduate of the University of Toronto, and a recipient of a Smith College fellowship to study at the Juvenile Research Institute in Chicago. Ruth felt obligated to give Margaret a report but decided to tell her only the bare minimum. She had no intention of telling her how thoroughly smitten—and ridiculous—Edward had become.

Apparently the letter Ruth had sent to Edward in response to his "news" of Jean had communicated her disapproval. When he wrote back, he sounded offended:

You say you can describe Jean in considerable detail. Would you care to set down your preconceptions? I should be willing to corroborate or set you right where necessary.

Ruth really didn't want to hear any more about Jean and she didn't encourage him to tell her more. He did anyway:

Jean is very pretty, often beautiful when you gaze into her calm, radiant eyes that have so much purity of feeling, much tremulous certainty of love and such kindness. No, Ruth, Jean is <u>not</u> a simple dear thing. She is all woman. Quite all, and she has an alert and sympathetic mind. Too wise to make any mumbo jumbo of a ragbag of intellectual goods. Her feelings are extraordinarily precise, unmarred, delicate . . . but hardly a taint of sentimentality.

He also seemed to be looking for opportunities to compare Jean to Margaret, in ways that would highlight the latter's shortcomings:

Jean has great psychological insight; false gestures and wrong accents can't pass her. She'd be shy and withdrawn with Margaret I suspect, but all the time her psyche would be crowding in on her and burning away all kinds of paper mache.

And, not surprisingly, Edward was already fantasizing about the future:

I have no true plans, Ruth—only dreams. Jean and I see each other rather frequently and have grown so closely together that the thought of a separation for longer than two or three days at a time seems difficult to bear. Neither Jean nor I are of the ambitious, planning type, and for that very reason are perhaps more likely to end up in wedlock than if we carefully scanned the future.

Certainly Ruth was not going to tell Margaret any of *this* now. Perhaps later, when her feelings weren't so raw. Instead, she reported what she could, saying that Edward had commented on the Christmas present Margaret had sent, a posed self-portrait, taken by a professional photographer before she'd left for Samoa. It had finally just arrived at Edward's office. He'd liked it, saying to Ruth "a strong wave of tenderness swept over me when I saw it." And then, because they offered a measure of solace, Ruth quoted Edward's final words:

> *Perhaps I have been terribly precipitate and brutal and yet some-*
> *thing keeps telling me that under Margaret's hurt pride there will*
> *be a cheerful little song of thanks, a glad relief at being disburdened*
> *of a relation and an irritation that her nature desires to taste rather*
> *than to feed on. Am I not right?*

During these months of separation from Margaret, Ruth had learned that some days of waiting were more difficult than others. Today was one such day. Perhaps it had to do with the fact that she'd spent the weekend researching hotel accommodations in Rome and Tuscany. Then, of course, there were the tickets she still needed to secure for their steamer journey home. She'd settled on the *Saturnia*, an Italian ship done in a Beaux Arts decor. Having heard that accommodations on the Italian liners were not to be trusted, she'd decided they couldn't "risk anything but first class." The cheapest first-class cabin would cost $234 and if Margaret had trouble covering the expense, Ruth had decided she'd make up the difference.

That night she found it almost impossible to sleep. She wrote to Margaret, "I almost weep at the thought. If this mood continues, it will be harder to wait the next months than all the time that's gone by."

By February, Margaret reported that she was thoroughly disenchanted with life at the dispensary. Her relationship with the Holts had broken down. She told her mother, "Mrs. Holt is the sort of old fashioned feminist who doesn't approve of my keeping my name but thinks 'women are so wonderful' and is furious while I dispense all my dreadful radical notions." Even worse, both Holts had "rebelled" at her having "mobs" of Samoans in her room. The final straw came while the USS *Tanager* was in the harbor. Members of the crew "jibed at Mr. Holt for having his porch covered with 'Samoan kids.'" Since then Margaret had been longing to "escape from that tiny island and the society of the tiny white colony on it."

Beyond this general atmosphere of unpleasantness, Margaret was finding it "practically impossible" to make any progress on her research. Now that hurricane recovery efforts had come to an end and services on Ta'u were restored, all the teenage girls had returned to school. Margaret complained there was little to keep her busy during the day. She wrote home to say that hearing the school gong and seeing the pupils with their "slate pencils" made her homesick "for New York or for the farm or for bathtubs or beefsteak."

Then Dr. C. Montague Cooke, a biologist whom she had met at Honolulu's Bishop Museum, showed up with two of his colleagues. They were on their way to collect land snails near Fitiuta, on the eastern end of Ta'u, and they invited Margaret to accompany them. The trip was a diversion—she had no reason to make it—but when the natives told her that Fitiuta's chief had paid her the great compliment of crowning her *Fusilelagi*, a *taupou* name meaning "Flower-in-the-Heavens," she accepted.

Margaret and the three biologists departed on February 20, trudging seven miles along a rough foot track that took them down "sharp descents into little canyons full of rocks" and through the kind of mud Margaret had only seen in "barnyards." When they arrived in Fitiuta, they found a "charming village," with houses spread out along either side of a high stone road.

Margaret and her party were greeted by the chief and she presented him with a case of canned salmon. In return the women presented her with a native dress to change into, and the youths of the village brought out ceremonial food offerings, including "platters of coconut leaves piled high with chickens and fish, land crabs, octopus and pieces of pork, all smoking hot from the oven."

After the feast the entertainment started up.

A dozen men began to pluck their ukuleles, and one of the chiefs walked over to Margaret and pulled her to her feet. With scarlet cordyline leaves tied around her wrists and ankles and coconut oil smeared over her arms and shoulders, Margaret danced before the assembled crowd.

Later that night she played *Sweepy* (Casino) to the tune of several ukuleles and bantered with the untitled men while the girls of the household made up the beds and hung the mosquito nets.

She was disarmed by the hospitality, enthusing, "Fitiuta is a gold mine and I have the whole village at my feet with dozens of high chiefs."

A few days later, when her friends from the Bishop Museum said it was time to return to Luma, she demurred, saying that she had more "ethnology" to do. The truth was she enjoyed being the center of attention. She wrote to Boas, "I haven't merely watched these procedures, I've been them!"

Moreover, she'd made the acquaintance of two young Samoans who were providing some much needed information. While they were not the adolescent girls she was supposed to be interviewing, she decided she could used them as informants anyway.

One, whose name was Fa'apua'a, was the twenty-four-year-old daughter of a high chief and reputed to be one of the most beautiful girls on the island. A *taupou* herself, Fa'apua'a had the habit of holding herself so aloof that she seemed "swathed in a cloak of dignity." The other was Andrew Napoleon, a twenty-two-year-old teacher at Fitiuta's government school. "Napo" as Margaret called him, spoke fluent English and was forthcoming on many subjects, including the behavior of young Samoan men.

During the ceremonies, Napo stood by Margaret's side, providing context for whatever she was observing. Much of what he said pertained to the sexual practices of married couples, possibly because he himself was a newlywed. One of his more far-fetched claims was that among young marrieds, he knew of "no impotence in any case nor of frigidity." He asserted that on *his* island, couples had intercourse "several times in one night, sometimes as many as fifteen." Napo was so informative that by the end of Margaret's ten-day stay, he had given her enough material to fill a thirty-six-page journal.

When the visit ended, Margaret reluctantly tramped back to the dispensary. She told Ruth, "Doing straight ethnology is just fun and so easy once the people love you." What excited her even more was that she'd finally heard stories that made it possible for her to tackle the question she'd been sent to investigate. On March 4 she wrote Ruth:

> *Getting the material was in a way what worried me most. I've got all the rest practically but Wissler and Ogburn both wanted the sex so much and it is so difficult to get at—and I doubted whether my results would have any point.*

Clark Wissler, a curator at the American Museum of Natural History, and William Ogburn, a sociology professor at Columbia, both had a vested interest in having Margaret prove the theory that adolescence was more heavily influenced by culture than by biology. She very much wanted to meet their expectations. She told Ruth, "But by lucky chance I've succeeded in getting enough so that it's now merely a question of verification."

The "lucky chance," of course, had been Napo. Although not an adolescent girl, he had provided an enormous amount of pertinent information.

She wrote to Ruth that finally she had a "sense of command" over her "problem" and felt "clear going ahead." She was ready to approach the adolescent girls she'd identified as informants—all sixty-six of them—hoping that they would confirm what she had already been told. She prepared her list of preliminary questions:

> Approximate age, rank, and schooling in government and pastor's school, amount of foreign experience, health and physical defect, date when puberty was attained, her training in etiquette, her skill in all of the domestic industries; her general personality traits, etc.

Margaret hoped that once acquired, this data would give her a better grasp of the "philosophical conflicts" that shaped a girl's teen years, particularly when it came to sex.

However, the very next day, before she could start these interviews, another invitation arrived. Dr. Charles Lane, her "old friend" from Pago Pago, had received a temporary posting to the nearby island of Ofu. He sent word that he and Mrs. Lane were enjoying themselves immensely and hoped Margaret would come for a visit.

At dawn on the morning of March 8, the boat from Ofu arrived. As Margaret was gathering a few provisions to take as gifts, Fa'apua'a and her best friend Fofoa "came tumbling head over heels" into her room, and announced that they wanted to join her.

Manned by nine Samoan oarsmen, their fifteen-foot whaleboat set sail under a broiling sun. The girls were desperately sick. During the three-hour pull Margaret lay in the belly of the boat, resting her head on a burlap bag filled with canned goods. "The Samoans chanted and shouted; after a little it poured and we could not see land at all."

By the time they reached Ofu the sun was setting.

Margaret joined the Lanes for a swim in the lagoon. Afterward, she attended a reception in the house of Misa, Ofu's high chief.

With her were Fa'apua'a and Fofoa, acting as attendants, making speeches, and tending to her personal comfort. Margaret thought of them as members of her "court," referring to them in letters as her "merry companions." The girls were so high-spirited that when they went to do Margaret's wash, "one carried the clothes but the other carried her ukulele."

In the eyes of their hosts, a visit from three unmarried women, far from home and traveling alone, was unprecedented. The young men, in particular, were thrilled. They taunted the girls with lighthearted banter. The spirit was contagious and that night, at bedtime, as Margaret was climbing under the canopy of a mosquito net, Fa'apua'a playfully asked her if there was one of the men that she favored.

Laughing, Margaret did not answer.

After a few days on Ofu, Margaret and her merry companions journeyed over land to the tiny village of Sili, on the adjoining island of Olosega.

In honor of the white *taupou*'s visit, the villagers of Sili killed and roasted a pig. In the balmy night air, under a crescent moon, the high chiefs shared anecdotes about cannibalism in bygone times.

The next day the girls were ferried, one at a time, by outrigger canoe to the eastern end of the island. From there the three made their way along the southern coast of Ofu. "It was a long walk skirting the sea, at places racing the tide, or leaping between high waves from one wet rock to another."

It was while they were on the trail, walking single file, with Margaret in the lead, and Fa'apua'a and Fofoa following behind, that Margaret worked up the courage to ask the questions she'd been too embarrassed to pose to any of her adolescent informants.

Directing her questions to Fa'apua'a, she asked, "At night, where do you go?"

"We go out at night," said Fa'apua'a with a mischievous smile.

"With whom?"

"We spend the nights with boys."

Margaret heard both girls laugh. "With boys?" she asked. "What do you do with the boys?"

The girls were laughing too hard to answer.

They seemed to be insinuating that they'd been sexually adventurous.

Margaret had assumed both young women were virgins. She knew that like all the highborn girls on the island, they'd been raised at the knee of a Protestant pastor, a religious official who all but guaranteed that his charges remained chaste. What's more, Fa'apua'a had been afforded the great honor of being named the ceremonial virgin of her village. But the way the girls were now acting belied everything Margaret thought she knew about them.

Was what they were saying the truth? Or were they playing a practical joke on her? Margaret wasn't sure.

She knew that Samoans loved playing practical jokes, or what they called "hoaxing." There were even several terms in their language—*ula*, *tausa*, and *taufa'ase'e*—that described this behavior.

Margaret was conflicted.

The fact was she'd come to Samoa with a preconceived idea—entertained by many Americans—that sensual enjoyment was a feature of life in the South Seas. This image had been fed by novels, travel literature, and the visual arts, and now the comments that Fa'apua'a and Fofoa were passing back and forth seemed to confirm everything that Margaret had heard. Besides, the notion that a young Samoan woman was free to enjoy carefree and casual lovemaking *before* marriage mirrored Margaret's own ideal of "free love." That ideal, when combined with Napo's tales about the robust sex lives of married couples, was a depiction of Samoan life that Margaret *wanted* to believe was true.

It was also the report Dr. Boas hoped she would be able to make to the NRC.

The more she thought about it, the more she decided to take what the girls had told her at face value.

Before she left Ofu, Margaret wrote to Ruth:

I haven't an ailment in the world except my arms and my eyes, to both of which I'm thoroughly accustomed—I can work all day with a will. And I've lost my dread of failure, with the conversations I've got what I was sent after.

For Margaret, succeeding in the eyes of Dr. Boas and Ruth was as important as it had ever been. To Ruth she said:

Once again my fear that you would decide however much you might love me that in science I was a bending reed, is stalled off. 40 years from now if I'm doing anything related to anthropology I'll still be doing it for you and worrying about what you will think about it.

Back on Ta'u, and relying exclusively on what she had learned from Napo and her merry companions Fa'apua'a and Fofoa, Margaret set down her findings in a lengthy letter to Boas:

Sexual life begins with puberty in most cases. Fairly promiscuous intercourse obtains until marriage and there is a good deal after marriage. It is the family and not the community (except in the case of the taupou) which attempts to preserve a girl's virginity—and this attempt is usually secretly frustrated rather than openly combatted by the adolescent.

In conclusion, she stated:

The neuroses accompanying sex in American civilization are practically absent, such as frigidity, impotence and pronounced perversions.

Convinced that she could substantiate her conclusions by writing up specific case histories, she added:

I feel absolutely safe in generalizing from the material I have. Aside from such matters, checking up my family cards, and getting a little more on individual sex experiences, I'm practically thru.

As far as Margaret was concerned, and she said as much to Boas, "my problem is practically completed."

Later, when Margaret was to reflect on her experience in Samoa, she would say that she had succeeded only by "losing her identity." Elaborating on her immersion into the life of the community, she singled out her walk along the trail with Fa'apua'a and Fofoa as the high point of the experience, saying that in this way she'd "been able to become acquainted with the Samoan girls, receive their whispered confidences and learn at the same time the answer to scientists' questions."

STRANGER FROM ANOTHER PLANET

Talking the old jargon is bringing it all back. Reo Fortune, this N.Z. boy, talks poetry, or radicalism or psychology— between the three I might as well be back with you all.
—MARGARET MEAD

May 1926

When Margaret left Pago Pago on May 7, 1926, she was setting out on a six-week ocean voyage that would end in Marseilles, France. The first leg was on the SS *Sonoma* heading to Sydney, Australia. From there, she was booked on the SS *Chitral*, a P&O luxury liner that was returning from its maiden voyage.

It seemed however, that all her carefully made plans were to be derailed. Within days of setting sail, the *Sonoma* encountered one of the worst storms to hit the South Pacific in decades. "Waves poured over the top deck and passengers went down like nine pins." Delayed by nearly a week, Margaret was resigned to the idea that by the time she reached Sydney, the *Chitral* would have sailed without her.

Upon disembarking, she heard the news that a dock strike in England had triggered a ripple effect, disrupting routes and steamer schedules across three continents.

There was the *Chitral*, still sitting in the harbor. For Margaret it was a beautiful sight. Writing to her mother she exulted, "I've had the most marvelous luck with every detail of my trip! I even succeeded in getting the dresses out of the mail at Pago Pago before my ship sailed!"

The *Chitral* was the newest passenger liner in the Peninsular and Oriental Steam Navigation Company fleet. During the last eighty years

P&O ships had carved out routes that reflected the expansion of the British Empire, sailing to Egypt, India, Australia, and the Far East. As soon as Margaret boarded, she went to inspect her starboard-side, first-class cabin. A first-class cabin had been expensive and, as a gesture to Dadda, Margaret had promised to save money in other ways. Writing home, she said this wouldn't be difficult. Each time the ship docked, while the other passengers disembarked to enjoy the port and its entertainments, she planned to remain on ship.

That first night in Sydney she did just that.

When the bell sounded for dinner, Margaret found herself waiting outside the grand salon, standing with a dozen other people, all, presumably like herself, anxious to economize. Doors opened to an enormous dining room, large enough to accommodate two hundred passengers at one sitting. At the far end of the room, assembled on a balcony, a small Dixieland jazz combo was playing "It Had to Be You."

It was then that Margaret noticed, standing apart from the others and holding a book in his hand, a tall and lanky young man with a thick shock of black hair. When he glanced in her direction, she noticed that his eyes were almost as dark as his hair.

Curious to know what he was reading, Margaret edged closer. The book was *Jude the Obscure,* a novel by the British writer Thomas Hardy.

When the rest of her shipmates made no move toward the dining room, Margaret walked to a large round table and pulled out a chair. The others followed, all taking seats near her. The tall young man was the last one in, and he joined them at the table. Throughout the meal he sat with his book open next to his plate, reading.

After dinner, Margaret went to see the Palm Court, a vast conservatory that had been designed to resemble a Burmese winter garden. In deference to the ship's colonial decor, great potted palms sat under open-work columns, and rattan easy chairs were scattered around small card tables. A lone bridge game was under way.

Margaret noticed the same boy sitting at one of the tables, nursing a cup of tea. His legs were stretched out in front of him in an insolent arc. His book was now lying facedown on his chest. He looked to be deep in thought. She took a moment to fluff up her hair and then, opening her bag, she fished around for a pack of cigarettes. They were the special cork-tipped, tin-packed Pall Malls that she'd asked her mother to send. She advanced toward the boy's chair.

"Excuse me," she said. "Can I trouble you for a light?"

Lifting the book off his chest and slowing rising to his feet, his eyes meeting hers, he said, "Of course." He towered over her. He bent down and struck a match.

Taking a drag of the Pall Mall she looked up at him and said, "I'm not smoking a lot, but when I do I like these."

Reaching over to pull out a chair, he said, "Would you care to join me?" She sat down.

"*Jude the Obscure*," she said, nodding toward his book. "That's one of Hardy's I haven't read."

"Not his best, I'm afraid." He spoke with an accent that she couldn't place.

A waiter brought more hot water for the tea and another cup.

When Margaret asked him where he was from, he said he'd been born in a village called Coromandel, a gold-mining boomtown on the North Island of New Zealand where his father, who had been a missionary in China during the Boxer rebellion, had settled to serve as the camp's cleric.

"The industrial story of New Zealand," he told her, "can be summed up in two words—wool and gold."

His parents had named him Reo, which he pronounced as Ray. The word "Reo" in Maori meant "logos" or "the word." His last name was Fortune.

He'd moved with his family four times before his father, at the age of fifty-two, had given up the holy orders and, with a personal capital of only forty pounds, had taken up dairy farming in the village of Paraparaumu, thirty miles north of the capital city of Wellington.

"Father was not one of those rich sheep farmers," he said. "Country gentry they called themselves. Burned off the bracken, cut and burned the forests just so they could sow the cleared land with their English grasses."

At age seventeen Reo had left home to attend Victoria University College in Wellington, earning his degree "under exceedingly frugal circumstances."

"What does that mean?" asked Margaret.

"Too poor to board," he said.

As the story unfolded, it turned out that he'd slept in the psychology lab in order to complete his master's thesis, which he'd finished in six weeks. Now he was sailing to England with a trunk full of his favorite books, including five volumes of Blake's poetry. He spoke of his admiration for George Bernard Shaw, whose socialist views used to send his father into a tirade. "If Father thought I admired anyone who was a radical, the whole house would ring with the sound of his voice, as he and I went at each other hammer and tongs."

"Poetry, radicalism and psychology," thought Margaret. This talk from Reo was certainly making her feel like she was home. Telling him that she'd spent the last nine months in Samoa, she said, "The shock of having anybody to talk to now is terrific."

Reo seemed nonplussed.

"Why are you going to England?" she asked.

When Reo said, with a modestly that wasn't a bit feigned, that he was on his way to attend university, on scholarship, as a prize for an essay he'd written on dreams, she nearly spit out her tea.

"Dreams?" She wanted to know more.

That this awkward but admittedly attractive young man was traveling *halfway around the world* to study dreams was astonishing.

Dreams and their interpretation were the holy grail of psychoanalysis. Margaret, like others in her circle, viewed psychoanalysis as the only viable tool for unlocking the unconscious, that most mysterious and inaccessible part of each individual. As such the study of dreams—the recording, analyzing, and visualizing of these sleep-induced dramas—was viewed as a near sacred endeavor.

How could a young man who'd been slopping out stalls on a dairy farm in Paraparaumu end up with a scholarship to a British university?

As Reo explained it, in 1923 he had taken a BA in advanced philosophy and the next year his college had submitted his thesis by mail to examiners in the United Kingdom. The following year they had awarded him one of New Zealand's first traveling fellowships. Then he said the most remarkable thing of all. He would be attending Emmanuel College at Cambridge.

Margaret was unable to hide her astonishment.

Cambridge, along with Oxford, was the Empire's most prestigious center of higher learning. Usually only the scions of upper-class families were offered admittance.

He told her he'd chosen Emmanuel College because W. H. R. Rivers had taught there.

This was really too coincidental. Remarkably, the now deceased Dr. Rivers was a man Margaret had first become interested in because of his work as an ethnologist in Papua, New Guinea.

Reo had been drawn to him for other reasons. As a Cambridge don Rivers had studied the connection between physiology and psychology, focusing on soldiers who had left the battlefield with deep psychological wounds. He had been the first doctor to pronounce "shell shock" a sickness that required treatment rather than an act of cowardice that deserved punishment.

When Margaret finally pried her attention away from Reo, she was surprised to see that the Palm Court was empty. Everyone except for one lone waiter had retired. Rising from her chair, she said good night. By the time she'd reached her cabin she'd decided this was going to be a very interesting voyage.

The next morning she didn't see Reo at breakfast. She kept looking for him, but he never appeared. The same thing happened at lunch and then again at dinner.

Then the following morning at breakfast he finally emerged, looking disheveled. He was more attractive than she remembered. She asked how he had occupied himself the night before.

"I fell asleep and missed dinner," he said. "When I finally came out of my room it was after ten and the only place to eat was that Palm Court."

"Colonial Burma," said Margaret, "that's the theme."

"It's fitting," said Reo. "I met a lone English woman from Kenya and India. She said she knew General Dyer—'poor dear old man'—he was dreadfully cut up at having to shoot those natives, but then he saved India, after all. She warned me, there are agitators in England who should be shot, also."

Margaret laughed. "Is she here this morning?"

Reo was looking around. "No, I don't see her. No doubt a late riser." Then turning back to Margaret. "You're a young lady, traveling alone?"

"Yes," said Margaret.

"She complained that a lady could go nowhere alone, even onboard ship. She was looking for an escort back to her cabin. However, I was intent on getting back to my own room to my writing, and was not to be deviated."

"Next she'll be inviting you to her hotel in Paris," said Margaret.

Reo laughed. "She already did. She showed me the address, a good one, she assured me. She said when I go to Paris, I'm to look her up."

That next morning while Margaret was eating oatmeal she felt a shadow over her shoulder. Then a hand was sliding a brown moleskin notebook in front of her.

She looked up. "Oh, hello," she said. "What's this for? Something I'm supposed to read?"

"No," said Reo. "Something you're to write." He sat down. "It's a journal for your dreams."

"You want to know my dreams?"

"No, I want you to know your dreams."

They picked up their conversation where they had left off.

It was Dr. Rivers, Reo pointed out, who had said that sleep was "much more than the negation of psychological activity," explaining that disturbed sleep only exhausts one's strength and makes "still more unequal the struggle between fear, horror, or shame." It was this work on sleep that led Rivers to "stand Freud on his head." Without changing any of Freud's precepts, Rivers had identified fear, instead of the libido, as the driving force in man. Margaret took all of this in. On the subject of psychology Reo obviously knew so much more than she did, and this made him enormously intriguing.

At the same time, Margaret was starting to understand that in spite of all his intellectual audacity, Reo was more rough around the edges than she could ever have guessed. Like a "cave man," he was innocent and inexperienced, and out of place. "He had never seen a play professionally performed; he had never seen an original painting by a great artist or heard music played by a symphony orchestra." Margaret was later to say, "It was like meeting a stranger from another planet, but a stranger with whom I had a great deal in common."

It was not long before the *Chitral*'s chief steward noticed that Margaret and Reo were so engrossed in conversation that the others at the table were "simply an impediment." He suggested that perhaps they might like a table to themselves. They accepted.

At the end of May, the *Chitral* docked in Adelaide, and Margaret suggested that they go ashore to visit the University Library. She wanted to introduce Reo to the groundbreaking work of the Polish anthropologist Bronislaw Malinowski. While Reo was reading one of Malinowski's monographs, Margaret went to post a few letters. Usually an indefatigable correspondent, over the last three weeks she'd barely put pen to paper. She wrote to her mother:

> I'm having a nice trip only very stormy. Too stormy to work any. There is a young psychologist on board who's trying to learn German and we egg each other on. It's an exceedingly comfortable boat, much food and wonderfully "squishy" couches.

To Ruth, Margaret had scrawled only a cryptic message:

> Talking the old jargon is bringing it all back. Reo Fortune, this N.Z. boy, talks poetry, or radicalism or psychology—between the three I might as well be back with you all.

The longest of Margaret's letters was addressed to her grandmother and it reflected her sanguine mood. It showed, too, that the subject of adolescent rebellion was very much on her mind. Beginning by acknowledging her upbringing in "a serene and untroubled household," she indicated that she saw herself as standing outside the cultural norm. Unlike most of her contemporaries, she had no quarrel with the essential thought of her parents, or her grandmother. This she said, was a rare privilege:

> . . . All the energies most of my contemporaries had to put into reconciling affection for their elders with honest revolt against their teachings I could conserve to use for my own development. It's very much owing to you that I've wasted so little time in life, made so few false moves, chased so few chimeras, extraneous to my personality.

Margaret and Reo were stretched out on deck chairs, gazing out at the smooth steel-blue sea.

"Lascars," said Reo, nodding toward two oilers, a sinewy East Indian and his older and bulkier companion, who were carrying some crates. "Usually they're confined below deck."

"Poor fellows," said Margaret, as the men passed.

The Lascars were sailors recruited from the Indian subcontinent, from ports in Bengal, Assam, and Gujarat. Living symbols of the Empire, in days past they'd spent their lives in indentured servitude, toiling in the engine rooms of ships that sailed for the British East India Company and then during the war for the King's Navy. With the advent of the British passenger liners, Lascars were still shoveling coal into the giant furnaces that drove the steam turbines. Referred to as the "*black gang*," not because of their skin color but because of the layer of soot that caked their faces, the Lascars on the *Chitral* were forbidden to appear above deck.

Margaret watched the pair turn and descend down the stairs into the steerage section.

"Heathcliff was a Lascar," said Reo.

"Really?" said Margaret.

"There was something about Heathcliff I always identified with."

Margaret took this in. Turning toward him, she said, "I have an idea."

Reo raised his eyebrows.

"The fancy dress ball . . ."

He cut her off. "You know I'm not going to that."

"No, hold on. We could go as Lascars."

On June 1, Ruth wrote to Margaret, "This month you'll be in Europe. The days do pass, and our year will be up."

Ruth had been marking off the days, much like one would with an advent calendar before Christmas. In less than three weeks now she and Stanley would be sailing for England. After they toured the British Isles, they would travel to Stockholm, where Stanley was scheduled to deliver a scientific paper. Then he'd be returning to New York, and from then on Ruth was free to tour Italy with Margaret. Exultant, she told Margaret, "Two whole months we'll have—think of it."

The school year was ending and, for Ruth, ending rapidly. There were loose ends to tie up, including one last visit to campus to clear her belongings out of the seminar room. Back in the city on Monday, she went directly there.

She found the campus in a celebratory state. Construction workers were busy erecting the graduation stage while students were setting up hundreds of folding chairs and draping colorful paper ribbons over the bleachers.

It wasn't until several hours later, after an afternoon of packing, that Ruth looked out the window and saw dark clouds filling the sky. Soon rain was falling. By eight in the evening, it was coming down in torrents. Carrying out her boxes, she passed through the quad, which was now one vast glistening field of mud and empty bleachers. When she returned to her room she wrote to Margaret:

> I've just come through the wrecked and decorated campus hung for "Campus Night." There are thousands of bright-seated chairs and heavy blue hangings with gold—lilies are they? for Columbia—over the speaker's platform, and hundreds of programs dropped into the puddles as the people ran. Ever since March one department of the university has been working on this program for tonight 6–10,—and the downpour began at 6:30.

It didn't occur to Ruth that the sodden ruins of graduation might be a foreshadowing of what could happen to her own carefully orchestrated celebration.

The knock came on her door, a rat-a-tat-tat. Margaret opened it. Reo was standing there, a grin on his face.

"*Entrez,*" she said, stepping aside with a flourish to let him enter.

He looked around. "Very elegant," he said, referring to her first-class accommodations, a class up from his own.

On the bed were their Lascar uniforms, washed, pressed, and neatly folded.

"Courtesy of the chief steward," said Margaret, placing one of the sets into his hands.

"Where'd he get them?"

"From some of the oilers," she said, referring to the boiler room crew. "Here, put these on."

She turned her back while he changed.

Turning back, she took him in. The baggy trousers, cut from a rough white cotton, reached to mid-calf; a long, dark, tapered tunic fell to his hips.

She walked over to him, reached around his waist, and wrapped the Lascar belt around him, fastening it on the tightest notch. She lingered there, standing just a few inches from him, adjusting his belt buckle, giving him every opportunity to pull her close. Certainly he had to know that she wanted him.

He stepped back. "Your turn," he said, picking up the other uniform and handing it to her. "I'll wait for you outside."

Alone in the room she smarted. What was stopping him? By the time she finished changing and let him back in she'd regained her composure.

To add to the verisimilitude of the disguise, they applied shoe polish to blacken their faces and exaggerate their lips.

The grand salon had been dressed for a carnival. Ropes of tiny glittering lights were wrapped around banisters and swayed from the ceiling, radiating color on the cream-colored walls. Women wearing elaborate gowns with sequined masks covering their eyes swept past them. In blackface, Margaret and Reo were distinctly out of place. They hesitated at the edge of the dance floor.

Suddenly Margaret saw the chief steward approach, a mischievous grin on his face. "I've seated you at the captain's table," he said. "Come with me."

When they arrived, only two people were already seated, an elderly and very proper English naval officer and his sister. The old man acknowledged their presence with an icy reserve.

Margaret smiled and introduced herself.

"We know who you are," said the officer, before turning his head away in disgust.

A few minutes later the captain appeared. He nodded in their direction, the look on his face impassive.

Near the end of the evening, when Margaret returned to collect her pocketbook, she found the naval officer seated at the table. His eyes met hers.

"It's an intolerable insult to the captain," he said. "You owe him an apology."

Margaret looked for Reo to tell him what had happened.

"Damn that man," said Reo, referring to the chief steward. "He knew what he was up to the whole time."

Margaret sighed. "I feel as if I have been accused, as in one of Mother's stories—of eating peas with a knife."

"That's about the gist of it," said Reo. "If you let it bother you."

"We ought to go to him to make our apologies," she said.

"To who?" said Reo, bristling.

"The captain, of course," said Margaret, whose upbringing dictated that one ought to apologize for an unintended discourtesy. "I'm going to send up our cards."

Later, as they were standing outside the captain's quarters, Margaret looked up at Reo and saw that his face was flushed. She reached over and squeezed his hand. "It's all right," she said. "It's all right to tell him we're sorry."

When the captain ushered them into his cabin, Reo made a stiff and unbending apology.

Uncertain and defensive over what he was hearing, the captain started to bluster.

Margaret, who had yet to say a word, jumped in. "I know covering our faces with shoe polish might have seemed excessive," she said, "and I must tell you, it was my idea. I'm an American and in America blackface is a kind of theatrical makeup."

"Well, I don't know," said the captain.

"It's a mainstay of the minstrel show," said Margaret. "You can see blackface on Broadway, any day of the week."

After the fiasco with the captain Margaret became aware that the other passengers were going out of their way to avoid them. It hardly mattered. Completely isolated on the big ship, eating three meals together, and so enthralled by what they were talking about, she was grateful not to have any interruptions. Apparently, everyone on shipboard thought they were having an affair, even though they weren't.

One June night after dinner they walked out to the bow of the ship, "where the spray came up around them and the sea seemed to be on fire."

Margret stood next to Reo. Their arms were nearly touching, their eyes focused on the ocean's shimmering phosphorescence.

Margaret could sense his hesitancy.

"I don't know if I've ever told you," he said. "I had a hard time when Barter was born." The Barter he was referring to was his brother, five years younger, and now his closest confidant.

"You mean because you weren't the only son anymore?"

"More than that. It was after Barter was born that my aunt left. My mother chased her off. She found out that it was she who my father really loved."

"Your father was in love with your aunt?"

"My mother's younger sister."

They stood side by side in silence. He said, "I haven't had much luck in love, either."

"Now it's coming," thought Margaret.

"Eileen," he said. "Her name is Eileen Pope."

Margaret thought she detected a change in his face when he said the name.

He told Margaret that Eileen's father was the headmaster of the Kaiwarra School and that Mr. Pope had been known throughout Wellington as a songwriter.

Margaret waited.

"An able cricketer, too," said Reo. "Opening batsman for the Star Club's Pearce Cup–winning team."

He turned and faced her. "I'd go there in the evenings. Sit at their kitchen table. Robert, her brother, played the fiddle, so did her sister Flora. But Eileen was the gifted one. And she could sing, too. It was a regular *ceilidh*."

"*Ceilidh?*" Margaret asked, not really caring what it was, but trying to cover her discomfort.

"Kitchen party," said Reo, looking out, over the sea. "I sent her my poems. She was encouraging. I asked her to marry me. She said no."

This Eileen must have had lots of other suitors, thought Margaret.

"You're a married woman," he said, reaching out and touching her arm. "But you don't talk about your husband. He's never in any of your dreams. Instead it's this Edward fellow who's always there."

"Luther's my best friend," she said. "Sometimes one tends to take one's best friend for granted."

THE ARENA HAS ALWAYS
BEEN ABOUT BLOOD

I'll not leave you unless I find someone I love more.
                                    —MARGARET MEAD

June 1926

The *Chitral* was due to dock in less than two hours, reuniting Luther with the wife he'd not seen in ten months. Since they'd said their good-byes at the Baltimore & Ohio railway station in Philadelphia, she'd kept in touch mainly through the group bulletins, offering him few clues to her state of mind and leaving him with a sense of vague misgiving.

That morning he'd explored the waterfront of Marseilles, making his way down narrow streets lined with terra-cotta buildings, their windows closed behind faded blue wooden shutters. His mission had been to secure the "nicest rooms in Marseilles" for Margaret. Somewhere along the way he passed a *boutique de modiste* and went in to buy a hat. Standing in front of the mirror, he tried on several berets until he found one he liked.

Two hours later he was at the pier looking up at the massive steel-sided *Chitral*. He thrust his hands into the pockets of his trousers, jingling a set of room keys.

At last the *Chitral*'s crew lowered the gangplank. As the passengers started to disembark, he ran halfway up the gangplank to intercept Margaret. Pushing his way through the crowd that was advancing toward him, searching the faces, he was surprised not to find her.

Returning to the foot of the gangplank, Luther waited, watching as the other passengers greeted their families and loved ones. Then, high above him, he saw a young woman in silhouette leaning on the ship's rail. He squinted up into the sunlight. She was too far away to recognize.

He waved and the figure waved back. Curiously, she did not move from her spot. He waved again and again she responded. After two or three more exchanges she walked away from her post.

Obviously it wasn't Margaret. He felt almost ill with disappointment.

Where was she? Why wasn't she there? The fear that something terrible had happened suddenly seemed possible.

Just then Margaret appeared at the head of the gangplank, along with a tall young man who stood at her side. Even at this distance Luther could see the man was good-looking. As soon as Luther spotted him, the man stepped out of sight.

Luther hurried up the gangplank. Margaret met him halfway.

"I'm sorry," she stammered. "I didn't realize the ship had stopped."

"Just so you're all right," said Luther. "I was beginning to worry."

"We need to get my luggage," she said, thrusting a baggage check into his hand.

Luther took the slip and went to retrieve her trunks. After she had cleared customs Luther hailed a taxi and gave the driver the address of their hotel.

Inside the cab Luther said, "I've found us a nice room."

He reached over to squeeze her hand. That's when he noticed that Margaret's fingers were closed tightly over the clasp of her handbag.

Their room in the hotel was on the third floor.

When Luther opened the door it was dark inside. Turning, he saw that Margaret had walked to the bed. He went to her and took her in his arms. Her shoulders were stiff, unyielding.

Afterward, after Luther finished dressing, he sat on the bed, watching Margaret as she fastened her skirt. Sensing her discomfort, he walked to her and pulled her back down on his lap.

Margaret started to cry, burying her face in his neck.

"There, there," said Luther, stroking her hair. "We have all the time in the world."

This seemed to make her cry, even harder.

"Mar," he said, continuing to smooth out her hair, "what is it?"

"Luther," she began, "do you remember how you said before our marriage that if . . .?"

He waited for a moment, then said, "Yes, of course. Go on."

Margaret stood up, straightened out her skirt again, and began to pace the room. "Well, I met someone onboard ship I love that way, and I want to be with him."

Taking this in, Luther went quiet. Then, in as neutral a tone as he could muster, "Tell me, Margaret, what's he like?"

She avoided meeting his gaze as she told him about the "brilliant young New Zealand student, on his way to Cambridge University on a two-year fellowship that had been awarded for his work on dreams."

"We talked and talked and talked," said Margaret. "For six weeks."

Luther said nothing.

"We were walking around the deck, talking, when the ship docked. Suddenly I sensed that the ship wasn't moving. That's when I saw you."

Luther stood and walked to the shuttered doors, stepped outside onto the balcony.

Standing at the iron railing he had a full view of the harbor. Moored sailboats bobbed on the water, their masts sticking up in the air like a thicket of nettles. He could hear the faint din of the fishmongers hawking their wares in the marketplace. He caught the slightly unpleasant odor of fish. Sunlight reflected off the surface of the water.

Thinking over the situation, allowing himself to calm down, he decided that it was not unreasonable that Margaret should have developed feelings for the young man she'd met on the ship. It was quite remarkable they had so much in common. And, after all, he himself had met an attractive British girl named Dorothy Loch. They'd become close friends. It might have turned into more had it not been for his commitment to his marriage. He resolved that he was not going to let this shipboard infatuation of hers ruin their time together. He'd come prepared with a list of interesting places, historic sites he really wanted to see. He was going to show her a marvelous time in France.

Walking back into the darkness of the room, Luther looked at Margaret. She was standing at the dresser, brushing her hair. Her back was to him.

He said, "I haven't changed my mind."

Margaret turned to him.

"I love you, and my love wants only your greatest happiness," said Luther.

Tears welled again in Margaret's eyes. "I know that."

"Okay," he said, "let's go to lunch. I think we both need it and will feel much better then."

Margaret spent her first days with Luther on the coast. The gentle breezes of the Mediterranean should have been a tonic to her troubled mind, but they were not. The effort to make sense of her conflicting relationships drained her of energy.

So she turned to dream analysis. For Margaret believed, as did many of her closest friends, that dreams were a window into the unconscious mind. Dreams—and what they told her—might provide a path through this difficult terrain.

Each morning, as soon as she opened her eyes, she jotted down the images from the night before. She had learned that if she didn't record them immediately, they'd vanish along with the morning dew. Some dreams she scribbled on scraps of paper, so illegible she could barely make out what she'd written. She labeled each dream with the date and time that it occurred, then placed it into the folder she was compiling for Reo.

Many of the dreams in this collection, not surprisingly, centered on how she might feel when she saw Ruth:

> *We are at a railway station waiting for Ruth. I don't know when she will arrive. Finally I see a large placard that reads "Mrs. R. Benedict." I see her approaching very eagerly. I am awkward in getting to her—have to go around several tables before I finally reach her and kiss her. . . .*

On June 28, before she and Luther left Marseilles, she sent Ruth a note saying, "I didn't write on the boat. There got to be so much to tell." Five days later she sent another rushed apology: "You won't know what all this is about. It's rotten of me to write this way—and yet there's too much to go into. I've the worst gnawing sense of failure." Finally, in a third letter, she had no choice but to give Ruth an explanation for her emotional distance:

> *Are you prepared to play nurse to a cranky invalid? I'm all of that. My sinuses are ghastly. I'm so tired I can't stay up for more than two*

or three hours at a stretch and just at present I'm cutting a wisdom tooth in a very wholesale fashion. It makes me sick. I did so want to enjoy Europe. I might just as well be in Kansas City. I've almost given up and gone home but I couldn't rest with my family and it's cheaper to live here. I haven't much money either. Only I'm not willing to spoil your summer with all my aches and pains and miseries. . . . I meant to bring you something better back.

Margaret and Luther traveled by train to Provence, where they joined their friend Louise Rosenblatt, who had spent the last year studying at a university in Grenoble. The three planned to tour the south of France and the Loire Valley together.

For Louise's sake, the unhappy couple pretended that things were fine between them but invariably conversations were strained and small disagreements erupted over sightseeing plans. As the three made their way through stunningly beautiful countryside, they seemed to be stuck under a smothering cloud of dejection.

On July 2, after they'd checked in at a pension outside the city of Nîmes, they reconvened for some tea on the balcony. Before them were the rolling hills and valleys that had, centuries before, been occupied by Caesar's army. The trees that covered the hills were chalky green, like desert plants, the land itself a pale and sandy limestone. From where she sat, Margaret could make out in the distance a long symmetrical shape. She reached for Luther's binoculars. A row of nine arches came into focus. It was the Pont du Gard, the ancient Roman aqueduct that crossed the Gardon River.

She glanced at Luther, seated across the table from her. A book about the Roman occupation of Gaul sitting open in front of him. She knew that few things excited him more than the achievements of the ancient engineers.

Sunset was a long time in coming. The sun remained suspended in the sky, showing a deep orange and scarlet between the dark branches of trees. The setting was a perfect foil for these newly reunited companions, all three trying to read one another's thoughts again and find some common ground. After what seemed to Margaret like an interminable interval, Louise rose from her chair and said, "I'm turning in."

Always the gentleman, Luther stood to kiss her on the cheek.

When he sat down, Margaret said, "I drove her off."

"Perhaps not," said Luther.

All of a sudden a bat flitted across the darkening sky, reeling into the unknown, a reminder of life's ominous and unexpected turns.

Luther leaned back in his chair. "Have I told you how I've always wanted to visit Nîmes? The arena, the gladiators?"

"Well, no gladiators anymore, I should hope," said Margaret.

After dinner they walked into the velvety blackness of the night. Following a sandy path that wound around the perimeter of a hill town, they reached an impasse, a wall that had been constructed out of limestone blocks, stacked one on top of the other, to form a haphazard fortress.

Suddenly Margaret felt that she could stand it no longer. She must bring him up. She said, "Reo must be in London by now."

"Oh?" said Luther.

"I have no plans to see him again," she said. "At least not for now."

Inside her head, feelings beat like the wings of that excited bat, a fluttering indecision that was nearly unbearable. At one moment she wanted to fly to Reo, the next to remain with Luther.

Since their initial lovemaking in Marseilles, which had been so desultory, Margaret and Luther had shared their bed as if they were brother and sister. Margaret was grateful that he put no pressure on her, but knowing him as she did, she was sure he was disappointed.

Then, of course, there was Ruth. The thought of Ruth, waiting and soon within close proximity, no doubt wondering why Margaret's letters were suddenly devoid of affection, was almost too much to bear.

Still the pull of desire for Reo, a man who had not yet committed to her, who had not taken any steps to consummate their affair, was irresistible.

Physically, he was holding her at arm's length.

Was it an aversion to something about her? Could his disinterest in sleeping with her be the result of what one friend called the "castrating effect" she seemed to have on men?

Or was it because he was still in love with Eileen Pope, the girl who had inspired so many poems?

Either way, Margaret was determined to overcome his reluctance.

More than anything she wanted Reo to make love to her.

The next day the three friends walked through Nîmes, stopping at the American Express office to collect their mail. Margaret found four letters from Ruth. She opened the one that had been postmarked the earliest, on June 26. Ruth had written it while still onboard ship:

I go up and stretch myself in my deck chair and close my eyes and warm my body and my soul at the thought of coming to you. It's always a delicious comfort just under my latest word, my latest movement. And I'm thinking of you these days landing in Marseilles. You will be with Luther and that will be home.

She'd ended her letter with, "Oh sweetness, I want you <u>now</u>."
Margaret stuffed the letter back in its envelope.

They wandered through Nîmes, stopping on a bridge that overlooked a pond of dark brackish water. Black swans floated across its surface and palm trees lined its edge. Luther pointed out the symbol of the crocodile that seemed to be embedded everywhere. He told them what he'd learned—that Nîmes was first cultivated by veterans of Caesar's Nile campaign who'd brought their beloved crocodiles with them when they came.

Barely able to contain his enthusiasm, Luther led them through the narrow city streets into the arena. His voice ringing out off the heavy stone walls he said, "The arena has always been about blood."

With notebook in hand, he pointed and gesticulated, trying to "recreate the sight of a festive afternoon when that huge arena was filled with fervent, yelling men and women, probably both the drunk and the sober, cheering as hungry lions were turned loose on a huddled band of Christian men and women." He went on to explain how the Roman engineers had designed a stadium that could hold 24,000 spectators and afford each one of them an unobstructed view of the blood sport.

Margaret looked for some shade, exhausted from the effort of sightseeing under the noonday sun.

Later that night she found the courage to write again to Ruth:

Oh if only you were somewhere nearby. I can't tell you things in letters. There's too much now. I'd have to write for a week. And my arms are playing a whole orchestra. . . . I am so tired I fall asleep on my feet. This restless touring of one night stands is maddening. We go and look at things which mean less than nothing to me. I've bitten my lips until I can't eat or sleep.

Feeling as she did, Margaret told herself, she must put an end to this indecision and do it soon.

The lobby of London's Russell Hotel was an ornate palace of gloom. Rose-colored marble panels lined the walls and a giant curved banister of matching marble ran up a wide staircase to a dark mezzanine. Ruth had chosen this establishment for its proximity to the British Museum and now she regretted it.

That morning she'd killed a few hours walking the halls of the museum, looking at the Greek statues and the powerful Assyrian bas-reliefs that those British lords of the universe had plundered for their own pleasure.

At a nearby tearoom Ruth sat before a pot of tea and a plate of seed cakes and scones. Margaret's letters had left her apprehensive. She knew Margaret so well. She was no doubt overextending herself, trying to please both Luther and Louise by giving them what she thought they wanted. Ruth wrote:

> Dear one . . . All I can write is that I love you. As for the rest I'm bound to talk beside the point. All I know is that you are miserable— that is all I'm conscious of. I know I can't touch the misery; all I can do is to hope that you'll come upon the technique of misery, which is mostly indifference, not to spend too much mental energy or the hours. And whatever weather and the charm of beautiful places can do, I wish them all to you.

Still, as much as Ruth tried to rationalize that Margaret was fatigued, even ill, there was an undercurrent in her letters that simply didn't "smell right."

In bed in their hotel room in Carcassonne, Margaret was turned on her side. On the white stucco wall, next to her, was a scorpion, its nose pointed downward. Its trunk was at least an inch long and slightly bloated, its tail curved with a spike on the end. Its pincerlike claws seemed to be grasping for something. Margaret felt if she were to make a sudden movement it would surely jump toward the sheets and onto her.

Luther was coming with a glass.

On silent bare feet he stepped close, clamping the glass against the wall, capturing the scorpion in the middle. Then he took a postcard and slid it along the wall, sealing off the opening of the glass. Now he had the scorpion trapped and could move it.

She watched him carry it outside.

Once again he had made things safe for her.

That night she chose Luther over Reo.

The next day she wrote the following to Ruth:

Letters from your sailing and landings came today. The war is temporarily over and I'm filled with a great repentance for all this meaningless hysteria I've been giving you. Just at the moment I'm calm and sane enough to confine myself to raging at these intervening weeks before we can be together. . . . And I love you so. . . .

A HOPELESS MUDDLE

"It's my punishment that I can never have one pure emotion that is not qualified by several others."

—MARGARET MEAD

July 1926

On the Left Bank the Hôtel d'Angleterre at 44 rue Jacob near St. Germaine des Prés was a small, semi-elegant establishment. As soon as she walked into the lobby, Margaret approved. Glancing over at Luther she saw that he was cheerfully conversing in French with Madame, the middle-aged concierge. Ever since she had let him know that she'd chosen him over Reo, the terrible tension between them had drained away. Even Louise, who had yet to hear a mention of Reo, was in better spirits.

While they were waiting for their luggage to be loaded into the lift, Madame suddenly reappeared, saying to Luther, she'd almost forgot, she had a letter for his wife.

Margaret recognized the handwriting as Reo's. Apparently so did Luther. He handed it to Margaret and she put it in her pocketbook. They rode the elevator in silence.

Later, when Margaret had some privacy, she took out Reo's letter and read it:

I am in trouble everywhere. My relatives have decided that my taste in the theater is impossible. Ibsen is being played and Chekov. They go to Gilbert and Sullivan. I am so discouraged with them that I have not gone.

He ended by informing her that in a few weeks he would be coming to Paris to see her. He didn't name a specific date.

The next morning, while they were dressing, Margaret considered how to break the news to Luther, who, at that moment, was sitting on the edge of the bed, pulling on his socks. She couldn't see his eyes. Hesitating for a moment, she turned and opened the door of the wardrobe. Looking at her blouses, hanging in a neat row, she fingered the material of one, then another. She turned and said, "I think I'll go to the Galeries Lafayette, and take Louise along."

"That's a good idea." Luther looked up and smiled.

Margaret had been commissioned to buy a wedding dress for her friend Fa'amotu, from Vaitogi. Fa'amotu had just gotten engaged and wanted Margaret to find her a Parisian gown that would make her look like "the bride on a wedding cake."

It had almost been a week since Carcassonne, when Margaret had put an end to the tug-of-war in her mind, choosing Luther over Reo.

She'd written to Reo of her decision. In an indirect way, she'd even informed Ruth, telling her that the war was over. This statement, made out of context, would be impossible for Ruth to understand; nevertheless, just saying it served to reinforce the position in her own mind.

But Reo's letters tested her. Things were said like, "Margaret I am lonely for you, more than everything I am alone . . ." and "Oh, Margaret, love. Little else would matter if you were by me."

But Reo's description of his new life in Cambridge was what really undermined her resolve:

These last days have passed in a whirl of teapots, saucers, tutors and strange meetings; and in becoming accustomed to the curious mores of the place, relics of medieval monastic education—the long Latin grace before meals, the wearing of cap and gown in visiting a tutor, in using the university library, after dark compulsory so that the Proctor and his bulldogs can detect any possible lapse.

Reo might think that these time-honored customs of an upper-class British university were antiquated and meaningless, but she, Margaret, did not. That Reo, a raw country boy, had won admission into this brotherhood of aristocrats still amazed her, not to mention that he was irreverent toward all of it.

It was this attitude of irreverence that made Reo so attractive. She could easily imagine him, walking along a moss-lined path with one of his peers, engaged in vigorous intellectual combat. In comparison, Luther's future seemed unexciting. Margaret found it almost unbearable that she was married to a man who was satisfied to teach sociology at a city college. She didn't want that dullness to rub off on her.

That day, shopping in the Galeries Lafayette, walking past the cosmetic counters so Louise could pick out a lipstick, Margaret told her about meeting Reo on the ship and his intention to visit her in Paris. Knowing that Louise considered Luther "their guardian angel," she did not reveal how she was *really* feeling, that she fantasized about Reo constantly, that she was tormented by the desire to make love to him.

That evening over dinner Margaret managed to tell Luther about Reo's impending visit. "He's written that he wants to see me."

Luther looked up from his plate. He leveled his steady gaze at her. "I thought we had an understanding and you ended it."

"We do," Margaret said, "and I did."

"Well," said Luther, looking at his fork, "I will have to handle it as best I can, won't I?"

Love and intimacy, when all is right, seem to flow between two committed individuals without effort. Under such peaceful circumstances, ordinary disappointments go unnoticed, work proceeds apace, and a general sense of well-being pervades the body and mind. But when doubt unsettles a marriage, it rises up as a monster, toppling one's construct of the future and devouring one's peace of mind.

Margaret now found herself confronting that monster.

Here in Paris she had to admit that the question of whether or not to remain with Luther was still not resolved. She was just as divided as she'd been when she arrived in Marseilles. Everything she was doing and saying during her waking hours had little to do with what was bubbling up from inside. Somehow she had to peel back the layers of social convention so she could hear what her unconscious mind was telling her.

The person Margaret really wanted to talk to was Ruth.

For the last few years, Ruth had been there to guide her through every crisis, big or small. Ruth understood what was in Margaret's heart better than she did herself. At present she knew Ruth was with Stanley, touring somewhere in the British Isles.

Surely Ruth could find a way—if only briefly—to come to Paris. On July 13, Margaret wrote:

> It seems just the final straw that I should have hurt you and so entirely without intent. I wasn't holding you at arm's length; I was just desolated that you were so far off—that instead of seeing you in a week at most it was to be six weeks. And I felt absolutely hopeless of trying to make all the confusion in my head clear to you. I didn't mean to erect walls or anything. And I thought I'd weathered almost the course. I'd thought about it and dreamt about it. And part of my despair over my tiredness was a fear that I wouldn't make it a success for you. . . .
>
> I know I should be properly punished for dumping a load of ambiguity on your head and I have been too, for when I begin hurting you it seems the peak of failure and demonstrates more clearly than anything else what a hopeless muddle I've made of my life.
>
> And holding you at arm's length is the last thing I'd ever do. It was I who was far off and you read into my desolation. I'm just writing the same thing over and over and whatever I say is probably wrong anyway. I'll try to pull my wits sufficiently together to write it all out—everything that's happened—only I hate to. I'll probably make another muddle of it all. But that my letters should "<u>bruise</u>" you! O Ruth . . . it just breaks my heart that I should have hurt you for a minute.

Ruth would see that her relationship with Luther was "falling to bits," that "she was failing all around." She'd see that she, Margaret, had made a "hopeless muddle of her life." Ruth would be able to tell her what she should do.

Margaret calculated that it would take five days for the letter to reach Ruth.

On a cloudless afternoon in late July, Ruth and Margaret sat on an iron bench in the small park on the Seine, directly across the river from the Cathedral of Notre Dame. From Ruth's vantage point she could see the side of the cathedral where its famous flying buttresses reached up their bony fingers to the roofline.

"There I was with Luther," Margaret said. "I'd had his letters, which were filled with an unclouded joy over my return. And at the same time a general depression because he hadn't a job and the church had gone quite by the boards."

Aware that Margaret's words were coming too fast, Ruth listened.

"He was far more unhappy than I knew. All that we had ever had seemed to be falling to bits and I had no explanation to offer except that I was a complete failure."

The two women sat for a moment, both ostensibly thinking about Luther and his uncertain future.

Margaret went on. "All the various accusations which Edward made were still fermenting in my mind." Her voice rose. "And from those, a tremendous distrust of myself. In trying to be all things to several people, wasn't I simply failing all round?" She paused. "And you had suddenly gone very far away."

Ruth shook her head. "I never went away."

"Then I'd planned to work and found I couldn't. Any attempt to work meant a violent headache. I woke with a major attack of conjunctivitis so that I couldn't read and I had to lie for hours with compresses on my eyes."

"Isn't it unbearable," said Ruth, looking then at the high and lofty outer walls of the cathedral bright in the sunlight, "that all of this is about nothing?"

Margaret stared at Ruth, as if to take her in for the first time.

Reflexively, Ruth ran her hand through her newly cropped hair. It had turned nearly white since the last time they'd seen each other.

"It's nice," said Margaret. "It suits you."

Ruth grimaced.

"If you got my letters from Australia," said Margaret, "you know in what a state of depression I started the voyage." She sighed. "Nothing seemed real to me."

"Dear girl," said Ruth, "I understood the mood. As much as I wanted, I couldn't do anything to save you from it."

Margaret looked away. "I wonder if I'm telling you all this to disarm you."

"Disarm me?" Ruth turned, her eyes widening, looking directly at Margaret now.

"I don't quite know any other way to say it, but to say it. I've fallen in love with someone new, the New Zealand boy I wrote you about."

Ruth stared. She had been blindsided.

"His name is Reo. Reo Fortune," Margaret said, pronouncing Reo the way he did it—as Ray.

And now Margaret was rushing headlong into the story. "He is a very clean-cut, essentially simple person—far less temperamentally complex than anyone I have ever known. I feel as though I'm a different person, I'm entirely skeptical of it lasting, but there it is."

"I see," said Ruth, a lump rising in her throat. How was it possible she didn't see this coming? "So I shouldn't be worried about you anymore?"

"I guess not," said Margaret. "In some ways he has the effect of a culinary knife on all my involved outer explanations."

"Well," said Ruth, rearranging herself on the bench. "I needed to be relieved. That's all."

Ruth looked down at the ground. Pigeons were walking back and forth in front of the benches. "Now that I know I imagine I should have understood from the London letters. You've no idea how many false scents I discovered in those letters."

When she looked up she saw that Margaret was crying.

Ruth rummaged in her pocketbook and pulled out a handkerchief. Handing it to Margaret she said, "And you *are* very happy."

Margaret blew her nose.

"Everything was just the surface misery of an essential happiness. Now, everything falls into place," said Ruth.

As to the practical consequences of all this, Margaret explained, there were very few for the present. Reo was studying at Emmanuel College at Cambridge for a doctor's degree in psychology. He had a two-year fellowship. During that time he would be working on his thesis, which he hoped would be published as a book. He planned to call it *The Mind in Sleep*. He intended to use some of Margaret's own dreams as examples that would underscore his hypothesis.

He'd written to Margaret to say that he wanted to come see her in Paris.

"In Paris? But Luther," said Ruth, "what about Luther?"

"Once he reaches New York he'll find us an apartment," said Margaret.

Ruth was silent.

Margaret stood up.

"It's my punishment that I can never have one pure emotion that is not qualified by several others."

"Punishment?" said Ruth. "I don't look at it that way."

She stood and, taking Margaret's arm, they started off across the park walking along the river.

"I've such a sense of having no right to this happiness that I fight it off with both hands—and yet at times on the boat I surrendered to it," Margaret continued, "as I shall for these few days this summer."

As Ruth watched Margaret enter her hotel, she felt ashamed of herself. She still yearned for her.

Later, when she'd had time to process the news she wrote the following to Margaret: "That was a vile adieu yesterday. It's rotten luck, but I hated seeing the last of you . . . and I'm bad at gentle tears." She ended by saying, "Yes, I love you my dear. I'd rather not write about it. Take it on faith."

Luther had been told to expect Reo's visit on a specific date. He found it annoying that Margaret had arranged a time and place for this rendezvous without bothering to consult him. When he confronted her she had apologized, saying there was no way to reach Reo to reschedule, even if she wanted to.

Near the appointed time, Luther said that he was going out for a few hours so Margaret and Reo would have time to conclude their conversation before he returned.

On his way out of the hotel, Luther stopped at the front desk to tell Madame that Miss Mead was expecting a gentleman caller.

Just at that moment a "tall good-looking young lad" stepped up beside him and, without apology, interrupted his conversation with the concierge.

"Tell Miss Mead that Mr. Fortune is here."

Turning to him Luther said, "I am Luther Cressman, Reo, and glad to see you. Margaret is expecting you."

Reo was speechless.

Madame looked from one young man to the other.

Seeing this, Luther spoke in French, telling her that Mr. Fortune was his wife's friend from the voyage from Australia and it was quite all right. Turning back to Reo, he said, "Go on up, Margaret is expecting you in room 12."

Saying to Madame, "*Merci bien*," Luther headed for the street.

With hands in his trouser pockets, Luther walked along the Seine, taking satisfaction in the fact that it had been Reo, and not himself, who had been thrown off-balance. Crossing the bridge to the other side, Luther walked into the Tuileries Garden and wandered down a sandy path shaded under plane trees. From time to time he checked his wristwatch.

When enough time had passed, Luther turned around and walked back along the same path.

Coming up the rue des Saints Pères, he turned at the rue Jacob. There, at the curving drive at the entrance of the hotel, he saw his wife in a close embrace with Reo. He quickly reversed course "without making waves," and took another turn around the block.

When he came back all was clear, and he bounded up the stairs.

Entering the room, Luther's eye quickly took in the neat, undisturbed bed and then Margaret, her back toward him, standing at the window, apparently looking out at the street.

"I suppose you want to know what happened?"

"Only if you want to tell me."

He had decided to say nothing about the embrace he'd witnessed out on the street.

"Nothing happened," she said, turning around. "Nothing at all."

"I see," said Luther, taking off his beret and tossing it on the bed. "If he's alone, why don't you invite him to the dinner?"

The dinner Luther was referring to was a small party he was throwing for Margaret and some of their New York friends who had all converged on the Left Bank.

When Margaret didn't say anything, he said, "Louise can look after him."

By the following week, Luther had put a plan into place. On the pretext of needing to prepare for his new teaching job at City College, he would return to New York as soon as possible.

On a morning in late July he was at the Paris office of the United States Lines, arranging his passage home. He reserved a second-class cabin on the SS *George Washington*. Half an hour later he was out on the street, slipping the ticket into the inside pocket of his jacket.

Luther had decided that the only way their marriage would survive was if Margaret was left free to make her own choice. Besides, the endless discussions about Reo had started to grind him down.

She had confided that during Reo's visit to Paris, they had not made love. The way she talked, it was unclear whether they ever would.

Luther found their relationship curious. Certainly Margaret was willing. "Why," he wondered, "hadn't Reo slept with her?"

Margaret told him, after he sailed for home, she planned to meet Reo in London. Then, if somehow circumstances changed, she would be in need of a contraceptive device. Knowing that Luther had made a study of women's health clinics, she asked if he could give her an address for a responsible source of birth control in London.

"You've always been careful with me, but Reo's not thinking that way," she said, "and I need your help."

Taking out a small notebook, Luther wrote out the address of a Dr. Stopes.

A look of anguish on her face, Margaret said, "What should I do?"

"You'll have to decide that for yourself," said Luther. He knew that Margaret, as much as she might protest otherwise, would not really welcome any advice on how she should behave.

Not satisfied with this answer, Margaret told him that if he wanted, she would run away from all of this with him.

"I'll leave with you now," she insisted.

Still in love with her, and tempted to take her away, Luther thought, "No, I'm not going to do that." He knew that she should have a choice of actions, decide between them, and accept the responsibility for her decision. She would never be satisfied until she discovered whether her dream was reality or fantasy.

Parting would be difficult and yet he felt a sense of relief at the thought of going. It was up to her to make a decision. For his part, he was grateful that he had a teaching job to return to.

On the day of his departure, he expected histrionics.

Contemplating the scene that might unfold, he decided it would be best if Louise accompanied them to the train station. Early on the morning of July 29, 1926, the three friends left by taxi for the Gare St. Lazare, where Luther would be catching a train to Cherbourg.

The cavernous train station was drafty. Particles of gray soot floated in the air.

A tearful Margaret leaned on Luther's arm. "Tell me what to do," she said.

"No," he said, "I can't tell you what to do."

He turned. With reddened nose and swollen eyes, she looked like a small child. He squeezed her arm. "You must make your own decision."

"My life is a hopeless muddle," she said.

The boarding whistle blew. Luther turned and, linking his arm through Margaret's, walked with her toward the train. For one last time, they embraced. Then, pulling back and holding her at arm's length, he looked into her eyes.

"I don't know what to do," she said, her eyes searching his.

A moment passed and then he kissed her deeply.

He swung himself up onto the train. The train lurched forward, its wheels starting to crank and groan.

He looked down. By now Margaret was pressed into Louise, her face the picture of misery. It would be the way he would think of her as he made his way by train, then by ship, back to New York.

"Take care of her, Louise. Take care of her!" Luther shouted.

The train pulled away.

Leaning out of the train, Luther watched. The women were standing still, their forms receding. Then, he saw them turn, Margaret still holding on to Louise's arm, and move back into the dark dome of the station.

EPILOGUE

Margaret Mead returned to New York City in the fall of 1926 and started work as an assistant curator at the American Museum of Natural History. At the age of twenty-five, and back on her home turf, she was still finding life confusing. Although married to Luther Cressman, she was writing love letters to Reo Fortune.

Under pressure to fulfill her obligation to the National Research Council, Margaret began her report on the experience of adolescent girls growing up in Samoa. At some point during her writing she hit upon an innovative idea. Why not gear her work for a general readership rather than a scholarly audience? Drawing upon the style she had used when composing her bulletins, a style that had so entranced family and friends, she took the gamble.

Ruth Benedict, who remained a staunch ally, said of Margaret's efforts, "She isn't planning to be the best anthropologist, but she *is* planning to be the most famous." In less than two years this prediction would prove true.

During the summer of 1928, Margaret traveled to Hermosillo, Mexico, where she filed for divorce from Luther Cressman. A few months later she was on her way to Papua, New Guinea, to begin fieldwork with her new husband, Reo Fortune.

That same year, William Morrow and Company published her report on adolescent behavior as a book, calling it *Coming of Age in Samoa*. From the very first page, its style was evocative:

> *As the dawn begins to fall among the soft brown roofs and slender palm trees stand out against a colorless, gleaming sea, lovers slip home from trysts beneath the palm trees or in the shadow of beached canoes. . . .*

As an example of anthropological method, Margaret's work failed to win the approval of several luminaries in her field, including A. C. Haddon, the don of British anthropology, and Edward Sapir. Sapir may have had an ulterior motive in finding fault with the research, but Haddon's criticisms could not be so easily dismissed. He accused Margaret of being a "lady novelist."

In spite of its academic detractors, *Coming of Age in Samoa* found favor with the general public. While Margaret was adjusting to life in the jungle, on the island of Manus, her book was turning into an unexpected bestseller. Not only did her description of child rearing and sexual attitudes in Samoa strike a nerve, but so, too, did her persona. Margaret Mead, the young lady who had been adventurous enough to live among the natives, became fixed in the public's imagination as the "Flapper of the South Seas."

Over the next five decades, Margaret proved that she had the ability to apply the methods and data she had used to study tribal cultures to speak about the problems and issues that Americans themselves faced. Thanks to her uncanny gift as a communicator, she managed to encourage millions of others to question societal conventions. By so doing, she ascended to the role of public intellectual and social commentator. The ideas she expressed over the radio, on television, and in the more than thirty books she authored, shaped the thinking of several generations.

Margaret's marriage to Reo Fortune lasted until 1935. A year later she married the anthropologist Gregory Bateson. The couple had one child, Mary Catherine Bateson, and were divorced in 1950. For the final twenty-five years of her life, Margaret lived with her partner, Rhoda Métraux. Margaret Mead died of pancreatic cancer in 1978.

ACKNOWLEDGMENTS

The person who launched this project, unwittingly, was Margaret Mead herself. My chance encounter with Mead occurred in 1972. She was in her early seventies, world-famous as an anthropologist, a social commentator, and an agent of change. I was a twenty-two-year-old college graduate, mostly unemployed, aimless, and desperate to find work that would engage me.

I was, at the time, working as a receptionist at a small publishing company in Cambridge, Massachusetts, xeroxing papers and answering phones. The work was tedious, the men who ran the company were all Harvard professors, aloof and condescending. Late one afternoon, while I was sitting at the switchboard and counting the minutes until closing time, I heard a noise in the foyer. Looking down the corridor, I saw an old woman struggling to get out of a heavy overcoat. Her hair was mousy gray, her shape squat and dumpy. Surprisingly, her mere presence was causing a commotion. The professors whom I knew to be cold and superior were swarming around her like a pack of fawning sycophants. I asked a coworker to tell me who she was. She said, "That's Margaret Mead."

Of course I'd heard of the famous Margaret Mead. Her name was synonymous with sexual liberation and the women's movement. She'd recently put out a memoir about her early life called *Blackberry Winter*. Soon after, I bought a copy to see what she was about and was struck by the way she talked about her own coming of age. Without my realizing it, a seed had been planted.

Ten years later I read Jane Howard's superlative biography *Margaret*

Mead: A Life and found I was still fascinated by those pivotal years when Mead was in her early twenties. What was it, I wondered, that had catapulted this seemingly ordinary, albeit determined, young lady onto a path that had led to adventure, self-realization, and world fame? During the next two decades my interest led me to other biographies about Mead and her colleague and close friend, Ruth Benedict. Books by Judith Modell, Margaret Caffrey, Lois Banner, and Hillary Lapsley were all comprehensive, and each brought a unique interpretation to my understanding of the lives of these two complicated women. As a writer I was discouraged from trying to add anything to this body of work as the ground had been so well covered. And yet I kept coming back to that narrow time frame—the handful of years before Mead left for Samoa. What had triggered her audacious trip into the unknown?

I don't believe I would have been able to undertake the kind of intensive research required to tell the story of her coming of age if it were not for the confluence of two unrelated events: In 2009, Margaret Mead's letters entered the public domain and, around the same time, archival libraries began the process of digitizing their collections.

The project was waiting for one more catalyst to bring it into being. That catalyst was Harvey Klinger, my agent of long-standing. Not only did he believe that Margaret Mead's coming of age was a worthy story, but he also had the patience to stand behind the project through several incarnations. Then, after he sold my proposal, he played the crucial role of smoothing my way at several challenging junctures.

Once I started serious research I realized that while the Margaret Mead letter collection was voluminous, it was also incomplete. Not only were there lapses in coverage, but the letters themselves were maddeningly circumspect. As a letter-writer she was a chameleon, at one turn deeply revealing, at another a cunning dissembler. Only when I started to read the letters that others had written to her, or about her, did a picture start to take shape. I decided that the best way to tell her story was from multiple points of view, specifically those of Luther Cressman, Ruth Benedict, Edward Sapir, and that of Margaret Mead herself.

Most of the correspondence that revolves around Margaret Mead is held within the Library of Congress, and I could never have penetrated the depths of this vast repository without the expertise of Candace Clifford, an indefatigable researcher and an able historian. Candace knows the Library of Congress the way others of us know our own bookshelves.

Armed with a digital camera, she went in and took high-resolution images of thousands of letters—the documents that would form the backbone of this book. Among those were ones penned by Ruth Benedict and Edward Sapir, small masterpieces that proved again and again that letter writing could be elevated to a high art.

I also owe thanks to several other institutions that safeguard the journals, oral histories, and other letters pertinent to this book. These include Vassar College (with a special thanks to Dean Rogers for his help with the Ruth Benedict collection), Columbia University, the American Philosophical Library, Marquette University (with a special thanks to Travis Williams for his help with Paul Radin's letters), and the Museum of History in Ottawa (with a special thanks to Benoit Theriault for his help with the Marius Barbeau collection).

Once my research had begun in earnest, there were several authors who gave me important insights into Mead's world. In particular, the late Luther Cressman who, in his memoir *A Golden Journey*, reconstructed incidents that occurred during his years with Mead; Regna Darnell, who brought Edward Sapir to life in her thoroughly engrossing biography *Edward Sapir: Linguist, Anthropologist, Humanist*; and the late Derek Freeman, whose provocative book *The Hoaxing of Margaret Mead* broadened my thinking about Mead's first foray into the field.

I wish to thank Julie Johnson-McGrath, Julien Vaubourgeix and Dr. Sanford Weinstein for helping me gain an understanding of how the chronically ill coped with lung infections during the early twentieth century.

I am especially indebted to my two editors at Thomas Dunne Books at St. Martins Press. Thomas Dunne bought my proposal, saying he could "see" the story, and Emily Angell guided me through several rewrites with a firm hand but gentle manner. Remarkably, like myself, both Tom and Emily are dachshund people.

I count myself extremely fortunate to have several like-minded friends who have been generous with their time and energy. Tony Ganz and Anne Stein read the manuscript at early stages and shared their insights. During the homestretch Mary Ann Abramowitz offered sound and invaluable counsel.

On the home front, my three sons, Tommy Herd, Andre Herd, and Theron Herd, all provided flashes of inspiration when I least expected them. And Dale Herd, my partner in all endeavors, put up with my constant interruptions, and proved again and again that he knows the central point to be reached, and that he has an unerring ear for the correct rhythm of words on the page.

NOTES

AUTHOR'S NOTE

ix. "This last night of waiting for mail is dreadful": MM to RB, Sept. 19, 1925, Library of Congress (herinafter LC), S-3.

ix. While in Samoa, Margaret set fire to the letters she had received from Edward Sapir: Darnell, 187 and Howard, 87.

EPIGRAPH

xi. "Sometimes sleep will not descend upon the village": Mead, *Coming of Age in Samoa*, 15.

1. SHOOTING STAR

1. "She was hitching her wagon to a star": Cressman, 131.
1. Margaret was known to be extravagantly talkative: Howard, 56.
1. For a description of Margaret's appearance: Banner, 6–7.
2. Margaret was starting a journey that would span nine thousand miles: Howard, 76.
2. Margaret expressed that she had "no feeling" and was "numb": MM to RB, Sept. 4, 1925, LC, S-3.
2. "Dear Grandma . . . Ruth left me last night at Williams and in three hours I shall be in Los Angeles": MM to MRM, Aug. 3, 1925, LC, A-17.
2. Margaret did not want to study the American Indian; she wanted to do her fieldwork in Polynesia: Lapsley, 101.
2. "We saw many Indians baling alfalfa into square blocks": MM to MRM, Aug. 3, 1925, LC, A-17.
2. Margaret was going to Samoa to study the behavior of adolescent girls in a primitive culture: Howard, 77.
3. "Ruth and I got different things out of the Grand Canyon": MM to MRM, Aug. 3, 1925, LC, A-17.

2. ONE FOR MY LADY LOVE

4. "Darling mine . . . , You are made up of . . . pretty eyes": LC to MM, Jan. 2, 1922, LC, A-2.

4. Luther rushed to Brentano's: LC to MM, Jan. 11, 1922, LC, A-2.

4. Luther's favorite bookstore: LC to MM, Sept. 22, 1921, LC, A-2.

4. Luther often quoted Aquinas: LC to MM, Dec. 24, 1921, LC, A-2.

5. "I am going to write a paper for Jenks that will make his hair crack": Ibid.

5. He purchased Romain Rolland and "one for his lady love": LC to MM, Jan. 4, 1921; Sept. 22, 1922, LC, A-2.

5. Memories of growing up: Cressman, 3.

5. "I remember when in high school we had a terrible blizzard": LC to MM, Jan. 11, 1922, LC A-2.

6. "Miss Mead has scarlet fever": Helen Page Abbott to EM, Jan. 8, 1922, LC, Q-2.

6. On the Scarlet Six: Ibid.

6. Hoping to keep a lid on the hysteria: Ibid.

6. "Dear family cannot contaminate the telephone am doing swimmingly": MM telegram to Mead Family, Dec. 25, 1921, LC, Q-2.

7. "My arms ache": LC to MM, Oct. 23, 1922, LC, A-2.

7. Margaret convinced Luther to switch to the Episcopal Church: Howard, 36.

7. "You should see how far Luther has swerved towards the left wing": MM to EM, March 7, 1921, LC, Q-2.

7. "They have me down for a Bolshevik Red": LC to MM, Dec. 22, 1921, A-2.

7. 400,000 British soldiers killed: Cressman, 52.

7. For the influence of Classic Greek legends on Luther: Ibid., 50.

7. He enrolled in the Citizens Military Training Camp: Ibid., 51.

8. Luther was commissioned to first lieutenant: Ibid., 53.

8. The Cressman family home burned to the ground: Ibid.

8. Luther met Margaret at dinner at the Mead's house: Ibid., 54.

8. Invited the "bright young student" Margaret to Christmas lunch: Ibid., 55.

9. "the rather intellectual Margaret": Ibid., 56.

9. For a description of Crack the Whip: Ibid., 19.

9. Luther told the story of Antigone: Ibid., 56.

9. "We had said little": Ibid.

9. A kiss sealed a secret engagement: Ibid.

9. They both knew Luther would be going off to war: Ibid.

10. "We found ourselves part": Ibid., 61–62.

10. "The haunting question of": Ibid., 58.

10. He would devote himself to *eliminating* war: Ibid., 63.

10. "thinks I am mostly a bother": LC to MM, Oct. 23, 1922, LC, A-2.

11. "I hope I didn't shock you": LC to MM, Jan. 2, 1922, LC, A-2.

11. "If you want to talk about devils": LC to MM, Jan. 2, 1922, LC, A-2.

11. "Dearest little girl": LC to MM, Jan. 7, 1922, LC, A-2.

11. The light made her hair look like a golden mist: Ibid.

11. "Now, that is the hair and face": Ibid.

11. "all hot and cold and weak": Ibid.
12. "Didn't you see me wave": Ibid.
12. "I dreamed about you last night": LC to MM, Jan. 3, 1922, LC, A-2.

CHAPTER 3: GIRLS, UNMARRIED AS YET

13. "I wish that you wouldn't tell me all the bribes": MM to EM, Dec. 9, 1919, LC, A-7.
14. "If I were a man I would probably be one of those bantam fighters": Margaret quoted in Banner, 189.
14. "I don't see how I ever could have gone anywhere else": MM to EM, Sept. 30, 1920, LC, Q-2.
14. Margaret was known among friends for asserting herself: Howard, 58.
14. "Girlie," "Little Girl" or "Dear Little Mar": Cited from accumulated letters to Margaret.
14. Dadda nicknamed Margaret "Punk": Mead in *Blackberry Winter*, 25.
15. "You girls sit up all night readin' poetry": Howard, 43.
15. "He made all the nonsense about dates": Mead in *Blackberry Winter*, 100.
15. "among the rejected and un-chosen": Ibid.
15. Margaret's vision of the future described: Howard, 40.
15. A description of the flapper and the cultural significance of the bob: Ibid., 42; Lapsley, 29.
16. "I haven't bobbed my hair": MM to EM, Jan. 10, 1921, LC, Q-2.
16. Dadda said he couldn't afford the tuition: Mead, *Blackberry Winter*, 34–37.
16. Emily Mead appealed to Dadda's vanity: Howard, 37.
16. "The invitations to the sorority": MM to EM, Sept. 19, 1919, LC, A-2.
17. Description of the dress that was designed to "represent a field of wheat with poppies": Mead in *Blackberry Winter*, 87; Howard, 37.
17. Margaret's social gaffe described: Howard, 37.
17. Ostracized by the popular girls: Mead, *Blackberry Winter*, 90, 94, 95.
17. "Don't let this fraternity thing": SM to MM, Oct. 6, 1919, LC, A-4.
17. "Mar . . . Really, Really, I can't make you out": SM to MM, Oct. 13, 1919, LC, A-4.
18. "Please let me come home": MM to EM, Nov. 19, 1919, LC, A-7.
18. "Dear Dadda . . . I am not to be tempted": MM to SM, Dec. 12, 1919, LC, R-6.
18. "it would be a moral defeat": MM to EM, Nov. 19, 1919, LC, A-7.
18. "I'm going out for the negative": MM to MRM, Feb. 6, 1922, LC, A-17.
19. "I have such a strong emotional bias": MM to EM, March 2, 1922, LC, Q-2.
19. "Write out every possible argument": SM to MM, Feb. 28, 1922, LC, A-2
19. "Look me in the eye!": Mead in *Blackberry Winter*, 37.
19. "Goodness knows whether I'll do well": MM to EM, March 7, 1922, LC, Q-2.
19. The Chair directed the speakers to move to the stage: *Columbia Bulletin*, March 1922.

20. "Those who are out of sympathy with": *Wellesley News*, March 23, 1922.
20. The Wellesley squad won: *Columbia Spectator*, March 21, 1922.
21. "Are the Reds Stalking Our College Women?": In *The Delineator*, June 1921.
21. They themselves were the agitators: Mead, *Blackberry Winter*, 103, 105.
22. Exploit your opponent's weakness: Ibid., 109–10.
22. On what one has to do to succeed in politics: Ibid.
22. Margaret was good at public speaking: Ibid.
22. Léonie was a real poet: Ibid., 107.
22. Léonie's poetry gave her celebrity status: Ibid., 109–11.
23. On the question of Margaret's future: Howard, 35.
23. Debating was dishonest: Mead, *Blackberry Winter*, 109–11.
23. A unique talent must be lurking within her: Ibid.
23. "like a missile waiting to be directed": Howard, 52.
23. When Margaret was a child, Grandma brushed her hair and told her stories: Mead in *Blackberry Winter*, 48.
23. "She told me about": Mead, *Blackberry Winter*, 50.

CHAPTER 4: A COURSE IN OLD MAIDS

25. "So much of the trouble is because I am a woman": Ruth quoted in Mead, *An Anthropologist at Work*, 120; Modell, 78.
25. On the benefits for Ruth of hard physical exertion: Mead, *An Anthropologist at Work*, 56–63; Banner, 7.
25. "resembled the platonic ideal of a poetess:" Bunny Bunzel quoted in Parezo, 107.
25. Ruth was described as shy and tentative: Modell, 144.
25. For a description of Ruth's mannerisms: Caffrey, 103.
26. For a sense of Ruth's affinity for her subject: Modell, 123–24.
26. "In spite of a diversity of local setting": Ruth quoted in Mead, *An Anthropologist at Work*, 18.
26. Some of Ruth's students felt embarrassed for her: Mead, *An Anthropologist at Work*, 4.
26. Margaret registered her concern: Ibid.
26. "Sometimes they would retire": Ruth quoted in Mead, Ibid., 21.
27. "'A suppliant goes out to a lonely part'": Ibid., 22.
27. "for the Cheyenne, the use of torture": Ibid.
27. Ruth was partially deaf: Modell, 38–39.
28. On Ruth's interest in the infliction of self-torture: Modell, 41, 124.
28. Frederick Fulton was stricken with a debilitating illness: Caffrey, 16–17.
28. "worn face, illuminated with the translucence": Ruth quoted in Mead, *An Anthropologist at Work*, 98.
28. Ruth's inattention as a child was caused by impaired hearing: Modell, 36.

28. Ruth's "cult of grief" described: Modell, 28; Mead, *An Anthropologist at Work*, 85.

28. Ruth made it a taboo to express emotion: Mead, *An Anthropologist at Work,* 105–6; Modell, 41.

28. "any longing to have any person love me": Ruth quoted in Mead, *An Anthropologist at Work*, 110.

28. Bertrice accepted a job at a secondary school in Missouri: Modell, 43.

29. Ruth moved to Pasadena to help her sister: Ibid., 71–72.

29. Description of Miss Orton's Classical School for Girls: Ibid., 73.

29. "What was my character anyway?": Ruth quoted in Mead, *An Anthropologist at Work,* 119.

29. "terrible destiny": Modell, 85.

30. "we women . . . have not the motive": Ruth quoted in Mead, *An Anthropologist at Work,* 120; Modell, 85.

30. For a discussion of Ruth's attitude toward old maids: Modell, 79.

30. Ruth brought up the unmarried teachers: Ibid.

30. "It really isn't a joke at all": Ibid.

30. "One is supposed to believe they're not old maids": Ruth quoted in Mead, *An Anthropologist at Work,* 120.

31. Stanley was a professor of biochemistry: Caffrey, 75.

31. "And Ruth—your mask is getting thicker": Stanley quoted in Mead, *An Anthropologist at Work*, 540.

31. Ruth returned to New York to marry Stanley Benedict: Caffrey, 77.

31. "the ennui of life without purpose": Ruth quoted in Mead, *An Anthropologist at Work,* 120.

31. "Last night Stanley and I talked": Ibid., 138.

31. Whatever the job she found, it would not hold her: Mead, *An Anthropologist at Work,* 138.

32. Ruth was unable to find a publisher for her biographies: Howard, 55.

32. The class was "Sex in Ethnology": Howard, 55; Caffrey, 95.

32. For a physical description of Boas: Mead in *Blackberry Winter,* 112.

33. "The whole face and head had in them something": Kroeber quoted in Cressman, 101.

33. For a description of Boas as a teacher: Modell, 120–21.

33. Boas was able to perceive the innate talents of his students: Ibid., 123.

33. Ruth would study diverse forms of religious experience: Ibid.

34. "Not only the means of obtaining the vision": Ibid., 18.

34. On Ruth's research and writing of "The Vision in Plains Culture": Modell, 124.

34. Esther Goldfrank was the anthropology department's secretary: Caffrey, 103.

34. Edward Sapir was in charge of ethnographic studies for *all* of Canada: Darnell, 17–20.

34. "Let me congratulate you": Edward quoted in Mead, *An Anthropologist at Work,* 49.

CHAPTER 5: THE PROMISE OF HIS BIRTH

36. "Sapir . . . is by far the most brilliant among the young men": Boas quoted in Darnell, 38.

36. General sense of Florence's health discussed: Benedict journal, Jan. 1923, Archives and Special Collections Library, Vassar College Libraries.

37. The Sapirs went to New York for a reliable diagnosis, Darnell, 133–35.

37. Edward was thrilled to feel the dullness of Canada dropping away: Ibid., 189.

37. Edward wanted to talk about books, politics, or psychotherapy: Ibid., 164–67, 189–93.

37. Dr. Lilienthal would prescribe the course of treatment: ES to RB, April 2, 1924, LC, S-15.

37. Edward Sapir was born in 1884, in Lauenburg, Prussia: Darnell, 1–2.

37. Jacob Sapir auditioned twice for the Berlin Opera: Ibid.

38. Edward won the citywide Pulitzer competition: Ibid., 4.

38. On Edward's appearance: McMillan, 94.

38. Edward took pride in projecting the aura of a Jewish intellectual of the bohemian sort: ES to RB, March 1, 1924, LC, l-90.

38. Edward possessed a sense of humor that was self-deprecating: As expressed in the over one hundred letters that have been preserved, LC.

38. While at Columbia, Edward mastered over a dozen languages: Darnell, 8.

38. On the quality of Edward's voice: McMillan, 93.

39. In 1903, Edward attended Boas's seminar in American Indian Languages: Darnell, 9.

39. "It's only a question of a few years": Cole, 204–5.

39. "polished and idiosyncratic perfection": Brady, 67.

40. "The time is late, the dark forces of invasion": Ibid.

40. During his early fieldwork in the Pacific Northwest, Boas had seen what the settlers had done to the native villages: Cole, 169–70.

40. "Your generation may be the last": Boas quoted in ibid., 205–6.

40. Boas and the Eskimos on Baffin Island: Cole, 65–82.

41. Boas chose the destination of The Dalles for Edward's fieldwork: Darnell, 19.

41. Edward's informant was Louis Simpson: Ibid., 17.

41. The early phonograph and Edward's reaction to using it: Brady, 21; Darnell, 19.

41. "A certain old man": Kroeber, 80.

41. The phonograph was damaged in the field and could not be repaired: Darnell, 19.

42. "getting such good information": Boas quoted in ibid., 20.

42. Boas made an effort to help Edward find employment: Darnell, 39–40.

42. Thanks to Boas, Edward was made the chief of anthropology within the Geological Survey of Canada: Ibid., 41–42.

42. "When you have a Jew": Barbeau, 622 F1, 10.

42. In 1911, Edward fell in love with Florence Delson: Darnell, 45.

43. "As to your well meaning attempt": Edward to Frank Speck, quoted in Darnell, 46.

43. Florence had already waged an eight-year battle with chronic lung disease: Darnell, 135.

43. As chief of Thoracic Surgery at Mount Sinai Hospital: www.ncbi.nlm.nih .gov/pmc/articles.

43. The precise nature of Florence's condition was not determined: Darnell, 135.

44. Florence was a candidate for drainage of her lung abscess: Ibid.

44. A lung abscess would be treated surgically: www.ncbi.nlm.nih.gov/pmc /articles; Darnell, 135.

44. "Something to consider": ES to RB, April 2, 1924, LC, S-15; Darnell, 135.

CHAPTER 6: A GLASS FULL OF CYANIDE

45. "She thought it took courage to die": MM to EM, Feb. 11, 1923, LC, Q-2.

45. "I still have two more exams": MM to EM, Jan. 31, 1923, LC, Q-2.

45. "No wonder your arm hurts!": Howard, 58.

46. "The rest of the section is so dumb": MM to MRM, Oct. 15, 1922, LC, A-17.

46. "awkward . . . intellectually eager but stiff": Mead in *Blackberry Winter*, 114.

46. From stories about Leonard Bloomfield: Despres, 1–5.

47. "You are a dummkopf": Hall, Part 2, 16.

47. "I've never studied so much": MM to EM, Jan. 19, 1923, LC, Q-2.

47. "got into the habit of writing down": Mead, *An Anthropologist at Work*, 10.

47. For Boas's undergraduate days in Heidelberg: Ibid., 9–10; Mead in *Blackberry Winter*, 112.

47. For Boas and his controversial antiwar sentiments: Mead, *An Anthropologist at Work*, 9–10.

48. "Dr. Boas excused you": MM to EM, Jan. 31, 1923, LC, Q-2.

48. "This morning was the Anthropology": Ibid.

48. Margaret was expected "to take some responsibility" for Marie: Mead in *Blackberry Winter*, 114.

48. Lee Newton became "hysterically blind": Ibid.

49. "in recognition of my helpful participation": MM to EM, Jan. 31, 1923, LC, Q-2.

49. Louise shared Margaret's left-wing sentiments: Rosenblatt, interview, OHP, 50–53.

49. Marie Eichelberg, the girl Margaret referred to as "the little freshman," and others called "Margaret's slave": Howard, 73.

50. It was obvious that Marie Bloomfield was dead: Rosenblatt interview, OHP, 50–53.

50. *The Journal of a Disappointed Man* on the bedside table: Ibid., 50.

50. "Marie Bloomfield, 18 years old": Obituary, *New York Times*, Feb. 8, 1923.

50. Margaret heard that Marie had killed herself by drinking cyanide: Caffrey, 186.

50. "Poor little lonely thing!": MM to EM, Feb. 11, 1923, LC, Q-2.

51. "It was such a shock,": MM to MRM, Feb. 22, 1923, LC, A-17.

51. "Marie's death is spread all over the newspapers": Mead in *Blackberry Winter,* 114.

51. "She could never be convinced that she was not totally inadequate": MM to EM, Feb. 11, 1923, LC, Q-2.

51. Gildersleeve expected a response Margaret could not give: Mead in *Blackberry Winter,* 114.

51. "You will be needed by the other girls": Quoted in Lapsley, 68.

CHAPTER 7: PAPER DOLLS

53. "Bought jam and cards!": Benedict journal, Jan. 23, 1923, Archives and Special Collections Library, Vassar College Libraries.

53. Ruth often chopped logs for firewood: Lapsley, 87.

53. "Stanley finds me sexually undesirable": Quoted in Modell, 131.

53. Stanley couldn't put his disapproval into words: Lapsley, 63.

54. "The greatest relief I know": Quoted in Lapsley, 96.

54. For the general sense that Stanley experienced her increasing independence of mind as abhorrent: Ibid., 63.

54. Stanley had work that absorbed him: Modell, 126.

54. "A good day to sit by one's own fire": Benedict journal, Jan. 1, 1923, Archives and Special Collections Library, Vassar College Libraries.

54. "played Go Bang": Ibid.

55. "We'll have no crumb in common": Ruth's poem, quoted in Mead, *An Anthropologist at Work,* 58.

55. "Anne Singleton," a pseudonym: Lapsley, 66.

55. The Anthropology lunches were held at the Hotel Endicott on Columbus and 81st Street and then were moved to the Stockton Tearoom: Lapsley, 74.

56. Edward's voice was low and rich: McMillan, 93.

56. "You produce a very fine piece of research": ES to RB, April 15, 1923, LC, l-90.

56. "you probably have half-done the job": Ibid.

56. The museum's exhibition cases sat empty: Darnell, 82–83.

56. "My wife Florence is very ill again": A theme running through Benedict journal, Jan. 1923. Archives and Special Collections Library, Vassar College Libraries.

57. "Bought jam and cards!": Benedict journal, Jan. 1923, Archives and Special Collections Library, Vassar College Libraries.

57. Description of Ruth cutting paper dolls with Edward's daughter: Ibid.

58. Edward experienced anti-Semitic resentments from the administrative staff: Barbeau, 622 F4, p. 87.

58. "Tonight I'm giving a lecture": Benedict journal, Jan. 1923, Archives and Special Collections Library, Vassar College Libraries.

58. "It's unbearable that life": Benedict journal, Feb 8, 1923, Archives and Special Collections Library, Vassar College Libraries.

58. For a general sense of Margaret's first visit to Ruth: Lapsley, 68.

59. On Ruth's "blue devils": Howard, 55.

59. "They've been determined to convince me": Mead in *Blackberry Winter,* 114.

59. The story of the suicide of the Fultons' servant: Ibid., 115.

60. For a description of how the administration dealt with Margaret: Ibid., 114.

60. "The one exception is Ruth Benedict": Ibid., 115.

60. Ruth hoped to be hired for the job opening in the Anthropology Department: Mead, *An Anthropologist at Work,* 65.

61. On Elsie Parsons's status in the Anthropology Department: Banner, 188; Goldfrank, 21; Peace, 40.

61. Although Ruth wanted the teaching job she wasn't surprised when it was given to Gladys Reichard: Benedict journal, Feb. 13, 1923, Archives and Special Collections Library, Vassar College Libraries.

61. "Gladys Reichard has accepted our teaching job": Benedict journal, Feb. 13, 1923, Archives and Special Collections Library, Vassar College Libraries.

61. Boas thought Gladys Reichard needed the teaching job more than Ruth: Howard, 55.

61. "Why don't you talk to Mrs. Parsons": Benedict journal, Feb. 13, 1923, Archives and Special Collections Library, Vassar College Libraries.

61. "Worst sick headache": Ibid.

61. "Said nothing to Mrs. Parsons": Benedict journal, Feb. 15, 1923, Archives and Special Collections Library, Vassar College Libraries.

61. "Wrote Mrs. Parsons I was interested": Benedict journal, Feb. 16, 1923, Archives and Special Collections Library, Vassar College Libraries.

62. "Lunch with Dr. Goddard": Benedict journal, Feb. 17, 1923, Archives and Special Collections Library, Vassar College Libraries.

62. Ruth accepted Parsons's offer: Modell, 169.

62. Fieldwork threatened Ruth's already fragile marriage: Ibid.

63. "At least there's something else to think of besides life and death": Benedict journal, March 12, 1923, Archives and Special Collections Library, Vassar College Libraries.

63. For a general sense of how Ruth felt about Edward, see Lapsley, 65–67; Modell, 127–35.

63. "Worked on texts AM.": Benedict journal, March 17, 1923, Archives and Special Collections Library, Vassar College Libraries.

CHAPTER 8: HELL'S KITCHEN

64. "Three nights running": Cressman, 90.

64. Luther liked to go hunting with his father in the country: LC to MM, Dec. 25, 1921, LC, A-2.

64. Luther preferred living in the country over the city: LC to MM, Jan. 8, 1922, LC, A-2.

64. "Such a life!": MM to EM, Nov. 19, 1922, LC, Q-2.

64. "I've been speaking to Father Sparks": LC to MM, Jan. 8, 1922, LC, A-2.

65. "I don't know if I want to live": LC to MM, Jan. 8, 1922, LC, A-2.

65. For a description of how Luther used to go out with the family dog: LC to MM, Dec. 27, 1921, LC, A-2.

66. "unbroken line of brick buildings": LC to MM, Jan. 4, 1921, LC, A-2.

66. Father Pomeroy warned Luther to be careful at the tenements: Cressman, 75–76.

66. "I have definite interests there": LC to MM, Jan. 11, 1922, LC, A-2.

66. "do you know anything about the law": LC to MM, Dec. 27, 1921, LC, A-2.

66. "Some young people": Ibid.

66. Luther and Margaret had decided to put off starting a family: Ibid.; LC to MM, Dec. 9, 1922, LC, A-2.

66. "I went along with Papa": LC to MM, Dec. 29, 1921, LC, A-2.

67. "Dearest little wife to be": LC to MM, Sept. 22, 1921, LC, A-2.

67. "She said she would cooperate": LC to MM, Dec. 20, 1921, LC, A-2.

67. "looked like 'the Faustus'": LC to MM, July 8, 1923, LC, A-2.

67. Luther was now a priest in the service of all people: Cressman, 82.

67. It was the culmination of four years of study at the seminary: Ibid., 79.

67. Luther chose for his thesis the life of John Wesley: Ibid.

67. Father Sparks arranged for him to split his time between two low-income parishes: Mead in *Blackberry Winter,* 119; Cressman, 87.

68. Luther was stunned to hear the woman had died: Cressman, 88.

68. Luther felt a sense of relief that he had not been present: Ibid., 88–89.

68. Luther was bothered by the inequality that deprived the poor of basic services: Ibid., 88–89.

68. For a description of the tenements of Hell's Kitchen: Ibid., 75.

69. For how Luther felt walking into the dead woman's home: Ibid., 88.

69. For a description of how Luther washed the dishes for the dead woman's family: Ibid., 89–90.

70. "What did the church have to say about this?": Ibid., 89.

70. For the next three nights Luther returned to the apartment: Ibid., 90.

70. For a description of Luther's journey to the cemetery in the Bronx: Ibid.

70. Luther felt he had won back his self-respect: Ibid.

70. Luther realized he had learned more about social responsibility from his parents than from the church: Ibid., 90.

71. Luther wondered, "could these tragedies have been averted?": Ibid., 88.

71. Luther's courses at Columbia raised questions about the role of the Church in regard to poverty: Ibid., 90.

71. "I have you to thank": LC to MM, Dec. 9, 1922, LC, A-2.

71. "Don't preach any more of that New Republic": Cressman, 90.

72. For Luther's feelings about the Pagan Bookstore: LC to MM, Jan. 3, 1922, LC, A-2.

72. "This woman Magdeleine Marx": Ibid.

72. "We'll make it go all right": LC to MM, Dec. 9, 1922, LC, A-2.

72. "Martha has a gas plate we can have": Ibid.

72. "I love every vibrant part": LC to MM, Oct. 19, 1922, LC, A-2.

72. For Luther's philosophy regarding marriage: Cressman, 88.

CHAPTER 9: A COTTAGE ON CAPE COD

73. "I'm going to be famous some day": Margaret quoted in Howard, 61.
74. "I haven't yet discovered": Marie quoted in Lapsley, 79.
74. "If only I could manicure your hands for your wedding day": Ibid.
74. Some called Marie her slave, but to Margaret, Marie was a godsend: Howard, 73.
74. Marie learned to tolerate Luther: Lapsley, 78.
74. Marie didn't like to be reminded that Margaret had other close friends: Lapsley, 79.
74. "How jolly that everyone is to turn up": LA to MM, July 14, 1923, LC, C-1.
74. "Your At-Home Cards": ME to MM, Aug. 22, 1923, LC, C-1.
75. "It looks, I don't know, a trifle immoral": ME to MM, Aug. 22, 1923, LC, B-4.
75. "A fantastic or garish note in the type effect": Post, 48.
75. For the story of why Emily Mead thought women should keep their own last names: Mead, in *Blackberry Winter,* 117.
75. "And the Cressmans weren't a bit shocked": MM to MRM, Dec. 7, 1923, LC, A-17.
76. "part of my college education": ME to MM, Aug. 22, 1923, LC, C-1.
76. "I'm going to be famous some day": Margaret quoted in Howard, 61.
76. "I'm going to get a job giving change in the subway": Ibid.
76. "Your industry makes me feel like a good-for-nothing": LR to MM, June 26, 1923, LC, C-1.
76. "If you'd been brought up": Howard, 42.
76. "That cost me ten thousand dollars": Ibid., 60.
76. "I have a proposition for you": Ibid.
77. "But I *want* to get married": Ibid., 60.
77. "he who pays the piper calls the tune": Sherwood quoted in Mead, in *Blackberry Winter,* 39.
77. She valued in Luther those abilities that Sherwood Mead lacked: Ibid., 83–84.
77. "He'll be riding up to marry you any time you want": Martha Ramsey Mead quoted in Howard, 60.
78. "Your family's not coming to the wedding in *those* clothes": Ibid., 61–62.
78. Father Pomeroy performed the nuptial Mass: Cressman, 91.
78. The Reverend Hollah performed the marriage ceremony: Mead, *Blackberry Winter,* 116.
79. "Damn those Meads, to them we Cressmans are outlanders": Luther quoted in Howard, 62.
79. "Hell's bells": Howard interview, Special Collections, Columbia University.
79. Margaret sent for a whisk broom: Mead in *Blackberry Winter,* 116.
79. Dr. Ostrolenk accidentally spilled coffee down the front of Margaret's dress: Ibid.
79. "Your inference is correct": Howard, 62.
80. On Ellis's theory regarding same-sex relationships between women: Lapsley, 319.

81. Ellis said sex was like a musical instrument that the participants learned to play: Mead, *Blackberry Winter,* 117.
81. Margaret wondered if Ellis was right about how to attain sexual satisfaction: Ibid.
81. "My flesh aches for the touch of love": LC to MM, Dec. 15, 1922, LC, A-2.
81. "My body is calling for yours": LC to MM, July 8, 1923, LC, A-2.
81. Over dinner Margaret told Luther about the paper she was working on: Howard, 62.
82. "Tonight I'm going to take the other bedroom": Margaret quoted in ibid., 62.
82. That night they did not consummate their union: Ibid., 62.
82. "We took Aunt Nellie, Cousin Elizabeth and Betty": MM to EM, Sept. 14, 1923, LC, Q-2.
82. Margaret described the monotony of the local architecture: Ibid.
83. On Margaret's "fear and hostility to the commitment of marriage": Howard, 62.
83. "willful at times, stubborn, sometimes quixotic": Cressman, 131.
84. "You'd better watch out": Luther quoted in Howard, 62.
84. "Our enjoyment of these long lazy": Mead, *Blackberry Winter,* 116.
85. For Luther's description of the end of the honeymoon: Cressman, 93; Howard interview, Special Collections, Columbia University.

CHAPTER 10: A WOMAN OF SPARE EFFECTS
86. "My main difficulty with this poetry": ES to RB, Feb. 29, 1924, LC, l-90.
86. "My wife wrote you, I believe, of how I broke my leg": ES to RB, Aug. 7, 1923, LC, l-90.
86. The next thing Edward knew he was in a cast: Ibid.
87. "I expect to be rid of the plaster cast": Ibid.
87. "Possibly the only kind of work that will ever interest the public": Ibid.
88. "All summer I've worked on the mythology": Ruth quoted in Mead, *An Anthropologist at Work,* 399.
89. "It isn't any laws people need": Stanley quoted in Benedict journal, February 25, 1923, Archives and Special collections Library, Vassar College Libraries.
89. "He has a fixed idea": ibid.
89. Stanley was driving her away: In Mead, *An Anthropologist at Work,* 83.
89. "For I am smitten to my knees with longing": Ruth quoted in Modell, 133.
89. "The great outdoors camp ground was filled with close-lipped people": Ruth quoted in Mead, *An Anthropologist at Work,* 149–50.
89. Ruth thought about the rigidity of her own religious upbringing: Mead, *An Anthropologist at Work,* 150.
90. Ruth contemplated a future without Stanley: Ibid., 120.
90. For Ruth's concerns about going into the field: Ibid., 150.
90. Ruth gave Margaret a $300 "no strings attached" fellowship: Howard, 59.

90. "Perhaps there is no accepted form": MM to RB, April 1923, LC, S-3.
91. Many in the department didn't like Margaret's assertiveness: Howard, 50, Howard interviews, Special Collections, Columbia University.
91. For Esther Goldfrank's description of Margaret: Howard interviews, Special Collections, Columbia University.
91. "She's afraid you're disappointed in her": Luther quoted in Mead, *Blackberry Winter*, 131 and Lapsley, 71.
92. For a description of Margaret's appearance when she walked: Mead in *Blackberry Winter*, 132.
92. On the friendship between Margaret and Ruth: Howard, 55–57.
92. "I say it's the zest of youth I believe in": Ibid., 57.
92. Ruth was made uncomfortable by the adulation: Banner, 220.
93. "I can't bear to think of your arms": RB to MM, Oct. 12, 1925, LC, S-4.
93. On what it meant to Ruth to have Edward as an ally: Modell, 125.
93. Ruth and Edward maintained an emotional distance between them: Mead, *An Anthropologist at Work*, 158.
93. The poets Ruth most admired were John Donne and Walt Whitman: Modell, 138–39.
94. "My main difficulty with this poetry": ES to RB, Feb. 14, 1925, LC, l-90.
94. Edward enjoyed obsessing over the subtle nuances of words arranged in verse: Darnell, 174.
94. "The best way to write a poem is to give up looking for a subject": Darnell 162.
94. On Edward's ideas regarding the writing of poetry: Ibid., 161–62.
94. "My verse comes back with the regularity of clockwork": ES to RB, March 24, 1924, LC, l-90.
95. Ruth had no intention of sharing her poetry: Mead, *An Anthropologist at Work*, 87.

CHAPTER 11: THE RIDEAU CANAL
96. "You are right in one thing. Death for myself does not seem such an evil": ES to RB, May 28, 1924, LC, T-3.
96. On Michael's piano lessons and practicing with the metronome: Darnell, 47, 154.
97. On the tension between Michael and Edward regarding piano practice: Ibid., 154.
97. On why Edward wanted to escape Ottawa: Ibid., 160, 164–68, 189–95.
97. On Florence's chronic illness and her unhappiness: Ibid., 133.
97. "I should have to mortgage my soul for 10 years": Edward quoted in Darnell, 134.
98. For the story of how Florence attempted suicide: Barbeau, 622 F3, p. 58.
98. "I seem to be in very poor trim psychologically": ES to RB, Dec 8, 1923, LC, 1–90.
99. Edward announced that he had been put in charge of the Anthropology

Program for the British Association for the Advancement of Science: ES to RB, Feb. 22, 1924, LC, l-90.

99. "I'm to be the local secretary for Anthropology": Ibid.

99. "We Canadians should not like to have the meeting fizzle": Ibid.

99. "Maybe I shall get some Indian agent to stage a war dance": Ibid.

99. "Anyway, you might think of a paper for the grand occasion": Ibid.

99. "I see you're running a typewriter": ES to RB, March 24, 1924, LC, l-90.

100. "Use a typewriter for a scientific manuscript": Ibid.

100. "I am old fashioned on a few things": Ibid.

100. "abnormally innocent when it came to the opposite sex": Bunny quoted in Banner, 186.

100. "Florence *is* quite right when she says of me that with all of my Bolshevistic fanfare": ES to RB, March 1, 1924, LC, l-90.

100. Edward was gratified that Ruth responded to his poems: ES to RB, March 24, 1924, LC, l-90.

101. "Send your verse. I feel it in my bones": ES to RB, Feb. 27, 1924, LC, T-3.

101. "I am delighted to hear that you are coming to Toronto": ES to RB, March 1924, LC, T-3.

101. "Maugham's book frightens me": ES to RB, March 27, 1924, LC, S-15.

101. "psychologically accurate but lightweight": ES to RB, April 16, 1924, LC, S-15.

101. "I wish I had a poem to send you": ES to RB, March 24, 1924, LC, S-15.

102. "but not the excision the New York doctor spoke of": Ibid.

102. Surgery was imminent: ES to RB, March 31, 1924, LC, S-15.

102. "Florence has pretty regularly recurring fever": ES to RB, April 2, 1924, LC, S-15.

102. "And I have peace. The moon at harvest is": Ruth's poem quoted in Mead, *An Anthropologist at Work*, 160–61.

103. Ruth's proposed topics for the conference sounded interesting: ES to RB, April 8, 1924, LC, T-3.

103. "I find myself at last somewhat in the mood": Ibid.

104. "The next . . . is to remove a few ribs and collapse the lung artificially": ES to RB, April 2, 1924, LC, S-15.

104. "So you see poor Florence has a great ordeal before her": Ibid.

104. Florence had been given morphine to lesson the pain: Ibid.

104. "Florence had an operation yesterday": Ibid.

104. Florence wanted to get her hair bobbed: ES to RB, May 19, 1924, LC, S-15.

105. "There is a mannerism of yours. An apologetic, conditional style of utterance": ES to RB, April 2, 1924, LC, S-15.

105. "There. You must send more": Ibid.

105. For the story of Edward using a Sarcee headdress to barter for Michael's camp fees: Darnell, 137.

106. "Mrs. Sapir is still very weak and has a good deal of fever": ES to RB, April 16, 1924, LC, S-15.

106. "Oh please": ES to RB, May 19, 1924, LC, S-15.

107. "The operation was in vain": ES to RB, April 24, 1924, LC, S-15.

107. "There's nothing deader than the past of physical personality": ES to RB, May 28, 1924, LC, l-90.

108. "Death for myself does not seem such an evil": Ibid.

108. "And the most terrible part of it all for me is the steady": ES to RB, May 19, 1924, LC, S-15.

CHAPTER 12: THEY DANCE FOR RAIN

109. "And now the clouds have listened to the insistent measure of the song": Ruth quoted in Mead, *An Anthropologist at Work*, 222.

110. "I can take down folktales and interviews in shorthand": Bunny quoted in ibid., 260.

110. "They make pottery there. Go with her to the pueblo": Boas quoted in ibid., 260.

110. Gallup was the last civilized stop before Zuñi: Bunzel, 4–5.

111. Ruth and Bunny rode in an old mail wagon to Zuñi: Ibid.

111. For a description of the landscape they traveled through: Ibid.

111. For a description of what happened when they reached Zuñi: Parezo, 260.

112. Margaret Lewis was no longer living in the town: Ibid., 262.

113. "Well two days—or is it two years": Ibid.

113. Bunny spent several hours a day with Catalina, Ibid., 261–62.

113. Ruth settled on Nick Tumaka as her primary informant: Lapsley, 107.

113. Nick recited the sacred stories in a singsong voice: Mead, *An Anthropologist at Work*, 29.

113. For a description of how Ruth worked: Ibid., 202–3.

113. Bunny called Nick "an old rascal who wants to see which way the cat jumps": Ibid., 292.

113. Ruth had a great fondness for Zuñi: Ibid., 291.

113. "Serpents lengthening themselves over the rock": Quoted in Modell, 172.

113. For a description of the Kachina ceremonies: Bunzel, 57.

114. "Most of my days and nights have been spent in numbness": ES to RB, May 19, 1924, LC, S-15.

114. "would pay out cash": ES to RB, June 22, 1924, LC, T-3.

115. For a description of the dance: Mead, *An Anthropologist at Work*, 222–24.

115. For a description of what happened when the rain started to fall: Ibid., 222.

115. "The song only rises a little louder": Quoted in Mead, *An Anthropologist at Work*, 222.

115. "Through the dry glitter of the desert sea": Edward's poem, quoted in Mead, *An Anthropologist at Work*, 88.

115. For a description of the men returning from their harvest: Bunzel, 7.

CHAPTER 13: HER HEAD WAS SPINNING

116. "At present my soul won't stop": MM to RB, Aug. 30, 1924, LC, S-3.

116. Grandma taught Margaret how to peel the skin off tomatoes: Mead in *Blackberry Winter*, 15.

116. "I don't like to think of you": MM to RB, Aug. 30, 1924, LC, S-3.

116. "At present my soul won't stop": Ibid.

116. "a list in her pocketbook of stories": MM to RB, Sept. 16, 1924, LC, T-3.

117. It was Margaret's first experience as a professional, on her own, in a foreign city: Mead in *Blackberry Winter*, 37.

118. "stories about people the other had never met": Mead, *An Anthropologist at Work*, 84.

118. Margaret met Erna Gunther, who had made an avant-garde "contract marriage" with Leslie Spier: Mead in *Blackberry Winter*, 124.

119. Margaret wanted to have a "people" of her own: Ibid.

119. Margaret spotted Goldie—the infamous Alexander Goldenweiser: Banner, 199.

119. "contain words that are unreadable by the old schoolmarms": This exchange is quoted in Barbeau, 622 F 4, pp. 88–89.

119. Jung's theories and their application to anthropology were under discussion at the conference: Banner, 228–29.

120. Diamond Jenness told a story about living with the Copper Inuit for a year: Jenness, 190–91.

121. For a description of how Margaret felt about not having chosen a field: Mead in *Blackberry Winter*, 124.

121. Margaret did not want to do her fieldwork in the American Southwest: Lapsley, 101.

121. "Here we are, dutifully waiting for another paper": ES to RB, Aug. 26, 1924, LC, T-3.

121. Edward was under the impression that Ruth considered him a "dainty man" because he wrote poetry: Banner, 201.

121. "Lately my muse seems": ES to RB, Aug. 26, 1924, LC, T-3.

122. Explanation of the Jungian theory of the anima and animus: Jung, 186–88;

122. Explanation of now the animus worked within a woman's unconscious: Jung, 198–207.

122. Margaret was waiting for something to propel her to greatness in the outer world: Mead in *Blackberry Winter*, 109–11; Jung, 198–207.

122. Margaret's feelings about reading her paper to her more senior colleagues, including Edward Sapir: Lapsley, 101–2; Banner, 227.

122. For a discussion of the impact that meeting Edward Sapir had on Margaret: Mead in *Blackberry Winter*, 109–11.

122. For a discussion of same-sex relationships at all girls' colleges: Banner, 95, 166–67.

123. For a discussion of Margaret's relationship with Lee Newton: Banner, 168–69.

123. Margaret and Lee created a fantasy life together based on their shared love of Shakespearean gender-bending comedies: Banner, 169.

123. Lee assumed a character named "Peter," while Margaret called herself "Euphemia": Banner, 169.

123. "The warmest glow just raced through me": Newton quoted in Banner, 169–70.

123. Margaret had doubts about whether she could be aroused by a man: Mead, *Blackberry Winter*, 117.

124. Margaret thought Edward was "the most brilliant person": Howard, 65; Lapsley, 101.

124. "The meeting at Toronto was": ES to RB, Aug. 23, 1924, LC, T-3.

124. "She is an astonishingly acute thinker": Ibid.

124. "This morning's mail brought your letter along": MM to RB, Sept. 8, 1924, LC, T-3.

CHAPTER 14: GUARDIAN ANGEL

126. "Dear George: I shall instruct all Navy personnel under my command": Rear Admiral Stitt to Dr. George Cressman, quoted in Cressman, 114.

126. Luther often had to guess who was using the bedroom: Howard interview, Special Collections, Columbia University.

126. Margaret and Luther often loaned their apartment out for trysts: Howard, 63.

126. Margaret believed in supporting her friends in their attempts to find love: Ibid.

126. Luther tried to be considerate of the lovers in the bedroom: Howard interview, Special Collections, Columbia University.

127. Margaret was interested in doing her fieldwork in the South Seas: Howard, 65.

127. "I was now escaped out of the shadow of the Roman Empire": Stevenson, 9.

127. "probably the part of the world which most urgently needs ethnological investigation": Haddon quoted in Howard, 65.

127. "the primitive cultures that would soon become changed beyond recovery": Mead in *Blackberry Winter*, 127.

128. Louise Rosenblatt had nicknamed Luther "Margaret's guardian angel": Mead in *Blackberry Winter*, 122; LR to MM, 1923, LC, C-1.

128. "another one of these affairs, that start out like firecrackers on the Fourth of July": Luther quoted in Howard, 66.

128. From Margaret's perspective, Boas seemed very old: Mead in *Blackberry Winter*, 127.

128. Gertrud Boas died in October of 1924: Boas, 228; Mead, *An Anthropologist at Work*, 347.

129. Gertrud died at Montefiore Hospital in the Bronx: Boas, 228.

129. For a description of the trip that Boas made to Baffin Island: Cole, 65–82.

129. For an explanation of why Boas refused to let Margaret go to Tuamotu: Howard, 70, Mead in *Blackberry Winter*, 129–30.

130. Boas told Margaret about the young men who had died or been killed doing fieldwork outside the United States: Ibid., 128.

130. Boas advised Margaret to take on a study of something that she'd lived through: Howard, 67.

130. In regard to the nature-nurture debate, Boas had published an article urging the National Research Council (NRC) to fund a study of an American Indian community: Freeman, 45.

130. For a discussion of how Boas viewed the phase of life called adolescence: Ibid., 68.
131. For a discussion of the nature-nurture debate: Ibid, 26.
131. "in the great mass of a healthy population": Boas quoted in Ibid.
131. "should behave like a liberal, democratic, modern man": Mead in *Blackberry Winter,* 129.
131. Before Boas suggested studying teenagers, Margaret had never given any thought to adolescence: Howard, 67.
131. Boas thought American Samoa might be safe: Ibid., 70.
132. "My new address, is rather a nice horse-hair-and-black-walnut kind of address": Bogan, 21.
132. "My entire exchequer is being ruined by visits to the dentist": Ibid.
132. For Edward's thoughts regarding the music of Sibelius: Howard, 66.
132. Luther felt the others had been condescending: Ibid.
133. "the tensions, indefinite as to cause perhaps a feeling of not communicating": Cressman, 129.
133. Luther told his father that Margaret wanted to do her fieldwork in the South Seas: Ibid., 114.
134. Luther told his father that Boas had suggested American Samoa because it was safe: Howard, 69–70.
134. Luther's father came up with the idea of contacting his old friend Edward Stitt, the surgeon general of the U.S. Navy: Cressman, 114.
134. Luther encouraged his father to contact Stitt to help Margaret: Ibid.

CHAPTER 15: THE OLD KING MUST DIE
135. "I am very eager not to take a false step": Edward quoted in Darnell, 196.
135. "It is high time I got on to a university job": Ibid., 192.
135. Edward was searching for a teaching position so he could escape Ottawa: Ibid., 193.
135. Securing a job at U.C. Berkeley was not possible: Ibid., 192.
135. Roland Dixon at Harvard couldn't promise a position in linguistics: Ibid., 193.
136. After Boas retired, the departments of Anthropology and Sociology at Columbia might be combined: Ibid.
136. Edward had to be careful about seeming too eager for Boas to retire: Ibid., 200.
137. "I have just received word from Nelson in which he states": ES to RB, Jan. 28, 1925, LC, S-15.
137. Ruth mailed the obituary from *The New York Times*: Obituary of Heinrich Boas, *New York Times,* Jan. 25, 1925.
138. "So you see teaching as the solution to your problems?": Boas quoted in Ibid., 192.
138. "I should give so much to be in contact with people": Edward quoted in Ibid., 194–95.

138. "I can appreciate your feeling that you lack congenial people: Boas quoted in Ibid., 194.

138. Boas offered Edward a position teaching two summer school classes at Columbia: Ibid., 195.

138. "I wrote Margaret yesterday and decided to tell her gently but frankly": ES to RB, Feb. 24, 1925, LC, T-3.

138. For Edward's reaction to Margaret: ES to RB, April 15, 1925, LC, T-3.

139. Margaret gave Edward a copy of *The Growth of the Mind* by Kurt Koffka: Mead in *Blackberry Winter*, 125.

139. "What forces shape personality, what forces determine behavior": Mead, *An Anthropologist at Work*, 201.

139. Margaret said that it was she who initiated the relationship with Edward: MM to RB, Sept 3, 1928, in Caffrey and Francis, 142.

139. Margaret and Edward were both interested in finding cultural patterns: Banner, 227; Mead, *An Anthropologist at Work*, 204.

140. Margaret thought Edward would respond to Koffka: Mead in *Blackberry Winter*, 125.

140. "I've been reading Koffka's 'Growth of the Mind' (Margaret's copy)": ES to RB, April 15, 1925, LC, T-3.

140. "If somebody with an icy grin doesn't come around to temper my low fever": ES to RB, April 15, 1925, LC, T-3.

141. "How is Margaret? It's too bad she has such a frightful time": ES to RB, April 15, 1925, LC, T-3.

141. "Until I actually get a black and white offer": Edward quoted in Darnell, 198.

CHAPTER 16: A SECOND HONEYMOON

142. "All competing affairs had been laid aside": Cressman, 130.

142. Aunt Fannie thought Margaret and Luther needed some special time together: Howard, 72.

143. "a second and true honeymoon": Cressman, 130.

143. "One of these clear northwest wind days we drove up through the White Mountains": RB to MM, July 11, 1925, LC. S-4.

143. For Ruth's attitude about Stanley: Mead, *An Anthropologist at Work*, 5.

143. "he always needs much waiting on when he's packing up for the summer": RB to MM, June 25, 1925, LC, S-4.

143. Margaret felt it was well worth the 370-mile detour to fill in this missing piece of Ruth's life: Ibid.

143. Ruth warned that West Alton was isolated: Ibid.

143. Telegrams were not delivered "unless they contain the words death or died." Ibid.

143. "You can put away your Blue Book when you strike the New Hampshire line": Ibid.

144. "I'd have been more lonely than you'd have guessed if you'd decided against coming": Ibid.

145. "Stanley has been immersed in Canadian Pacific literature": RB to MM, July 3, 1925, LC, S-4.

145. "He'd never have started if I'd been here to stay on with all summer": Ibid.

145. Stanley devised a plan so Ruth and Margaret could travel together by train across the country: Ibid.

145. "I'm to meet him in Cincinnati and travel with him across country": Ibid.

145. For Ruth's explanation about how she and Goddard had planned to travel together: Ibid.

145. "It's his contribution that in due time I write Goddard": Ibid.

146. Ruth took Margaret and Luther on her favorite walk: RB to MM, June 17, 1925, LC, S-4.

146. "How is Elizabeth? My mind has been so full of her lately": RB to MM, July 7, 1925, LC, S-4.

146. "They've consulted a specialist near Pittsfield": MM to RB, July 5, 1925, LC, S-3.

146. "I wonder when you'll have any conclusive word": RB to MM, July 7, 1925, LC, S-4.

146. "Stanley is inspired. His scheme is unequaled": MM to RB, July 16, 1925, LC, S-3.

146. "Stanley is a born crook politician": MM to RB, July 7, 1925, LC, S-3.

147. "It's an excellent scheme to get Goddard's plans": Ibid.

147. "He wants to be sure I need him": Ibid.

147. "I find myself trying to break all the threads that bind me to this life": Ibid.

147. "I don't know why, but you always seem to sympathize with my obscure vagaries": MM to RB, Oct. 14, 1925, LC, S-3.

147. Lately Margaret's feeling of self-sufficiency had gone to pieces: MM to RB, July 11, 1925, LC, S-3.

148. Edward was a "a convenient personification" of all Ruth's interests apart from him: RB to MM, Nov. 5, 1925, LC, S-4.

148. "he always believes that whenever we're separated awhile": Ibid.

148. For a discussion of the sexual relationship between Margaret and Ruth: Lapsley, 93–96.

148. "It seems absurd to keep secrets from him anyway": MM to RB, July 9, 1925, LC, S-3.

148. "I worry so about you. Do the arms still shriek?": RB to MM, July 11, 1925, LC, S-4.

149. "It's my curse, I suppose, but to me it seems perfectly natural": MM to RB, July 15, 1925, LC, S-3.

149. "I'm beginning to think that I'm incapable": Special Collections, Columbia University.

149. "Luther is a *perfect* husband": RB to MM, Nov. 5, 1925, LC, S-4.

149. "He, like Stanley, provides comfortable companionship": Ibid.

149. Ruth wanted Margaret to realize that being married to Luther was critical to her happiness: RB to MM, Aug. 11, 1925, LC, S-4,

149. Ambition was Margaret's strongest impulse, the motivating force in her life: Cressman, 131.

150. Ruth knew it was necessary for Margaret to pursue her career: Lapsley, 93.

150. "you're fortunate to have a husband like Luther": RB to MM, Nov. 5, 1925, LC, S-4; RB to MM, Aug. 11, 1925, LC, S-4.

150. "Be true to your instincts, dear, and drink sharply from them": RB to MM, Aug. 6, 1925, LC, R-7.

150. On the visit to the pond: Howard interview with Luther, Special Collections, Columbia University.

150. "Elizabeth's a little better and the Doctor says there are no 'positive sounds' in her chest": MM to RB, July 7, 1925, LC, S-3.

151. ". . . all this should be hearty prelude to a proper expression of our gratitude for your hospitality": MM to RB, July 1, 1925, LC, S-3.

151. "Enclosed you will find the result of several hours intensive examination of all known time tables": MM to RB, July 5, 1925, LC, S-3.

151. "Will you check your preference and send it back so I can put it through, please": Ibid.

151. "Does it mean we go all the way together?": RB to MM, July 7, 1925, LC, S-4.

152. ". . . then I'll telegraph him after we're started ": RB to MM, July 11, 1925, LC, S-4.

152. "You see how I'm taking care of myself?": MM to RB, July 16, 1925, LC, S-3.

152. Margaret felt free to leave for Samoa without worry or guilt: Ibid.

CHAPTER 17: ARIEL

153. "Of the heedless sun you are an Ariel": Edward quoted in Mead, *An Anthropologist at Work*, 88.

153. "We call this Rabbit Run": Mead in *Blackberry Winter*, 74.

153. "I'm not buoyantly pleased about it, yet not depressed": ES to RB, June 22, 1925, LC, l-90.

153. "For years I'd been placing my hopes in Columbia and Boas": Ibid.

154. "I suspect Boas merely goes through a few innocent motions": Ibid.

154. "I decided there was no use waiting any longer": Ibid.

154. "You and Ruth would have been my chief reason for preferring New York": Ibid.

154. "Once this farm had over a hundred acres planted in wheat and rye and oats": Mead, *Blackberry Winter*, 74–75.

154. As a child, Margaret and her mother sometimes served their farmhands their midday meal: Ibid.

154. Sherwood Mead was known to be disinterested in the running of the farm: Ibid., 30–31.

155. For a description of the pigeon lofts: Ibid.,74–75.

155. "This haymow floor was just the right height for giving plays": Ibid.

155. "Sometimes you're like a child. An absurd little girl": ES to RB, Sept. 1, 1925, LC, S-15.

155. For a discussion of how Luther and Margaret viewed the institution of marriage: Cressman, 87–88.

156. Margaret's mother discovered Margaret and Edward making love in the barn when she went there to call them for dinner: Lapsley, 119.

156. Edward was aware of the many obstacles that stood in the way of his relationship with Margaret: ES to RB, Aug. 5, 1925, LC, S-15.

156. "Find a reason to come into the city for a day": ES to RB, Aug. 11, 1925, LC, S-15.

156. At first Margaret told Edward that it was impossible for her to meet him in the city: Ibid.

157. "I love you beyond words": Ibid.

157. "Perhaps I'll hear today about the weekend": RB to MM, July 15, 1925, LC, S-4.

157. "Sapir's visit was most delightful": " MM to RB, July 7, 1925, LC, S-3.

157. Ruth was anxious to talk to Edward to find out what had *really* happened on the farm: Lapsley, 123.

158. Edward did not sense that Margaret was concerned with the practicality of their affair: ES to RB, Aug. 5, 1925, LC, S-15.

158. "Of the heedless sun you are an Ariel": Edward quoted in Mead, *An Anthropologist at Work*, 88.

158. Margaret told Edward that she had decided to meet him in the city: ES to RB, Aug. 11, 1925, LC, S-15.

158. Margaret said that she had the perfect excuse for going into the city: Ibid.; Lapsley, 119.

158. Margaret told Edward to book a room at a hotel for them: ES to RB, Aug. 11, 1925, LC, S-15; Lapsley, 119.

158. Edward was unable to think about anything except his assignation with Margaret: ES to RB, July 18, 1925, LC, T-3.

158. Margaret had reawakened Edward's "capacity to love which he thought had died for all time": ES to RB, Jan. 26, 1926, LC, S-15.

159. "It's easy to blame everything on sex differences": MM to RB, July 7, 1925, LC, S-3.

159. "Well, there is a situation I'd like to speak to you about, if I may": ES to RB, July 17, 1925, LC, l-90.

159. Edward questioned why Margaret was going to Samoa, Ibid.

160. "It's the latent neurotic situation": Ibid.

160. "Don't you think you should do something to stop this whole infernal business": Ibid.

160. "I communicated my uneasiness to Boas today": Ibid.

160. "Sapir had a long talk with me about Margaret Mead": FB to RB, July 18, 1925, *An Anthropologist at Work*, 288.

162. "I shall kidnap you some day and subject you to full TB regimen": RB to MM, July 11, 1925, LC, S-4.

162. "All these things that have alarmed Sapir I have known for a long time": RB to FB, July 16, 1925, *An Anthropologist at Work,* 290.

162. "She has written me about the offer of the museum for next year": Ibid.

163. "I credit her with a great deal of common sense": Ibid.

163. "I'm sorry you're going with Goddard": ES to RB, Aug. 23, 1924, LC, T-3.

163. "Of course Elizabeth is wonderful. A regular Saint of the Primitives": Ibid.

163. "I am reserving Tuesday, the 28th, for you": Ibid.

CHAPTER 18: HOTEL PENNSYLVANIA

164. "Margaret, we must have a little child together someday: ES to RB, Aug. 11, 1925, LC, S-15.

164. "I feel it in my bones that you should refuse that offer": Ibid.

164. "You would be opposed to anything Goddard had to say": Ibid.; MM to RB, July 16, 1925, LC, S-3.

165. "I think you left your razor strap at my parents' house": MM to RB, Dec. 13, 1925, LC, R-6.

165. "My mother told me 'Dr. Sapir' left something here": Ibid.

165. "Margaret, we must have a little child together someday": ES to RB, Aug. 11, 1925, LC, S-15.

165. "In or out of wedlock. I just feel the mystical necessity": Ibid.

165. According to Edward, Margaret said that that she wanted to have a child with him: Ibid.

165. Margaret called Edward, "My beloved": Ibid.

165. "Are you happy? Is the nervous tension lessened?": Ibid.

165. Margaret told Edward that her nervous tension had lessened: Ibid.

165. "Why do we have to do anything about Luther?": ES to RB, Aug. 5, 1925, LC, S-15.

166. "She lives intensely in the outer world and it will all mean a great deal to her": ES to RB, May 2, 1925, LC, l-90.

166. "Margaret's younger sister Elizabeth is wonderful": ES to RB, Aug. 23, 1924, LC, T-3.

166. "Whatever did you mean, Margaret seemed 'so much bigger' there?": Ibid.

166. "what exactly is Margaret's attitude toward Luther?": ES to RB, Aug. 5, 1925, LC, S-15.

166. "Margaret and I are lovers. No doubt she will tell you": Lapsley, 122; ES to RB, Aug. 11, 1925, LC, S-15.

166. "She gave herself completely. She was completely happy": ES to RB, Aug. 11, 1925, LC, S-15.

166. "I even called her 'little wife,' once or twice": Ibid.

166. "I don't understand, though. Just what is her relationship with Luther?": ES to RB, Sept. 1, 1925, LC, S-15.

167. "I do not believe in the love of Luther and Margaret": Ibid.

167. "I'm afraid my bewilderment, fear for her, and aching desire for her presence": ES to RB, Aug. 8, 1925, LC, S-15.

167. "Tell me what to do, Ruth": ES to RB, Aug. 11, 1925, LC, S-15.

167. Ruth called the day she found out that Margaret and Edward were lovers "the worst day of my life": Lapsley, 122.

167. Margaret knew that Ruth had strong romantic feelings about Edward: Ibid., 122–23.

167. Ruth had an overwhelmingly strong sexual desire for Margaret: Ibid.

167. Ruth yearned for a physical relationship with Margaret: Ibid., 123.

168. Edward wanted to take Margaret away from Luther. He even wanted to persuade Margaret to leave New York City: ES to RB, Aug. 18, 1925, LC, S-15.

168. Ruth had to make Margaret realize that that Edward's plans for her were wrong: RB to MM, Nov. 5, 1925, LC, S-4.

168. "Believe me I shall be well-informed about the exact moment": RB to MM, July 25, 1925, LC, S-4.

168. Margaret had arranged with a friend in Cincinnati to send Goddard a telegram in Ruth's name: Ibid.

168. "Have cancelled Santa Fe reservations": Ibid.

168. Edward was so possessive that he would put restrictions on Margaret: RB to MM, Nov. 5, 1925, LC, S-4.

168. If Margaret was with Edward, that would put an end to the relationship Ruth had with Margaret: RB to MM, Aug. 1, 1925, LC, S-4.

169. Luther and the Meads took Margaret to the train station: Cressman, 131.

169. "You're hitching your wagon to a star": Ibid.

169. "You will meet her in Marseilles next spring, Luther?": Ibid.

169. "You made my visit so pleasant with all the somberness that overhung": LC to EM, July 26, 1225, LC, R-6.

170. Edward Sapir, with his ardent lovemaking and frantic attempts to stop her was not going to succeed: RB to MM, Aug. 11, 1925, LC, S-4; RB to MM, Sept. 25, 1925, LC, R-7.

170. Edward couldn't remember the name he used to check into the hotel: Howard, 67.

170. The hotel clerk looked up Edward's room number: Ibid.

170. "don't think of it as a cultural symbol; those symbols are meaningless to me": ES to RB, Aug. 8, 1925, LC, S-15.

170. "It's meant to say that I'm giving you all the love that had once been Florence's": Ibid.

170. "Another interesting problem is that of crushes among girls": FB to MM, July 14, 1925, in Freeman, *Fateful Hoaxing*, 219–20.

CHAPTER 19: A NEED FOR SECRECY

172. "Ruth . . . was the most impressed by the effort of the river to hide": MM to MRM, Aug. 3, 1925, LC, A-17.

172. Margaret and Ruth took the train trip together: Ibid.

172. Margaret knew that Ruth was upset and expected a scene: Lapsley, 122–24.

172. Ruth's train connected with Margaret's in St. Louis: RB to MM, July 25, 1925, LC, S-4.

173. Ruth told Margaret that she knew the exact moment their trains were due to connect: RB to MM, July 25, 1925, LC. S-4.

173. Margaret told Ruth that she'd initiated the relationship with Edward. She also claimed that part of her attraction to Edward was his "symbolic association" with Ruth. For her full disclosure see Margaret's letter of Sept. 3, 1928, quoted in Caffrey and Francis, 142.

173. "I can see your eyes are dizzied with this other love": RB to MM, Nov. 5, 1925, LC, S-4.

173. Both Margaret and Ruth knew that the death of Florence had left Edward vulnerable and Margaret didn't want to cause him any more pain: Lapsley, 125.

173. "Trust love to be sheer gain": RB to MM, Nov. 5, 1925, LC, S-4.

173. "The warping goes deep, deep, deep": RB to MM, Sept. 2, 1925, LC, R-7.

174. "He will say many things that sound plausible": Ibid.

174. "There will be letters from him, words fused by his love": RB to MM, Aug. 1, 1925, LC, S-4.

174. "It's the one thing I know out of the extra years": Ibid.

174. "Well, you came to Edward, too. You've done more for him than you imagine": RB to MM, Nov. 5, 1925, LC, S-4.

174. Margaret and Ruth planned the train trip knowing they would be sharing the same berth: MM to RB, July 5, 1925, LC, S-3.

175. "Now you know everything I could ever say to you": RB to MM, Aug. 1, 1925, LC, S-4.

175. "we might have loved each other with all our hearts and not had this, too": Ibid.

175. "When I'm earthborn this year": MM to RB, Aug. 3, 1925, LC, S-3.

175. "If I was less selfish": MM to RB, July 19, 1925, LC, S-3.

175. Ruth told Margaret she must "develop all the expedients she could against weeping": Howard, 80.

175. "I will be traveling to Europe myself": RB to MM, July 3, 1925, LC, S-4.

175. Ruth planned to attend the Congress of Americanists, in Rome in September of 1926: RB to MM, July 3, 1925, LC, S-4; Howard, 99.

175. "It's always been one of my dreams to see Italy with you": MM to RB, July 7, 1925, LC, S-3.

176. "What have the meetings to do with it really?": RB to MM, July 3, 1925, LC, S-4.

176. Margaret and Ruth worked out a code that would enable them to communicate by cable: MM to EM, Aug. 18, 1925, LC, R-6.

176. As part of this code, there were some secret letter combinations: Ibid.

176. "There must be a letter that stands for Edward": RB to MM, Aug. 1, 1925, LC, S-4.

176. "And there must be one that means, 'I'm sending this just because'": Ibid.

176. "The desert has charms of its own": MM to MRM, Aug. 3, 1925, LC, A-17.

177. Margaret pointed out some gray, gaunt cattle grazing in a field: Ibid.
177. When they passed juniper trees, Margaret said, "They smell like evergreens": Ibid.
177. "The part I love the best are the endless possibilities": Ibid.
177. "there's a castle, with a great white horse of mythical stature": Ibid.
177. "The river had to hide": Ibid.
178. "We had everything": MM to MRM, Aug. 3, 1925, LC, A-17.
178. Margaret began making her way down the aisle. In a moment she was rushing, moving from car to car: MM to RB, Aug. 3, 1925, LC, S-3.
178. "And then I get no further for my tears": Ibid.
178. "You and I were both moving, both moving fast": Ibid.
178. "I got on the train at eight o'clock and found the berth all made up": RB to MM, Sept. 21, 1925, LC, S-4.

CHAPTER 20: QUICKSILVER LOVE
179. "Now the theory of polygamy that Margaret evolved": ES to RB, Sept. 1, 1925, LC, S-15.
179. For Luther's visit to Halifax: Cressman, 133.
179. Luther traveled steerage class to England: Ibid.
179. "I'll not leave you unless I find someone I love more": Margaret quoted in ibid., 132.
179. "far more a device to facilitate M's Samoan plans": Luther quoted in Howard, 75.
180. "It seemed to me sometimes that one of the options was suicide": Ibid.
180. Edward was so obsessed with Margaret, he felt "useless": ES to RB, Aug. 5, 1925, LC, S-15.
180. "I'm so sorry our visit together was so fleeting": Ibid.
180. "I don't understand Margaret's point of view at all": ES to RB, Aug. 11, 1925, LC, S-15.
180. "She seems to me to expect the impossible": Ibid.
180. According to Margaret, a "polygamous love" was not bound up with ideas of monogamy, exclusiveness, jealousy, and undeviating fidelity: Howard, 86.
181. "Now the theory of polygamy that Margaret evolved": ES to RB, Sept. 1, 1925, LC, S-15.
181. "She cannot give her body to another": ES to RB, Aug. 18, 1925, LC, S-15.
181. Margaret told Edward that the "generation gap" between them made it difficult for him to understand her ideas: Mead in *Blackberry Winter*, 128.
181. "Your letter from Williams Arizona cut me to the heart": ES to RB, Aug. 8, 1925, LC, S-15.
182. "You must stand by us both, dear Ruth": ES to RB, Aug. 11, 1925, LC, S-15.
182. "My table has been fun": MM bulletin, Aug. 10, 1925, LC, R-15.
183. For a description of the approach to Honolulu: Ibid.

183. "The principle of this country is endless folds": MM bulletin, Aug. 14, 1925, LC, R-15.

183. "Edward's long letter . . . still is too much to read peacefully": MM to RB, Aug. 14, 1925, LC, S-3.

183. "It's no use, dear friends, I just can't write you a nice long": MM bulletin, 5th day at sea, bulletin, 1925.

184. For Margaret's description of her crossing between Hawaii and Pago Pago: Mead in *Blackberry Winter*, 146.

184. For a description of Margaret's landing at Pago Pago: Mead, *Letters from the Field*, 25.

184. "The presence of the fleet today skews the whole picture badly": Ibid., 26.

184. On the way to the hotel, Walters told Margaret about life in Pago Pago: MM bulletin, Aug. 14, 1925, LC, R-15.

184. For a description of Pago Pago as a naval base: Freeman, 78.

184. For a description of the Mau, a Samoan protest movement: Howard, 67.

185. "Do we navalize or civilize it?": Ripley in *The Nation*, 393–95.

185. Somerset Maugham had stayed in this same hotel, and had used it as the setting for his story "Rain": Howard, 79.

185. "Stitt had the Superintendent of Nurses write Miss Hodgson": Mead, *Letters from the Field*, 26.

185. Miss Hodgson arranged for Margaret to have a language tutor: ES to RB, Aug. 25, LC, S-15 and ES to RB, Aug. 11, 1925, LC., S-15.

185. For a description of the first ceremony Margaret attended: MM bulletin, Sept. 2., 1925, LC, R-15.

186. "gorgeous in full regalia, a high grass headdress": Ibid.

186. The Samoans gauged "a visitor's importance by the rank of the naval officers with whom he or she associated": Freeman, 80.

186. "This last night of waiting for mail is dreadful. I can't read, I can't write coherently": MM to RB, Sept. 19, 1925, LC, S-3.

186. "It is difficult to exaggerate the importance of 'Steamer Day'": MM bulletin, Sept. 20, 1925, LC, R-15.

186. For a description of the distribution of mail: Ibid.

187. "The emotional effect of having all one's news spread out": Ibid.

187. Margaret had a system for opening her mail: Ibid.

187. "Today was one of the days when I took the next boat": RB to MM, Aug. 11, 1925, LC, S-4.

187. "my fingers tangling in your hair": RB to MM, Oct. 12, 1925, LC, S-4.

187. "I've been lying awake making love to you": RB to MM, Aug. 25, 1925, LC. R-7.

188. "if you were here, your eyes and hands would tell me much": ES to RB, Aug. 25, 1925, LC, S-15.

188. "growing up like weeds without a mother": ES to RB, Aug. 18, 1925, LC, S-15.

188. Edward's letters were full of accusations: MM to RB, Aug. 22, 1925, LC, S-3.

188. "water-tight system of rationalizations": ES to RB, Sept. 1, 1925, LC, S-15.

188. Edward told Margaret she had a "prostitution complex": ES to RB, Aug. 11, 1925, LC, S-15.

188. "cowardly and contemptible": MM to RB, Aug. 22, 1925, LC, S-3.

188. "get no stronger in dealing with it": Ibid.

188. Margaret described Ruth's words as a "benediction": Ibid.

188. "The gifts you bring me are too heavy for my hands": MM to RB, Aug. 6, 1925, LC, S-3.

188. Margaret received an invitation to attend a dinner party at the home of Commander and Mrs. Mink: MM bulletin, Sept. 2, 1925, LC, R-15.

189. "Jopani, our cook boy, had to leave": Ibid.

189. "Jopani, that scoundrel," said Dr. Mink, "has got my wife wrapped around his little finger": Ibid.

189. For Margaret's attitude about the station wives: Ibid.

189. "This sweet little group of gossips are just seething": Ibid.

189. "I've learned that if people lack both personality": MM bulletin, Sept. 14, 1925, LC, R-15.

190. Margaret's attitude about the ladies of the station: Ibid.

190. "who although mightily spoiled and childless": Ibid.

190. For a description of Margaret's journey to the Atauloma Boarding School for Girls: Freeman 11, 85; Mead, *Letters from the Field*, 28.

190. For a description of the feast and the ceremony that followed: Freeman, 85.

190. On the importance of physical chastity in Samoa: Ibid., 93–94.

190. "This is a lonely job and I do value having a decent": MM to RB, Sept. 9, 1925, LC, S-3.

191. For a description of G. F. Pepe: MM bulletin, Sept. 4, 1925, LC, R-15.

191. "She dictates to me in Samoan and then I try to give it back to her": MM bulletin, Sept. 4, 1925, LC, R-15.

191. Pago Pago had been "overrun with missionaries, stores and various intrusive influences": Margaret quoted in Freeman, 87.

191. On the importance of finding a more isolated culture to study: Ibid.

191. Margaret needed to establish an intimacy with her informants: RB to MM, Aug. 24, 1925, LC, R-7.

191. "I'm in a state of despair at present": MM to RB, Sept. 22, 1925, LC, S-3.

191. For the reasons why Margaret did not want to reside in a native's house: Freeman, 88.

192. "At present this whole task seems utterly fantastic and impossible": MM to RB, Oct. 22, 1925, LC, S-3.

CHAPTER 21: THE TELEGRAM

193. "Margaret is a far more typical woman": ES to RB, Sept. 1, 1925, LC, S-15.

193. Margaret learned that Edward Holt and his family lived on Ta'u, a remote

island in the Manu'a group of American Samoa: MM to RB, Oct. 4, 1925, LC, S-3.

193. Mrs. Holt was in Pago Pago, returning to Ta'u after the birth of her baby: MM bulletin, Oct. 13, 1925, LC, R-15.

193. Dr. Owen Mink, the chief medical officer on the base at Pago Pago had to give his consent in order for Margaret to reside with the Holts on Ta'u: MM to RB, Oct. 4, 1925, LC, S-3.

194. Margaret wasn't sure if living with the Holts would be conducive for conducting research: Ibid.

194. "Oh how terribly I need your loving arms!": MM to RB, Oct. 22, 1925, LC, S-3.

194. Ruth Holt agreed to let Margaret live with them at the naval compound on Ta'u: MM to RB, Oct. 4, 1925, LC, S-3; Freeman, 80.

194. Margaret was optimistic that Dr. Mink would agree to let her go to Ta'u: MM to RB, Oct. 4, 1925, LC, S-3.

194. "It's also optimum from an ethnological": Ibid.

195. For a description of Margaret's visit to Mrs. Wilson in Leone: Mead, *Letters from the Field,* 29.

195. Margaret's chief purpose in making the acquaintance of Mrs. Wilson was to learn more about the upbringing of teenage girls: Ibid.

195. For more about the importance of chastity for unmarried girls in Samoa: Freeman, 94.

195. For an explanation of the role of the *taupou* in Samoan culture: Ibid., 93.

195. After her interview with Mrs. Wilson Margaret understood that a Samoan girl was expected to be a virgin when she married: Ibid., 94.

195. Edward was packing up his Ottawa office to move to the University of Chicago: ES to RB, Aug. 25, 1925, LC, S-15.

195. "Ever since Margaret and I found ourselves": Ibid.

196. Leaving Ottawa represented the end of a chapter in Edward's life: Ibid.

196. "Cole has taken an apartment for me": Ibid.

196. Chicago had advantages but Edward fretted that Margaret would not be there: ES to RB, Oct. 29, 1925, LC, T-3.

196. "There's no one on God's earth": ES to RB, Sept. 14, LC, S-15.

197. Edward worried that the harsh words in his letters made Margaret feel lonely and ill: ES to RB, Sept. 19, 1925, LC, T-4.

197. Edward composed a telegram to send that told Margaret how much he loved her: Ibid.

197. Once Edward knew the cable was on its way, he felt relieved: Ibid.

197. "Has there been a cable": MM to RB, Sept. 11, 1925, LC, S-3.

197. For a description of how agitated Edward became waiting for her response: MM to RB, Sept. 11, 1925, LC, S-3.

197. Based on Margaret's complaints, Edward worried that she was undergoing a physical breakdown: ES to RB, Sept. 19, 1925, LC, T-4.

197. Edward remembered that Dr. Owen Mink had been asked to look after Margaret: Ibid.

197. Edward sent the cable he had written to Margaret care of Dr. Mink: Ibid.

198. Margaret went to the court to gain practice hearing Samoan translated into English: Freeman, 86.

198. "believes with all Americans here that the Samoans": MM bulletin, Sept. 27, 1925, LC, R-15.

198. Dr. Mink assumed the cable was from Margaret's father: MM to RB, Sept. 19, 1925, LC, S-3.

198. "I thought you said your father was at the University of Pennsylvania?": MM to RB, Sept. 9, 1925, LC, S-3.

198. "He must be doing some work in Ottawa": MM to RB, Sept. 19, 1925, LC, S-3.

199. "and then to cap the climax Edward cabled me": Ibid.

199. "It's more than generous of you to take up my letters with such beautiful interest": ES to RB, Aug. 15, 1925, LC, T-3.

199. For a description of Edward's encounter with Ruth in Chicago: ES to RB, Aug. 25, 1925, LC, S-15.

199. "When I get into certain moods": ES to RB, Aug. 14, 1925, LC, T-3.

199. "Margaret is a girl of extraordinary power": ES to RB, Sept. 1, 1925, LC, S-15.

199. "Loves? Loves us *both* you say?": ES to RB, Aug. 25, 1925, LC, S-15.

200. "Am I to accept Margret's philosophy of love without a wink": ES to RB, Aug. 18, 1925, LC, S-15.

200. "Please, Ruth, try to see things a little my way": Ibid.

200. "The image of little Margaret actually *loving*": ES to RB, Aug. 14, 1925, LC, T-3.

200. "Now I realize the hopelessness of moving such cultivated girls": ES to RB, Aug. 25, 1925, LC, S-15.

200. "You know, Ruth, there is a real element of comedy": ES to RB, Aug. 14, 1925, LC, T-3.

200. "Someday I may discover that a woman can love": ES to RB, Aug. 25, 1925, LC, S-15.

200. "She is so much younger": ES to RB, Aug. 18, 1925, LC, S-15.

200. "Margaret is a far more typical woman": ES to RB, Sept. 1, 1925, LC, S-15.

201. "There's dynamite latent in it all": ES to RB, Aug. 18, 1925, LC, S-15.

201. For Ruth's dream after she left Edward: RB to MM, Sept. 13, 1925, LC, R-7.

201. "Darling, everything is a nice dark conspiracy": Ibid.; RB to MM, Sept. 25, 1925, LC, R-7.

201. Ruth knew if the museum job came through Margaret would stay in New York: MM to RB, Nov. 26, 1925, LC, S-3.

201. Ruth decided to talk to Goddard to push him to give Margaret the job: RB to MM, Nov. 12, 1925, LC, S-4.

202. "But don't think we didn't enjoy each other too": RB to MM, Sept. 25, 1925, LC, R-7.

202. "Dear love, write me that you love me": RB to MM, Sept. 25, 1925, LC, R-7.

CHAPTER 22: A CEREMONIAL VIRGIN

203. "In my three months down here I don't think I've made a single friend except the Samoans in Vaitogi": MM to RB, Nov. 26, 1925, LC, S-3.

203. For a description of Vaitogi and Margaret's visit there: Mead: MM bulletin, Oct. 31, 1925, LC, R-15.

204. Margaret allowed her hosts in Vaitogi to assume that she was a virgin: MM bulletin, Oct. 31, 1925, LC, R-15: Freeman, 96–98.

204. "America excels in the making of machinery": MM bulletin, Oct. 31, 1925, LC, R-15.

204. For a description of Ta'u and the medical dispensary: MM bulletin, Nov. 14, 1925, LC, R-15.

205. For a description of the different people living within the medical compound: Ibid.

205. "There is the most peculiar sensation one gets": MM bulletin, Dec 11, 1925, LC, R-15.

205. For a description of sunset in Siufaga on the island of Ta'u: Ibid.

205. For a description of what happened when the curfew-angelus began to sound: Ibid.

206. "I am furious that I didn't come sooner": MM to RB, Oct. 22, 1925, LC, S-3.

206. "Thanksgiving was a turkey-cranberry celery-mince pie sort of a day": RB to MM, Nov. 24, 1925, LC, S-4.

206. Margaret's love for Edward was taking a toll on Ruth: Ibid.

206. "I do wonder what living with the Holts will be like": Ibid.

206. "His present point is that I must come to Chicago—on any terms. I see no clear path": MM to RB, Nov. 3, 1925, LC, S-3.

206. "The bittersweet fact remains that I love Margaret and cannot bear the thought of indefinite separation": ES to RB, Oct. 29, 1925, LC, T-3.

207. Edward had begun to grudge Ruth's knowledge of the affair: RB to MM, Nov. 12, 1925, LC, S-4.

207. "Sometimes I have a nightmare that I'm risking your love in this same role, and I wonder if I could take courage to go on": RB to MM, Nov. 12, 1925, LC, S-4.

207. "I pray that you may draw every drop of sweet the gods will allow out of your love for each other": RB to MM, Nov. 24, 1925, LC, S-4.

207. ". . . he was so jealous he couldn't bear": RB to MM, Nov. 5, 1925, LC, S-4.

207. "Darling, by all the rules I should not be writing": Ibid.

207. Edward had no control over the "cruel warping" of his psyche: Ibid.

208. For a description of what happened when Ruth went to Goddard's office: RB to MM, Nov. 12, 1925, LC, S-4.

208. "I hold that knowledge close": RB to MM, Nov. 12, 1925, LC, S-4.

208. For a discussion of how Edward met Jean McClenaghan: Darnell, 204–5.

208. Jean was studying at the Chicago Institute for Juvenile Research: Ibid.

209. On the reaction of Edward's students to Jean: Ibid., 206–7.

209. Edward was not good at managing his time: Ibid., 204.

209. "Ruth, dear, I may be horribly unjust in all this": ES to RB, Nov. 22, 1925, LC, S-15.

209. "Margaret has given me more than any woman has given me": ES to RB, Dec. 5, 1925, LC, S-15.

209. "Only life and years can teach Margaret. Certainly not I": ES to RB, Dec. 21, 1925, LC, S-15.

209. Margaret felt ill and asked Mrs. Holt to take her temperature: MM to RB, Nov. 26, 1925, LC, S-3.

209. "you're so full of complaints. I'm beginning to wonder if you're not a hypochondriac": Ibid.

210. "I got into a terrific mood—which fortunately I spared you": Ibid.

210. "very comfortable it would be to die": Ibid.

210. As a girl Margaret had always demanded that her family make a fuss over her birthday: Howard, 49.

210. "in my three months down here I don't think I've made a single friend except the Samoans in Vaitogi": MM to RB, Nov. 26, 1925, LC, S-3.

210. Margaret felt more appreciated by the villagers in Vaitogi than by the whites in the naval enclave: Freeman, 98.

210. Margaret's relationship with the Holts deteriorated into a "lovely fiasco": Ibid.

211. "Go a little slow on the racket, Miss Mead": Ibid.

211. "He's a frightful prude, the psychology of his simper was simple enough": Ibid.

211. As a result of her altercation with the Holts, Edward Holt wouldn't let Margaret use her cable code until she registered it: MM to RB, Dec. 15, 1925, LC, S-3.

211. "Oh Ruth, I am so damnably lonely ": Ibid.

211. "And it's the eve of my birthday": Ibid.

212. For a discussion of why Margaret felt obligated to give the NRC what they wanted: Freeman, 45.

212. Edward thought Margaret placed too much importance on external accomplishment: ES to RB, Nov. 22, 1925, LC, S-15.

212. On December 24, 1925, Margaret received a cable informing her that she had been appointed assistant curator at the American Museum of Natural History: Freeman, 106.

212. Margaret was thrilled to have the job, which paid a salary of $2,000 per year and ended her insecurity about her future: Ibid.

212. Margaret wrote to Ruth to say she was "counting and weighing the minutes of the days" that were left in Samoa: ES to RB, Dec. 12, 1925, LC, S-15.

CHAPTER 23: A BONFIRE ON THE BEACH

213. "You see I've never stopped loving anyone whom I really loved greatly": MM to RB, Jan. 28, 1926, LC, S-3.

213. Margaret's New Year's Day began with her working on her report for the NRC: Ibid.

213. For a discussion of the role of the Protestant Church and the London Missionary Society in Samoa: Freeman, 111.

214. Margaret felt pressure to begin her report for the NRC but she hadn't interviewed any informants and didn't have enough information to begin: MM to RB, March 4, 1926, LC, S-3.

214. A storm was building and Margaret decided against leaving the dispensary: MM bulletin, Jan. 12, 1926, LC, R-15.

214. Edward Holt and Sparks were in the yard, gauging the strength of the coming storm: Ibid.

214. For a description of the intensifying hurricane: Ibid.

214. Using "butter that hadn't seen ice for weeks," Margaret made the hard sauce for the fruitcake: Ibid.

214. "Pieces of tin banged on the roof and the palm over the engine shed lashed its tin roof in a perfect fury of chastisement": Ibid.

214. Margaret noticed that Mr. Holt was chewing on a matchstick, a sure sign that he was worried: Ibid.

214. The buildings were kneeling down in "a long thatched line": Ibid.

214. For a description of the force of the wind: Ibid.

214. The calm lasted less than a minute: Ibid.

214. "And then the other edge of the storm, charging straight over the sea from Ofu": Ibid.

215. Edward Holt gave the order for everyone to take shelter inside the water tank: Ibid.

215. For a description of how Margaret and the others climbed into the water tank: Ibid.

215. The village had been completely decimated: Ibid.

215. The navy sent in William Edel, the hurricane relief administrator: Howard, 84–85.

215. Margaret complained "Informants were not to be had for love or money": Freeman, 114.

216. Margaret wrote to Dr. Boas to say that she was sending a preliminary report to the NRC that covered a period of fieldwork "too short to justify even tentative conclusions": Ibid., 113–14.

216. Margaret asked Boas for advice on how to organize her material: MM to FB, Jan. 5, 1926. Quoted in Freeman, 114.

216. "It is very sad that anyone as willing to take advice as I am should be so far beyond the reach of it": MM to FB, Jan. 16, 1926.

217. "There was no way of knowing what lay ahead in the many months": Mead, Letters from the Field, 6–8.

217. "This letter is about clothes": MM to EM, Jan. 24, 1926, LC, R-6.

217. "I've no mind to land in Sydney in the middle of winter in dotted Swiss": MM to EM, April 30, 1926, LC, R-6.
218. "I would like Mrs. Stengel to get me a smart silk traveling suit or dress": MM to EM, Jan. 24, 1926, LC, R-6.
218. "I would like it to be either black or dark blue or dark green (not brown)": Ibid.
218. "Crêpe de chine would be nice and it's not too expensive": Ibid.
218. "a pongee blouse . . . or a tricolette one": Ibid.
218. Margaret instructed Luther to find them an apartment for the next year: Ibid.
218. For more about Margaret's concern about her wardrobe for the ship: MM to EM, Dec. 24, 1925, LC, A-2.
218. Edward wrote to Margaret to tell her that he'd fallen in love with another woman: ES to RB, Jan. 23, 1926, LC, S-15.
219. "hysterical enough to conjure up any demon": MM to RB, Jan. 28, 1926, LC, S-3.
219. "No doubt I'm being unjust," he wrote, "But I seem to feel little necessity to do otherwise": ES to RB, Jan. 23, 1926, LC, S-15.
219. Margaret burned all of Edward's letters in a bonfire on the beach: Darnell, 187; Howard, 87.
219. Margaret reawakened Edward's "capacity to love," which he thought had died: ES to RB, Jan. 23, 1926, LC, S-15.
220. "When circumstances and the clash of our temperaments": Ibid.
220. Margaret wrote to Edward telling him that she hoped he would be happy and to let her know that he was: ES to RB, March 11, 1926, LC, T-3.

CHAPTER 24: A PRACTICAL JOKE
221. "Doing straight ethnology is just fun": MM to RB, March 4, 1926, LC, S-3.
221. For Ruth's reaction to the news about Jean: RB to MM, March 7, 1926, LC, S-4.
222. "You say you can describe Jean in considerable detail": ES to RB, Jan. 23, 1926, LC, S-15.
222. "Jean is very pretty, often beautiful": ES to RB, March 11, 1925, LC, T-3.
222. "Jean has great psychological insight": ES to RB, April 15, 1925, LC, T-3.
222. "I have no true plans, Ruth—only dreams": ES to RB, Jan. 23, 1926, LC, S-15.
223. "Perhaps I have been terribly precipitate and brutal": ES to RB, Feb. 4, 1926, LC, S-15.
223. Ruth chose an Italian steamer for her return trip back from Italy with Margaret: MM to EM, April 8, 1926, LC, R-6.
223. "I almost weep at the thought": RB to MM, Feb. 28, LC, S-4.

223. "Mrs. Holt is the sort of old fashioned feminist": MM to EM, Feb. 17, 1926, LC, R-6.

223. The crew of the USS *Tanager* "jibed at Mr. Holt for having his porch covered with 'Samoan kids'": Ibid.

223. "escape from that tiny island and the society of the tiny white colony on it": Margaret quoted in Freeman, 134.

223. Margaret was finding it difficult to make any progress on her report: Mead, *Letters from the Field*, 59.

224. When Margaret and the scientists from Honolulu's Bishop Museum arrived at Fitiuta, they were greeted by the chief, who brought out ceremonial offerings of food: Freeman, 55–56.

224. For a description of Margaret as she danced for everyone: Freeman, 124.

224. Margaret "played *Sweepy* (Casino) to the tune of several ukuleles": Mead, *Letters from the Field*, 56.

224. "Fitiuta is a gold mine and I have the whole village at my feet": MM to RB, March 4, 1926, LC, S-3.

225. "I haven't merely watched these procedures, I've been them!": Freeman, 129.

225. Fa'apua'a seemed "swathed in a cloak of dignity": Ibid., 123.

225. For a description of Napo's role during the ceremonies: Ibid., 125.

225. Napo asserted that in Samoa, couples had intercourse "several times in one night, sometimes as many as fifteen": Ibid.

225. "Doing straight ethnology is just fun and so easy once the people love you": MM to RB, March 4, 1926, LC, S-3.

225. "Getting the material was in a way what worried me most": Ibid.

226. "But by lucky chance I've succeeded": Ibid.

226. Margaret wrote to Ruth that finally she had a "sense of command" over her "problem": Ibid.

226. "Approximate age, rank, and schooling in government and pastor's school": Freeman, 120.

226. Fa'apua'a and Fofoa accompanied Margaret on her trip: Ibid., 136.

226. For a description of the boat trip to Ofu: Ibid., 135.

227. For a description of why Margaret referred to Fa'apua'a and Fofoa as her "merry companions": Freeman, 136

227. "The girls were": Freeman, 136.

227. Fa'apua'a asked Margaret if there was one of the men that she favored: Freeman, 147.

227. Margaret and the Samoan girls journeyed over land to the tiny village of Sili, on the adjoining island of Olosega: MM bulletin, March 26, 1926, LC, R-15.

227. "It was a long walk skirting the sea": Freeman, 138.

227. Margaret worked up the courage to ask the girls questions about their sexual behavior: Freeman, *Fateful Hoaxing*, 3.

228. Margaret wondered if what Fa'apua'a and Fofoa were saying was the truth: Ibid., 140–41.

228. Margaret had gone to Samoa with a preconception that sensual enjoyment was a feature of life in the South Seas: Ibid., 140–61.

228. Boas was an avowed cultural determinist and hoped that Margaret would return with information that confirmed his theory that culture played a more important part than biology in shaping an individual's behavior: Ibid., 25–27.

228. "I haven't an ailment in the world except my arms and my eyes": MM to RB, March 11, 1926, LC, S-3.

228. "Once again my fear that you would decide however much": Ibid.

229. "Sexual life begins with puberty in most cases": MM to FB, March 14, 1926, in Freeman, 230.

229. "The neuroses accompanying sex in American civilization": Ibid.

229. "I feel absolutely safe in generalizing from the material I have": Ibid.

229. Margaret wrote that her success in Samoa was due to the fact that she lost her identity while immersed in the culture: Freeman, 141.

CHAPTER 25: STRANGER FROM ANOTHER PLANET

230. "Talking the old jargon is bringing it all back": MM to RB, May 27, 1926, LC, S-3.

230. "Waves poured over the top deck and passengers went down like nine pins": Mead, *Blackberry Winter,* 156–58.

230. "I've had the most marvelous luck with every detail!": MM to EM, May 19, 1926, LC, R-6.

231. Margaret made up for the cost of the first-class cabin by economizing in other ways: Mead, *Blackberry Winter,* 157.

231. For a description of the return passage on the SS *Chitral:* Mead, *Blackberry Winter,* 156.

231. For a description of Margaret's first impressions of Reo Fortune: Ibid., 157; and Howard, interview with Barter Fortune, Special Collections, Columbia University.

231. The cigarettes Margaret had with her were the special cork-tipped, tin-packed Pall Malls that she'd asked her mother to send: MM to EM, Jan. 7, 1926, LC, R-6.

232. "I'm not smoking a lot, but when I do I like these": Ibid.

232. For a description of Reo's childhood: Howard, 92.

232. "The industrial story of New Zealand can be summed up": Howard interview with Barter Fortune, Special Collections, Columbia University.

232. For the origins of Reo's name: Howard, 92.

232. For background on Reo's father: Ibid.

232. "Father was not one of those rich sheep farmers": Howard interview with Barter Fortune, Special Collections, Columbia University.

232. Reo attended Victoria University College in Wellington "under exceedingly frugal circumstances": Howard, 92.

233. "If Father thought I admired anyone who was a radical": Howard, 92

233. "Poetry, radicalism and psychology": MM to RB, May 27, 1926, LC, S-3.

233. "The shock of having anybody to talk to now is terrific": Mead, *Blackberry Winter,* 158.

233. For a discussion of Reo's work on dreams: Ibid., 157.

233. For a discussion of Reo's accomplishments: Ibid., 158.

233. Reo would be attending Cambridge University: Howard, 92.

233. Reo wanted to attend Cambridge because W. H. R. Rivers had taught here: Ibid.

234. Margaret would have liked to study under Rivers because of his work as an ethnologist in Papua New Guinea: Mead, *Blackberry Winter,* 158.

234. Reo was interested in Rivers because he had made a connection between physiology and psychology, which he had applied to a study of shell shock during the Great War: Howard, 92.

234. "I met a lone English woman from Kenya and India": RF to MM, Oct. 7, 1926, LC, R-4.

234. For a discussion of the travails of young ladies traveling alone: Ibid.

234. "She was looking for an escort back to her cabin": Ibid.

235. "She showed me the address, a good one, she assured me": Ibid.

235. Without changing any of Freud's precepts, Rivers had identified fear, instead of the libido, as the driving force in man: Mead, *Blackberry Winter,* 158; Howard, 93.

235. Margaret said that she was enormously intrigued by a man who knew more than she did: MM to RB, Sept 3, 1828, in Caffery and Francis, 143.

235. "It was like meeting a stranger from another planet": Mead, *Blackberry Winter,* 158.

235. The *Chitral*'s chief steward noticed that Margaret and Reo were so engrossed in conversation that the others at the table were "simply an impediment": Ibid., 157.

236. "I'm having a nice trip only very stormy": MM to EM, May 31, 1926, LC, R-6.

236. "Talking the old jargon is bringing it all back": MM to RB, May 27, 1926, LC, S-3.

236. ". . . All the energies most of my contemporaries": MM to MRM, May 20, 1926, LC, R-6.

237. The Lascars were forbidden to appear above deck on the *Chitral*: Mead, *Blackberry Winter,* 160–61.

237. It was Margaret's idea to go to the costume ball as Lascars: Howard, 95.

237. "This month you'll be in Europe": RB to MM, June 1, 1926, LC, S-5.

237. Stanley was scheduled to deliver a scientific paper in Stockholm and then would be returning to New York: Ibid.

238. "I've just come through the wrecked and decorated campus": RB to MM, June 1, 1926, LC, S-5.

238. The chief steward got the Lascar uniforms from the oilers: Mead, *Blackberry Winter,* 160–61.

239. Margaret said that in regard to her relationship with Reo, she was the aggressor: MM to RB, Sept. 3, 1928, in Caffrey and Francis, 143.

239. Margaret and Reo were seated at the captain's table, along with an old British naval officer: Ibid.

239. "It's an intolerable insult to the captain": Ibid.

240. For Margaret's apology to the captain for appearing in blackface: Dream folder, LC, July 1926 to December 1926.

240. The other passengers on the ship though that Margaret and Reo were having an affair: Ibid., 185.

240. For a description of what was said between Margaret and Reo when they went out to talk on the bow of the ship: Ibid., 160–62.

240. For a description of what happened when Reo's brother Barter was born: *Blackberry Winter*, 161–62.

241. For Reo's confession about Eileen Pope, his first love: Ibid., 160–62.

241. For the description of Eileen Pope's father: Ibid., 162.

241. "Luther was not in Margaret's dreams": Dream folder, LC, July 1926 to December 1926.

CHAPTER 26: THE ARENA HAS ALWAYS BEEN ABOUT BLOOD

242. "I'll not leave you unless I find someone I love more.": Cressman, 132.

242. Luther's mission was to secure the "nicest rooms in Marseilles": Howard, 97.

242. Luther's love of berets: Ibid.

242. For a description of what happened when the *Chitral* docked in Marseilles: Cressman, 175–76.

243. Luther spotted a young man who turned out to be Reo, onboard the ship: Ibid., 176.

243. "I'm sorry. I didn't realize the ship had stopped": Margaret quoted in ibid.

243. For a description of what happened when Margaret and Luther were inside the hotel room in Marseilles: Howard, 97.

244. "I met someone on board ship I love that way . . .": Cressman, 176.

244. For Luther's reaction to hearing that Margaret had fallen in love with Reo: Cressman, 176.

244. For what Margaret told Luther about Reo and his accomplishments: Ibid.

244. "We talked and talked and talked": Margaret quoted in Ibid., 177.

244. For a description of how Luther composed himself after learning about Reo: Cressman, 177.

244. "I love you, and my love wants only your greatest happiness": Howard, 97.

245. "let's go to lunch. I think we both need it and will feel much better then": Cressman, 177.

245. Margaret believed that dreams were a window into the unconscious mind: Lapsley, 156–57.

245. Margaret developed the habit of writing down her dreams: Ibid.

245. "We are at a railway station waiting for Ruth": Margaret quoted in ibid., 157.

245. "I didn't write on the boat": MM to RB, June 28, 1926, LC, S-3.

245. "Are you prepared to play nurse to a cranky invalid?": Margaret quoted in Lapsley, 156.

246. Margaret and Luther had planned to meet Louise Rosenblatt for a sight-seeing tour of France: Howard, 97.

246. The mood between the three friends was full of tension: Cressman, 176–77.

246. For a description of the time Margaret and Luther spent together in Nîmes: Ibid., 177.

247. Margaret told Luther that she had no plans to see Reo while they were in Europe: Ibid.

247. Margaret had different theories why Reo hadn't tried to make love to her: Howard, 50, 99.

248. "I go up and stretch myself in my deck chair and close my eyes": RB to MM, June 26, 1926, LC, S-5.

248. "Oh sweetness, I want you now": Ibid.

248. For a description of Luther's knowledge of ancient engineering and the Roman gladiators: Cressman, 155.

248. "Oh if only you were somewhere nearby": MM to RB, July 3, 1926, LC, S-3.

249. Ruth knew something was wrong with Margaret, but she thought that Margaret had overextended herself: RB to MM, July 10, 1926, LC, S-5.

249. "Dear one . . . All I can write is that I love you": Ibid.

250. Ruth sensed an undercurrent in Margaret's letters that didn't "smell right": RB to MM, June 30, 1926, LC, S-5.

250. Luther made Margaret feel safe: Howard interview with Luther Cressman, Special Collections, Columbia University.

250. "Letters from your sailing and landings came today": MM to RB, July 7, 1926, LC, S-3.

CHAPTER 27: A HOPELESS MUDDLE

251. "It's my punishment that I can never": MM to RB, July 15, 1926, LC, S-3.

251. "I am in trouble everywhere": RF to MM, Oct. 7 and Oct. 9, 1926, LC, R-4.

251. "The war was over": MM to RB, July 7, 1926, LC, S-3.

252. "Margaret I am lonely for you, more than everything I am alone . . .": RF to MM, Oct. 9, 1926, LC, R-4.

252. "These last days have passed in a whirl of teapots, saucers, tutors and strange meetings": RF to MM, Oct. 12, 1926, LC, R-4.

252. Margaret went to the Galeries Lafayette to buy a wedding dress that she could send to Fa'amotu: Lapsley, 153.

252. While in Carcossonne, Margaret chose Luther over Reo: MM to RB, July 7, 1926, LC, S-3.

253. For a discussion of what happened when Margaret told Luther that Reo was going to visit her in Paris: Cressman, 178.

254. "It seems just the final straw that I should have hurt you": MM to RB, July 15, 1926, LC, S-3.

254. "I'd had his letters which were filled with an unclouded joy over my return": Ibid.
255. "All the various accusations which Edward made were still fermenting": Ibid.
255. "Then I'd planned to work and found I couldn't": Ibid.
255. "Isn't it unbearable that all of this is about nothing?": Ruth quoted in Howard, 100.
255. "If you got my letters from Australia": MM to RB, July 15, 1926, LC, S-3.
255. "I understood the mood": RB to MM, July 7, 1926, LC, S-5.
256. "He is a very clean-cut, essentially simple person": MM to RB, July 15, 1926, LC, S-3.
256. "Now that I know I imagine I should have understood from the London letters": RB to MM, Aug. 2, 1926, LC, S-5.
256. "Everything was just the surface misery of an essential happiness": Ibid.
256. "It's my punishment that I can never": MM to RB, July 15, 1926, LC, S-3.
257. "I've such a sense of having no right to this happiness that I fight it off with both hands": MM to RB, July 15, 1926, LC, S-3.
257. "That was a vile adieu yesterday": RB to MM, Aug. 26, 1926, LC, S-5.
257. "Yes, I love you my dear": RB to MM, Sept. 3, 1926, LC, S-5.
257. "Take it on faith": RB to MM, Sept. 1, 1926, LC, S-5.
257. In the Hôtel d'Angleterre a description of what Luther did when a "tall good-looking young lad" stepped up beside him: Cressman, 178–79.
258. When Luther returned to the hotel he bounded up the stairs: Ibid., 179.
258. Luther decided not to mention that he'd seen Margaret embracing Reo: Ibid.
258. Luther suggested that Margaret invite Reo to the dinner party they were giving for their friends who were visiting Paris: Ibid.
258. Luther planned to return to New York earlier than expected: Ibid., 181.
258. Luther reserved a second-class cabin for himself on the SS *George Washington*: Ibid.
259. Margaret confided that if she were to meet Reo in London, she would need a contraceptive device: Ibid., 180.
259. For Luther's theory about giving Margaret the freedom to choose: Cressman, 180.
259. For Luther's feelings about leaving Margaret behind in Paris: Ibid.
259. Margaret told Luther she was still torn about what to do and asked him for advice: Howard, 99.
260. For a discussion of Margaret's profound confusion about her life when Luther bid her farewell at the train station: Ibid., Howard, 99.

EPILOGUE
261. Margaret found ways to widen the audience for her report on adolescence in Samoa: Howard, 105.
261. "She isn't planning to be the best anthropologist": Howard, 111.

261. During the summer of 1928, Margaret traveled to Hermosillo, Mexico, where she filed for divorce from Luther Cressman: Ibid.

261. After her divorce, Margaret joined Reo: Ibid., 106.

262. "As the dawn begins to fall among the soft brown roofs": Mead, *Coming of Age in Samoa,* 12.

262. A. C. Haddon considered Margaret's report about life in Samoa to be worthy of a "lady novelist": Howard, 124.

262. Mead's last partner was the anthropologist Rhoda Métraux: Caffrey and Frances, xxix, 171–72.

262. Margaret Mead died of pancreatic cancer in 1978: Howard, 424–25.

BIBLIOGRAPHY

BOOKS

Anderson, Barbara Gallatin. *First Fieldwork: The Misadventures of an Anthropologist*. Long Grove: Waveland Press, 1990.

Banner, Lois W. *Intertwined Lives: Margaret Mead, Ruth Benedict, and Their Circle*. New York: Alfred A. Knopf, 2003.

Bateson, Mary C. *With a Daughter's Eye: Memoir of Margaret Mead and Gregory Bateson*. New York: Harper Perennial, 1994.

Benedict, Ruth. *Patterns of Culture*. Boston: New American Library, 1953.

Berton, Pierre. *The Impossible Railway: The Building of the Canadian Pacific*. New York: Alfred A. Knopf, 1972.

Blum, Stella. *Everyday Fashions of the Twenties*. New York: Dover, 1981.

Boas, Franz. *Anthropology and Modern Life*. New York: Dover, 1987.

Boas, Franz, and Ronald P. Rohner, eds. *Ethnography of Franz Boas: Letters and Diaries of Franz Boas Written on the Northwest Coast from 1886–1931*. Chicago: University of Chicago Press, 1969.

Boas, Norman Francis. *Franz Boas, 1858–1942: An Illustrated Biography*. Mystic: Seaport Autographs Press, 2004.

Bogan, Louise, and Ruth Limmer, eds. *What the Woman Lived: Selected Letters, 1920–70*. New York: Houghton Mifflin Harcourt, 1974.

Bowman-Kruhm, Mary. *Margaret Mead: A Biography*. Amherst: Prometheus Books, 2011.

Brady, Erika. *A Spiral Way: How the Phonograph Changed Ethnography*. Jackson: University Press of Mississippi, 1999.

Bunzel, Ruth. *The Zuñi*. Internet Archive: Forgotten Books, 2008.

Caffrey, Margaret M. *Ruth Benedict: Stranger in This Land*. Austin: University of Texas Press, 1989.

Caffrey, Margaret M., and Patricia A. Francis, eds. *To Cherish the Life of the World: Selected Letters of Margaret Mead*. New York: Basic Books, 2006.

Cole, Douglas. *Franz Boas: the Early Years, 1858–1906*. Seattle: University of Washington Press, 1999.

Cole, Douglas, and Ira Chaikin. *An Iron Hand upon the People: The Law Against the Potlatch on the Northwest Coast*. Seattle: University of Washington Press, 1990.

Cressman, Luther S. *A Golden Journey: Memoirs of an Anthropologist*. Salt Lake City: University of Utah Press, 1988.

Daniel, Thomas, M. *Captain of Death: The Story of Tuberculosis*. Berlin: BOYE6, 1999.

Darnell, Regna. *Edward Sapir: Linguist, Anthropologist, Humanist*. Berkeley: University of California Press, 1990.

Driver, Susannah A. *I Do I Do: American Wedding Etiquette of Yesteryear*. New York: Hippocrene Books, 1998.

Frazier, Sir James George. *The Golden Bough: A Study of Magic and Religion*. Greenwood: Suzeteo Enterprises, based on the 1922 edition.

Freeman, Derek. *The Fateful Hoaxing of Margaret Mead: A Historical Analysis of Her Samoan Research*. Boulder: Westview Press, 1999.

Fortune, R. F. *The Mind in Sleep*. London, Kegan Paul, Trench, Trubner & Co., LTD., 1927.

———. *Sorcerers of Dobu: The Social Anthropology of the Dobu Islanders of the Western Pacific*. Oxford: Routledge, 2004.

Goldfrank, Esther Schiff. *Notes on an Undirected Life*. Queens: College Publications in Anthropology; no. 3 Queens College Press, 1978.

Golla, Victor, ed. *The Sapir-Kroeber Correspondence: Letters Between Edward Sapir and A. L. Kroeber, 1905–1925*. Berkeley, University of California, 1984.

Hall, Robert A., ed. *Leonard Bloomfield: Essays on His Life and Work*. Amsterdam: John Benjamins Publishing Company, 1987.

Hill, Thomas W. *Native American Drinking: Life Styles, Alcohol Use, Drunken Comportment, Problem Drinking, and the Peyote Religion*. Los Angeles and Las Vegas, New University Press, 2013.

Howard, Jane. *Margaret Mead: A Life*. New York: Simon & Schuster, 1984.

Jenness, Diamond. *Dawn in Arctic Alaska*. Chicago: University of Chicago Press, 1984.

Jung, C. G. *Man and His Symbols*. New York: Dell Publishing, 1968.

Kroeber, Karl. *Native American Storytelling: A Reader of Myths and Legends*. Hoboken, Wiley-Blackwell, 1991.

Kuklick, Henrika. *The Savage Within: The Social History of British Anthropology, 1885–1945*. Cambridge: Cambridge University Press, 1993.

Kyvig, David E. *Daily Life in the United States, 1920–1939: Decades of Promise and Pain*. Chicago: Ivan R. Dee, 2001.

Lapsley, Hilary. *Margaret Mead and Ruth Benedict: The Kinship of Women*. Amherst: University of Massachusetts Press, 1999.

Lutkehaus, Nancy C. *Margaret Mead: The Making of an American Icon*. Princeton: Princeton University Press, 2008.

Mark, Joan. *Margaret Mead: Coming of Age in America*. New York: Oxford University Press, 1999.

Maugham, W. Somerset. *Of Human Bondage*. New York: Pocket Books, 1968.

McMaster, Fanny Fogg. *A Family History*. St. Joseph, Mich.: Privately printed, 1964.

Mead, Margaret. *An Anthropologist at Work: Writings of Ruth Benedict*. Boston: Houghton Mifflin, 1959.

———. *Blackberry Winter: My Earlier Years*. New York: Touchstone, 1972.

———. *Coming of Age in Samoa*. New York: Harper Perennial, 1973.

———. *Letters from the Field, 1925–1975*. New York: Harper Perennial, 2001.

———. *Ruth Benedict*. New York: Columbia University Press, 1974.

Mead, Margaret, ed. *The Golden Age of Anthropology*. New York: George Braziller, 1960.

Miller, William H. Jr. *The Fabulous Interiors of Ocean Liners in Historic Photographs*. New York: Dover, 1985.

———. *The First Great Ocean Liners in Photographs*. New York: Dover, 1984.

Modell, Judith Schachter. *Ruth Benedict: Patterns of a Life*. Philadelphia: University of Pennsylvania Press, 1983.

Müller-Wille, Ludger. *The Franz Boas Enigma: Inuit, Arctic, and Sciences*. Montreal: Baraka Books, 2014.

Müller-Wille, Ludger, ed.; William Barr, trans. *Franz Boas Among the Inuit of Baffin Island, 1883–1884: Journals and Letters*. Toronto: University of Toronto Press, 1998.

Nowry, Laurence. *Man of Mana: Marius Barbeau, a Biography*. Ottawa: Canadian Museum of Civilization, 1998.

O'Connor, Richard. *Hell's Kitchen: The Roaring Days of New York's Wild West Side*. Cranbury: Old Town Books, 1993.

Oren, Dan A. *Joining the Club: A History of Jews and Yale (The Yale Scene: University Series, Vol. 4)*. New Haven: Yale University Press, 1988.

Parezo, Nancy J., ed. *Hidden Scholars: Women Anthropologists and the Native American Southwest*. Albuquerque: University of New Mexico Press, 1993.

Peace, William J. *Leslie A. White, Evolution and Revolution in Anthropology*. Lincoln: University of Nebraska Press, 2004.

Post, Emily. *Etiquette: Manners for a New World*. New York: William Morrow, 2011.

Radin, Paul. *The Autobiography of a Winnebago Indian: Life, Ways, Acculturation and the Peyote Cult*. Berkeley: University of California Press, 1963.

Rivers, W. H. R. *Medicine, Magic and Religion*. London: Routledge Classics, 2001.

Sackman, Douglas Cazaux. *Wild Men: Ishi and Kroeber in the Wilderness of Modern America*. New York: Oxford University Press, 2010.

Sapir, Edward. *Edward Sapir, Culture, Language and Personality Selected Essays*. Berkeley: University of California Press, 1956.

Sinclair, Keith. *A History of New Zealand*. Auckland: Penguin, 1991.

Stevenson, Robert Louis. *In the South Seas*. New York: Penguin, 1999.

Tone, Andrea. *Devices and Desires: A History of Contraceptives in America*. New York: Hill & Wang, 2001.

Wilson, Edmund; Leon Edel, ed. *The Twenties: From Notebooks and Diaries of the Period*. New York: Farrar, Straus & Giroux, 1975.

Woodforde, John. *The Strange Story of False Teeth*. London: Routledge, Chapman & Hall, 1983.

PERIODICALS
Columbia Spectator, Volume LXVI, Number 127, March 21, 1922.
Coolidge, Calvin. "Are the Reds Stalking Our College Women?" in Enemies of the Republic, in *The Delineator,* June 1921.
Despres, Leon, "My Recollections of Leonard Bloomfield": Histographia Linguistica, Volume 14: Jan. 2, 1987.
Ripley, Madge. "Samoa: Shall We Navalize or Civilize It?".
Wellesley News, Volume 30, Number 22, March 23, 1922.

NEWSPAPERS
New York Times, Marie Bloomfield, Obituary, Feb. 8, 1923.
New York Times, Gertrude Boas, Obituary, Oct. 6, 1924.
New York Times, Heinrich Boas, Obituary, Jan. 25, 1925.

ARCHIVES AND ORAL HISTORIES
American Philosophical Society, Philadelphia. Typescript letters between Ruth Benedict and Franz Boas, and between Franz Boas and Margaret Mead. Letters between Franz Boas and Marie Boas, Franz Boas Papers.
Canadian Museum of History, Ottawa. Letters of Edward Sapir and Memoirs and Letters of Marius Barbeau; *Les Memoires de Marius Barbeau*; transcriptions from the interview, reels 107–19, 1957–1958; Marius Barbeau Correspondence (1911–1944).
Columbia University, Oral History Project. Interview with Louise Rosenblatt.
Columbia University. Rare Books and Manuscripts Library, Butler Library, Jane Howard Papers; Jane Howard interviews with approximately two hundred of Mead's friends and associates.
Library of Congress, Manuscript Division. Jean Houston interview with Margaret Mead.
Library of Congress, Manuscript Division. Margaret Mead Papers and the South Pacific Ethnographic Archives.
Marquette University, Milwaukee. Raynor Memorial Libraries, Special Collections, Paul Radin Papers: Correspondence, 1901–1962.
University of California, Berkeley. Bancroft Library, Alfred L. Kroeber Papers; Robert H. Lowie Papers.
Vassar College, Archives and Special Collections. Ruth Fulton Benedict Papers: journals and letters.

PAPERS/DISERTATIONS
McMillan, Robert Lee, The Study of Anthropology, 1931 to 1937, at Columbia University and the University of Chicago.
PhD York University, 1986
Sacharoff, Mary. "Paul Radin: The Struggle for Individuality."
Anthropology 891
Sacharoff, Mary, Radin and Sapir: Friendship and Influence, 2/4/39

INDEX